TACTICAL TREND TRADING

STRATEGIES FOR SURVIVING AND THRIVING IN TURBULENT MARKETS

Robert Robbins

Apress®

Tactical Trend Trading: Strategies for Surviving and Thriving in Turbulent Markets

Copyright © 2012 by Robert Robbins

All rights reserved. No part of this work may be reproduced or transmitted in any form or by any means, electronic or mechanical, including photocopying, recording, or by any information storage or retrieval system, without the prior written permission of the copyright owner and the publisher.

ISBN-13 (pbk): 978-1-4302-4479-0
ISBN-13 (electronic): 978-1-4302-4480-6

Trademarked names may appear in this book. Rather than use a trademark symbol with every occurrence of a trademarked name, we use the names only in an editorial fashion and to the benefit of the trademark owner, with no intention of infringement of the trademark.

President and Publisher: Paul Manning
Acquisitions Editor: Morgan Ertel
Editorial Board: Steve Anglin, Mark Beckner, Ewan Buckingham, Gary Cornell, Louise Corrigan, Morgan Ertel, Jonathan Gennick, Jonathan Hassell, Robert Hutchinson, Michelle Lowman, James Markham, Matthew Moodie, Jeff Olson, Jeffrey Pepper, Douglas Pundick, Ben Renow-Clarke, Dominic Shakeshaft, Gwenan Spearing, Matt Wade, Tom Welsh
Coordinating Editor: Rita Fernando
Copy Editor: Tamsin Willard
Compositor: Bytheway Publishing Services
Indexer: SPi Global
Cover Designer: Anna Ishchenko

Distributed to the book trade worldwide by Springer-Verlag New York, Inc., 233 Spring Street, 6th Floor, New York, NY 10013. Phone 1-800-SPRINGER, fax 201-348-4505, e-mail orders-ny@springer-sbm.com, or visit www.springeronline.com.

For information on translations, please contact us by e-mail at info@apress.com, or visit www.apress.com.

Apress and friends of ED books may be purchased in bulk for academic, corporate, or promotional use. eBook versions and licenses are also available for most titles. For more information, reference our Special Bulk Sales–eBook Licensing web page at www.apress.com/bulk-sales. To place an order, email your request to support@apress.com

The information in this book is distributed on an "as is" basis, without warranty. Although every precaution has been taken in the preparation of this work, neither the author(s) nor Apress shall have any liability to any person or entity with respect to any loss or damage caused or alleged to be caused directly or indirectly by the information contained in this work.

*This work is dedicated to those
who have helped make it possible.*

*To my wife Nicole and my son Logan:
You both mean everything to me and I'm truly
lucky to have such a great family.*

*To my brothers Mike and Jimmy,
and my mother and father: Thank you for
your support and love through the years.*

*To Luciano, Rich, and my investment brothers
in arms: Thank you for the ideas, the camaraderie,
and your trust.*

*To my mentor Ralph Bloch: Thank you for
taking a chance and sharing your wisdom.*

Contents

About the Author vii
Introduction ix
Chapter 1: Tactical Trend Trading 1
Chapter 2: The Market Backdrop 13
Chapter 3: Setups and Chart Patterns 41
Chapter 4: Technical Tactics 73
Chapter 5: Market Considerations 101
Chapter 6: Systematic Trend Following 117
Chapter 7: Discipline and Risk Control 133
Chapter 8: Pitfalls 147
Chapter 9: Philosophy 165
Chapter 10: Summing It All Up 207
Appendix A: Resources 217
Index 219

About the Author

Robert Robbins, CFA, started his financial career in 1994 in stock market research. From 1995 to 1999, he worked as a stock market strategist, using technical analysis to drive sector strategy, investment ideas, equity strategy, and macro research. In 1999, he started Robbins Capital, LLC, an investment adviser and fund manager, and he served as its portfolio manager. Since 2011, Robbins has been the sole principal, portfolio manager, and president of everTrend Global, LLC, a systematic macro investment fund. Robbins has been quoted in *Barron's* and the *St. Petersburg Times* and has provided his insights and knowledge into the stock market on several television newscasts.

Introduction

It was April of 1994, and the market was in a correction. The S&P 500 was in a waterfall decline that had carried it down 10% from its first-quarter peak. Under the surface, the action was far worse. Small-cap stocks were being obliterated, with bids falling away and 20-30% drops common across a broad spectrum of industries. I was working in the research department of a large brokerage firm, and, as I walked out of my office and turned into the hallway, the sight of half a dozen fundamental analysts huddled around the quote machine with a palpable look of anxiety splayed upon their faces will be forever etched in my mind.

I joined the group in watching the blinking red lights signaling the slaughter as clearly as cannon smoke did a few centuries ago. It was a mess; stocks were in full retreat, panic was in the air. The source of the analysts' confusion centered on the fact that, while the market was coming apart at the seams, their stocks and industries were reporting no fundamental problems. Business was good, outlooks were fine—or so their CFO and CEO contacts were telling them. The dichotomy between the fundamental situation and the market situation couldn't have been starker, and their confused looks and anxious tones confirmed that they couldn't make sense of the situation. It was cognitive dissonance writ large. They had both failed to foresee the sell-offs in stocks they were intimately acquainted with, and they had no sense as to when the bloodletting would end.

At the far end of the hall, the situation was far different. Our technical analyst, Ralph Bloch, was widely known in Wall Street circles and a veteran with over 30 years of experience. His stock market method was altogether different from that of the fundamental analysts. Instead of battling against the reality of the prices on the quote machines, he was in tune with them, and his method analyzed the core supply/demand situation of the macro marketplace itself. He had correctly called the sell-off and, based on the high put/call readings that he was seeing, was now looking for a quick end to this steep drop. I had been reading Ralph's daily missives for a few months, and his work intrigued me enough to lead me to start a dialogue with him and to read Edwards and Magee's classic Technical Analysis of Stock Trends. He was a forceful personality and confident in his technical abilities.

Some days later, I asked him why these fundamental analysts seemed so lost in analyzing the prices of the stocks they were close to. He laughed and then told me a joke. "An American was on vacation in New Zealand, and as he drove down a small, winding road, he came upon an incredibly large herd of sheep. He stopped his car and looked out over the rolling hillside. The owner of the sheep came up to him after a few minutes and saw the look of wonder on his face, so he said to him, 'If you can tell me how many sheep I have, then you can pick one out and keep it.' The man laughed arrogantly and began counting. After only a few minutes, he turned to the shepherd and said, 'Sir, you have 1,133 sheep.' Amazed, the shepherd stood back, then proceeded to tell the man that there were five grades of sheep and he could now pick his sheep. The man climbed up the hillside, picked his sheep, and returned. He saw that the shepherd was now smiling. 'What's so funny?' the man asked. The shepherd then posed a challenge to him, saying, 'If I can guess your occupation, will you give me my sheep back?' The American quickly agreed, thinking, 'There are literally thousands of occupations out there. How would he possibly be able to guess correctly?' The shepherd cleared his throat and guessed, 'You're a fundamental stock analyst, aren't you?' Perplexed, the man queried, 'How could you possibly know?' In an even tone, the shepherd replied, 'Well, you're obviously very good with numbers, but then you picked the worst one!'"

Ralph's joke, which highlights the differences between fundamental and technical analysis, stayed with me, and I eventually switched to the technical method that I now employ in my trading. Technical analysis has been the core of my investment philosophy for many years now, and I continue to see the advantages of this pragmatic approach to analyzing the supply and demand dynamics that shape the prices we see every day in markets, ranging from stocks to bonds, from commodities to currencies. But as trustworthy as this investment style has proved to be over the years, my methodology has evolved and grown over time, and I now use a blend of technical analysis and trend trading, an approach I like to refer to as *tactical trend trading*.

Tactical trend trading, in my view, is the most reliable way to increase your net worth and gain financial freedom in an uncertain world. It entails significantly less risk than long-term buy-and-hold investing in individual stocks. It takes commitment, discipline, and the right psychological makeup, but for those willing and able to make the journey, it is the truest path to financial freedom.

Here are the primary benefits to tactical trend trading: at any given time your assets will be at work in the leading stocks and futures markets or will be safely in cash, your stop-loss sell discipline will protect your hard-earned capital during the inevitable times when you are wrong, and you will be in tune with the broader stock market and macro environment. The long-term buy-and-forget investor, on the other hand, will typically enter the market on an upswing and mentally commit to a conservative investment program. When the bear market comes to maul his portfolio, he will either cower in fear, hoping his investments rebound, or sell his "long term" holdings into the bad news of a slumping stock market and incur a terrible loss. I've seen it happen time and time again. Most investors simply do not have the stomach for the gut-wrenching 20-40% drops that are inevitable over a full market cycle. There is a better way.

The simple aim of this book is to illuminate the path to that better way. The methodology I share with you in the pages of this book will work over the course of any investment cycle. In broad terms, you can divide the goals of this book into three major themes. The first is generating returns and finding the stocks, market environments, and futures markets that are conducive to meeting that goal. The second is risk control, discipline, and avoidance of common pitfalls that await the amateur and seasoned trader alike. The third is a philosophical and epistemological framework that correctly reflects and works with the real world—not the theoretical world taught by academics and Wall Street talking heads.

I have divided the book into ten sections, each of which covers a specific element necessary for successful tactical trend trading. They are as follows:

1. Tactical Trend Trading – What is it, what are its primary benefits, and what kind of commitment is required?

2. The Market Backdrop – Looking at the big picture, then working down to the leading sectors and stock market indicators.

3. Setups & Chart Patterns – Using technical analysis and relative strength to find the profit-generating ideas we seek.

4. Technical Tactics – A guide to trading tactics to aid your work and round out the investment process.

5. Market Considerations – Taking account of the big picture and incorporating the macro outlook into your work.

6. Systematic Trend Following – Using trading rules, risk management, and portfolio selection to create a systematic trading system.

7. Discipline and Risk Control – The concepts and practice of implementing risk control, which is the most important rule in investing.

8. Pitfalls – The psychological and emotional obstacles that hinder the journey to profit generation and risk control.

9. Philosophy – The epistemological framework that serves as a basis for successfully dealing with the markets and change.

Introduction

10. Summing It All Up – A reiteration of important points and an encouraging word.

I wish you well on your journey to a successful trading career. It is a dynamic, fast-paced, and exciting field that will test your mental fortitude and acumen every step of the way. Apart from its financial benefits, the emotional rewards for competing successfully make it a fulfilling and worthwhile endeavor. You can gain financial and geographic freedom, as you can trade from anywhere in the world. Once you learn the steps necessary to compete, you can trade for as long as you are committed to it. In short, the freedom that comes from trading successfully is tough to match. Best of luck and enjoy.

CHAPTER 1

Tactical Trend Trading

Tactical trend trading can be defined as positioning yourself in those markets that are moving in defined up trends while shorting those markets moving in down trends. It involves using macro, intermarket, and technical analysis to identify those markets that are trending and may begin new trends in the future. It requires using strict risk-control measures so that you size positions in line with your risk tolerance and maintain stop-loss controls and diversification. It takes patience, a love of the markets, a positive attitude, and the mental flexibility to analyze and profit from change and trends. It requires an open mind and a sturdy work ethic to apply yourself to your craft and commit yourself to adopting both a trading-to-win mentality and a risk-averse posture when proven wrong.

The rewards for success are both financial and mental, as trading in a macro style is the ultimate money game. Being able to see 100 moving parts and create an image of the world that makes sense of this view is a never-ending game that carries its own rewards. Being able to sidestep the next bear market and profit from it is an incredibly rewarding experience that will boost your confidence and separate your investment style from that of ninety-nine percent of the investing world. In the world we live in, with all of its inherent instability and its boom/bust nature, tactical trend trading is a robust method designed to increase your odds of success and financial survival.

The real power behind tactical trend trading is the long-term gains that come from the power of compounding. Yes, you'll be trading in a shorter-term time frame than most investors, but you will be doing it with every intention of satisfying two larger goals: one, achieving the long-term growth of capital that comes from consistent performance, and, two, gaining financial freedom and independence. Worthwhile goals, but let's put pencil to paper and show the very real growth that can happen when one compounds solid investment results. Table 1-1 highlights a $100,000 portfolio growing at 15% per year. You can see that in 17 years, the portfolio grows in value over tenfold! At 20% growth, this same $100,000 would increase in value by 22 times!

Table 1-1. The Power of Compounding

Year	15% Growth Ending Value	20% Growth Ending Value
1	115,000	120,000
2	132,250	144,000
3	152,088	172,800
4	174,901	207,360
5	201,136	248,832
6	231,306	298,598
7	266,002	358,318
8	305,902	429,982
9	351,788	515,978
10	404,556	619,174
11	465,239	743,008
12	535,025	891,610
13	615,279	1,069,932
14	707,571	1,283,918
15	813,706	1,540,702
16	935,762	1,848,843
17	1,076,126	2,218,611

This kind of growth can be yours if you combine the alpha generating ability of stock and market selection with the discipline of using a strict stop-loss discipline to control your risk.

Stock Trading vs. Investing

The benefits of buying leadership stocks will quickly be obvious to those with some experience with investing. By buying only markets that are showing relative strength, you stay in tune with the companies displaying the healthiest growth in earnings and revenue. You automatically avoid the laggards that may look cheap but are usually on their way to a lengthy period of stagnation or possibly on the road to the La Brea tar pit of extinction to join the other dinosaurs. Another benefit is that you stay in tune with the stock market as a whole. There are times when attractive investment opportunities will be scarce or nonexistent. During those periods, you should remain in cash, awaiting your next opportunity. And never fear; another opportunity will come, on its own terms and in its own time. When that time comes, you will be ready to take full advantage of it with a positive mental outlook and your capital intact. You will keep your objectivity and, most importantly, your ability to enjoy the financial freedom that comes with the power of compounding.

At this point, the academic in you is enraged. "Trading is risky, and no one can predict the market!" you say. "Investing is the way to go!" You've heard the media, academics, and talking heads on Wall Street pound the idea of long-term buy-and-forget investing into your head. But never forget that the mutual fund companies are talking their book, and the way they maximize profits is by closet indexing and growing assets. Let's look at reality. Investing is far riskier than trading, as one is gambling on an uncertain future. This is less so with index vehicles or mutual funds, but with individual stocks, long-term holding is sheer lunacy. One only has to remember that not one member of the current Dow Jones Industrial Average (DJIA) has remained continuously in the index from its inception. Not one—and the DJIA is supposed to be a low-risk index of large "blue chip" corporations meant to withstand the test of time!

Things change, and any investment method that cannot change with the world, the economy, and the whims of human nature is doomed to mediocrity at best and failure at worst. Look at former market-leading stocks that now either are out of business or have had stunning declines in both stock price and future prospects over the last 20 years. Lehman Brothers, AIG, Fannie Mae, General Motors, Enron, Wachovia, Delta Airlines, Eastman Kodak, Bear Stearns, Chrysler, MF Global, Washington Mutual, American Airlines, Circuit City, CIT Group, Conseco, and WorldCom were all once considered safe long-term investments. Real change happens every day, rendering companies and whole industries obsolete in the blink of an eye. Buy-and-hold investing does not take this type of change into account.

"Okay," you concede. "Maybe investing isn't the best way to go, but trading is tax inefficient, and I already pay enough taxes!" My old boss used to joke that if you hold your stocks long enough, your tax problem will go away. After all, many long-term holders don't need to pay taxes, because their investments aren't profitable in the first place. But you're better off paying the man on your winnings and moving forward. What matters is not trading costs or payment of taxes. What matters is your net return after these costs at the end of each year. Is your investment strategy working? Are you making money in the stock market? If so, continue as you are, but if not, it's time to formulate a new plan, a new way.

Let's look at the benefits of a sound stock trading strategy. First, the trader analyzes the state of the stock market, investing only when the market is in a favorable position. Then he identifies leading sectors and growth stocks to maximize his risk/reward equation. The trader only buys stocks under this method as they are breaking out of sound technical patterns, a practice that naturally allows him to focus on the market's leading stocks and sectors. By doing this, the tactical trend trader is in tune with the market's best-performing stocks, allowing him to avoid the laggard 70% of the market that is either going sideways or in downtrends. By buying leaders and avoiding these laggards, he steers clear of the big risks associated with industry obsolescence, impending bankruptcy filings, and the large multiple contraction that occurs from serial earnings disappointments. By employing this method, the trader is also in tune and flowing with the market instead of fighting against the investment trends of his day.

As to risk, it's the most important consideration in the investment game. Risk control is the toughest practice to implement and yet the most vital aspect of executing a successful investing career. Selling your stocks when they reach your predefined stop point is the only infallible rule. You must accept that you will be right only 50-60% of the time and plan accordingly. Does that sound pessimistic? It's not. Ben Franklin once stated, "Do not fear mistakes. You will know failure. Continue to reach out." If you follow this rule, you will succeed over the long term and be able to continue to reach out with your capital intact. The best traders at leading hedge funds, the top pros in their fields, are right only 50-60% of the time, yet they consistently profit over time. Compare this situation to that of the All-Star baseball player who will hit the ball into play safely only 33% of the time. That is enough to make the Hall of Fame, yet he will go back to the dugout two-thirds of the time without success. That's life, so deal with it and plan accordingly. The alternative option is the position the long-term investor takes when confronted with a sell-off—the fetal position. By remaining both inflexible and lazy, the long-term buy-and-hold investor incurs enormous risk and is sure to catch every downturn.

If you cannot get over this hurdle and handle your losses, put this book down and move on. I've found that risk control is the toughest thing to master, even when you accept the premise. You will sometimes be wrong on individual trades, but if you see the big picture, you will be right and successful over the course of a year and certainly over the course of your investment career. Each time you enter a trade, place a hard stop so that you will sell and take your loss at a predetermined price. I'll touch on this more in Chapter 7, but for now remember that this strategy is your most important defense and ensures long-term success and preservation of capital during adverse periods. The good news is that once you commit to this program and see the benefits during the next inevitable bear market, you will feel the real power of trading freedom and independence that this method of risk control brings.

Futures Trading

Futures trading requires many of the same tools for success as stock trading and offers several distinct advantages, but it requires greater discipline and risk-controlling rigor. If trading stocks keeps you connected to the leading sectors in the economic engine at any point in time, then trading futures will keep you connected to the global financial markets and macro market environment. Trading futures will hone your ability to spot intermarket relationships. It will give you the opportunity to participate in the "big picture" shifts that occur in different futures sectors. Futures markets are pure supply/demand–led markets, so technical analysis works very well from a trading standpoint. Furthermore, you do not face the same degree of corporate and fundamental interference that you do with individual stocks. There are no buybacks, stock splits, dividend cuts, or CEO conference calls. Instead, the interaction of supply and demand in the marketplace determines the trading and price action, giving the technical approach a significant advantage in futures trading.

There are four main futures sectors: currencies, bonds, equities, and commodities. You can further break commodities futures into four sectors: energy, metals, softs, and grains. While there are several hundred individual futures markets globally, you can effectively gain exposure to the bulk of the heavily traded markets and sectors by focusing on 30-40 markets. Scanning these markets and looking at their daily and weekly charts will give you a good picture of what is happening in the macro landscape at any point in time. As an example, if bonds are trading poorly, while metals, equities, and oil are rallying, you can assume that the economic environment is strong, with increased demand for oil and metals and increased earnings for stocks. This same environment would likely be bullish for growth currencies like the

Australian dollar and Canadian dollar, whereas it could be negative for a flight-to-safety currency like the Swiss franc.

Intermarket and technical analysis will greatly aid the futures trader in determining which sectors to trade from the long side and which to trade from the short side. Grains and softs are more specialized sectors, generally trading on their individual supply/demand characteristics. Every year, two to three of these markets get very interesting and can provide the trend trader with an outstanding opportunity to capture a more significant price trend. This occurs because these markets are subject to large price swings when there is a fundamental supply shortage. The price action in the second half of 2010 is a prime example, as many agriculture markets advanced over 40% in a few short months. Cotton was the star performer, rallying from $20/lb to over $160/lb from August of 2011 to March of 2012!

The same thing is true within the four main futures market sectors. In most years, one or two of the main sectors should command the bulk of your trading attention. One year, energy will provide hefty long-side profits as the economy heats up while supply is constrained; the next year, bonds will be an excellent shorting opportunity, as rates rise in response to collapsing faith in central banks and sovereign budgets. There is usually a larger opportunity from a macro standpoint, and a trader must attempt to ride the profitable trend as it unfolds.

Macro trading in this way gives the technical trend trader several advantages not readily available in a traditional stock/bond portfolio. For example, a futures trader gains diversification through exposure to currencies and commodities. He also has the ability to participate in special situations throughout the trading year as larger trends develop, and he can participate just as easily on the short side as he can on the long side, as there is no downtick rule and no borrowing requirements. Trading futures markets allows one to see the overall macro picture more clearly and to stay in sync with these big-picture trends, giving futures traders more connection to economic cycles as well as the toolkit to take advantage of that connection through up and down cycles.

The relative strength of a given sector is key to discovering the early clues that will highlight leadership long-side and short-side opportunities in the futures market. When it comes to putting your capital to work, identify relative strength and follow it within the futures market's four broad sectors. As an example, if grains begin to enter downtrends, seek to short the weakest market within the group. If the group is beginning to challenge support areas but wheat begins to break down early, then wheat should be your first foray into the short side as its support area is violated.

Futures markets should be traded with patience and discipline, with the trader avoiding marginal trades altogether. Patiently waiting for a market to break through identifiable technical patterns increases the odds of a successful futures campaign. Trades should not be forced but instead entered into only when price action aligns with a well-defined trading plan. Risk control is extremely important, and you should enter your fixed stops as soon as your trade entry is completed. I advocate sizing trades and using stop-loss levels at points that fix the portfolio risk per trade at 1% for conservative traders and up to 5% for very aggressive traders. Most technical traders use 1-3% as their portfolio risk level when trading futures, but each of us differs in our risk tolerance. The key is finding the risk/reward level that suits your trading goals and personality.

Trading to Win

There are several overriding themes and philosophies that I wish to impart throughout this book, but trading to win is one of the most important points I wish to stress. Trading to win is an approach advocated by Ari Kiev in his great book of the same name, and it involves commitment, concentration, recovery, and preparation. It enables you to trust your true self. The core of the approach is to let go of ego, be proactive and forceful with winners, and get out of losing positions fast.

When your indicators and your method trigger a buy signal, the trading-to-win approach means that you trade with a positive offensive mindset and commit to the opportunity. If your position moves against you and violates your defined stop point, it means selling your position quickly and without fail. It means keeping your ego out of the process and staying in flow with the markets and your method. It is not a passive approach. To compare it to a football team's offense, it means you are looking to put seven points on the board when the ball is in your hand. You are not looking to run out the clock or score a field goal. You may end up doing that, but it is not your initial intention. It does not mean that you operate in a reckless manner or hold a position until it provides a large gain or bust. It does not mean that you won't accept a small loss on a trading position. It means simply that you go into a situation only when the odds clearly favor the trade's being a solid and large winner.

When you enter a position, there are only five possible outcomes: (1) a large gain, (2) a small gain, (3) breakeven, (4) a small loss, or (5) a large loss. In trading to win, you are taking a proactive, positive mental and business approach to trading. You are going in with the expectation of the first outcome—a large gain. At the same time, you are actively managing risk in order to stay disciplined and cut your losses at a predetermined price so that you avoid the large losses that come from staying with losing positions. You rely on your indicators and your method to generate your ideas and on your risk control and discipline to handle the losers so that you can remain in sync with the markets and in control of your portfolio.

The bulk of your investment gains in any given year will come from a small percentage of your trades. By operating in this fashion, you ensure that a few large losses don't hold you back from your annual and long-term goals. You then have the courage to stay longer with your winning trades, riding them for bigger profits, and to sell your losers quickly so they don't tie up your capital and drain your mental energy. This is the secret to remaining in the flow and enjoying your trading to the fullest. Losing trades, especially large losses, hurt you in more places than your pocketbook. They sap your mental strength, steal your ability to remain in the present so that you can spot new investment opportunities, tie up capital, and waste precious time that could be spent on more productive activities.

A trader who is trading to win is looking to play offense and defense with equal enthusiasm. He's looking to put points on the board and is not afraid to go for it because he knows he can forcefully back out of a situation if it's not going well for him. This keeps the winning trader playing with a positive mindset that carries over into the next trading day. Strength begets strength, and the trader who is trading to win stays strong by winning big when things are going well and losing little when things are not.

Choose Leaders Only: Buy the Best

There are thousands of stocks and index vehicles available to today's trader, there are over 100 global futures markets, and the growth in investment vehicles has been explosive over the last ten years. But all of this won't help someone any more than having ten extra jogging tracks will help them run a faster mile. To succeed in investing, you must buy the best. What is the best from a trading standpoint? The best stocks are the companies leading any current market rally. Typically, those companies will have earnings growth of over 30% annually, revenue growth of at least 20%, positive earnings revisions, and excellent relative strength versus the broad market indices, and they will trade with active volumes. There are numerous research services that have shown a long-term ability to identify these potential winners. You can find many of these names in *Investor's Business Daily*, *Zacks Investment Research*, and in *Value Line*. You can use one of these services along with other research products as long as they fit in with your investment method.

The reasoning behind buying stocks from among the leaders is relatively straightforward. If a stock or sector is going to generate attractive long-term returns, it will have to ultimately hit new highs and exhibit the strong fundamentals that it takes to attract investment interest. By choosing from among a list of attractive leading stocks, you improve your odds of staying in touch with the leaders of the current economy. You will then tend to own those stocks showing solid revenue and earnings growth, expanding margins, upward earnings revisions, and new highs in price. By default, you will also tend to avoid those stocks and industries undergoing secular decline, slowing revenue growth, and negative earnings revisions. You can see that the benefits are twofold: keeping you in potentially large winners and allowing you to avoid the most obvious large losers.

Risk vs. Reward: A Business Approach

It is imperative that you approach the trading arena with a logical mind that can accept the inherent risk/reward trade-off that investing in stocks and futures entails. There are no guarantees, and no one will bail you out from your mistakes. It takes a businesslike approach to risk and reward to succeed in this and in many other worthwhile endeavors in life. To enjoy the potential upsides that come with trading, you must be able to accept and protect against the potential downsides. Doing so is what makes tactical trend trading work. It is a proactive approach that encourages you to pursue profits aggressively when the opportunities are available at the same time that it advocates moving to cash and a defensive posture when they are not.

The philosophical framework that I'll discuss in Chapter 9 of this book postulates a more pragmatic and fundamentally sound approach to the cyclicality in the stock market and economy. Stocks are inherently volatile and sectors inherently cyclical, so the philosophical framework I advocate works with that reality. Meanwhile, futures markets are typically traded with leverage, and market performance is inherently cyclical, which is why playing defense and approaching investments as one part of a larger cycle are so important. Consensus thinking, which assumes steady market returns, efficient markets, little risk of business obsolescence, and bell-curve distributions, puts you in a theoretical world that does not exist. That model is flawed, and yet it's followed by the vast majority of investors and business schools. This epistemological gap between how the world should be and how the world is causes extreme stress and exposes traders to numerous long-term risks.

You must enter each trade and each investment endeavor with the risk-control mindset of a businessperson. There is potential loss and potential gain. Weigh both the positive and negative factors before you enter a trade, place stops so that you limit your downside, and hedge against the worst outcome in any situation. You should seek out and understand viewpoints that run counter to your own so that you are aware of the potential flaws in your investment thesis. You should maintain a flexible mind with few fixed assumptions etched in the proverbial stone. Remember: the blade of grass is stronger in a hurricane than the 100-year-old oak tree. When you are "wrong and strong" in the markets, rigidity will punish you mercilessly. It will also keep you from seeing the world as it is and adjusting to any eventuality. You must remain in step and flow with the markets as often as possible. Take your losses quickly, stay with your winners, and keep your mind sharp, alert, and flexible to new developments.

Method and System: You Need an Edge

What is your edge? Let me ask this question another way. How do you intend to make money in the markets? Is there a method to your madness, or is it just madness? Let's break down what it means to have a trading system and the edge that you need to profit in the markets that you trade. A trading system should address the following seven questions:

1. What are the long-term goals of my trading?
2. What is my working philosophical framework?
3. Which markets or stocks should I buy and sell?
4. How do I size positions?
5. What are my entry rules?
6. Where do I place stop-loss levels?
7. Where do I take profits?

You should be able to answer these questions so that you are not operating in a haphazard fashion and flitting about from one style to another. If you don't have a plan, you will more easily be pulled in multiple directions and end up chasing a style just as its popularity is at its peak while its usefulness is at its low. Every style goes into and out of favor, but the key is to know your style so that you can maximize its profit-making potential when it is working and manage your risk effectively when it is not. If you simply jump around aimlessly, you virtually ensure your own trading failure.

By answering these questions and formulating a game plan, you put yourself in a formidable position by establishing a framework for success. You will know what to buy and sell, how large to make each position, how and when to enter a trade, where to place a stop to limit losses when you are wrong, where to take profits when you are right, and what the long-term goals of your trading are so that your short-term moves fit within this plan. You'll also be able to define your working philosophical framework for how markets operate so that you can evaluate the strengths and weaknesses of your method. If you can answer these questions and function within your game plan, you have a much better chance of fulfilling your long-term trading goals.

You Must Commit—Time, Discipline, Thought, Balance

Trading is hard work. You can succeed at it, but you must fully commit your time and energy to it. You must cultivate the correct mindset so that you can succeed in the ultimate mental game. You will be competing against other traders and investors and must ride through numerous market cycles. Many come to the trading arena with little preparation or planning. They assume that because it is easy to enter a buy and sell order, it must be easy to pull profits from the market. These lazy players will typically enter at the tail end of a bull market run, enjoy short-term success, and then flame out with spectacular losses during the next down cycle. There is an old joke that these amateurs never make money in the markets, they just borrow it for a while. Having come into an alien field with nothing but false hopes and dreams, how can they expect anything else?

There are many reasons that trading is a tough endeavor. We are used to absolutes in life and in most academic fields. In math, adding two and two will always give you four. In the markets, however, adding the same group of fundamentals will sometimes equal eight and sometimes two; only rarely will it work out to a given expected level. The only absolute in the financial markets is that there are no absolutes. The only thing you can count on is change. You must continue to learn and remain mentally flexible. You must also maintain a disciplined approach, as managing your losses is one of the few things you can control. Markets tend to cycle, and no two up or down cycles are the same. In any bull market, the leadership will tend to be completely different from the previous bull market, so a good trader must continue to learn about and spot the leaders in the current market cycle. This ability to adapt to change and stay in flow with the current environment at all times is critical to profiting over the long term.

The good news is that it can be done. You have the ability to hone your craft and get better with each passing year. You will gain more knowledge from those times when you are wrong, so you must approach setbacks and short-term losses as learning opportunities. Learn from your mistakes so that you can profit from the wisdom they impart for the future. Continue to cultivate your patience and your ability to spot winners so that you can maximize your profit-making ability when things are going well. If you commit enough time and energy to the trading field, you will be able to reap the rewards that come from succeeding in this exciting arena.

CHAPTER 2

The Market Backdrop

In this chapter I'll cover stocks and futures, with an emphasis on finding the right market environments and technical set patterns to trade. I'll highlight the characteristics of these markets and suggest methods to hone in on the best risk/reward markets for trading.

Stocks

With thousands of listed stocks, the stock market is an exciting domain where something is always happening. Large bull and bear markets will unfold in select securities even in flat stock market environments. Each decade is witness to both meteoric rises and falls, with young companies growing into titans and former Wall Street darlings plummeting into bankruptcy. Whole sectors will march to their own tune if investor sentiment is swayed enough. Capturing these moves and focusing on the most potentially profitable market areas is the goal of this chapter.

Don't Fight the Trend, Flow with It

The goal of tactical trend trading is to identify and trade in concert with the primary trend of a market. Think of the major trend as a river flowing strongly in one direction. Will your boat go faster if you embark on its downstream current or if you fight and thrash with great effort and little intelligence against it? Most investors must be either masochists or egotistical, as they prefer the less profitable and ruinous path of flailing against the tide instead of flowing with and adjusting to its currents. In *The Art of War,* Sun Tzu states that a great

Chapter 2 | The Market Backdrop

general is one who can modify his tactics in relation to his opponent. The same applies when trading markets, and an intelligent operator must know the state of the macro market before he sets his trading course.

The benefit of investing with the trend has been highlighted in research done by Mebane Faber.[1] From 1901 to 2008, when stocks traded above their ten-month moving average, the annualized return was 14.4%, while annualized volatility was 14.3%. As shown in Table 2-1, in years when the market was trading under its ten-month moving average, returns dropped to 3%, while volatility increased to 24.2%. These results confirm the power of investing with the trend for great returns and less portfolio volatility. The main reason this is possible is that one avoids the secular bear markets, like those of 1973–74, 2001–02, and 2008–09.

Table 2-1. Stock Return and Volatility (Source: Mebane Faber)

	Market Above 10-Month MA	Market Under 10-Month MA
Stock Return	14.4%	3.0%
Volatility	14.3%	24.2%

First, let's define what I mean by a trend. A trend is the general direction of movement in the current market. A market can trend in one of three directions—up, down, or sideways. An uptrending market is defined by a series of higher highs and higher lows, while a downtrending market is defined by a series of lower lows and lower highs. A sideways trend occurs when a market trades in a fixed range and makes little progress up or down. Each market should be traded very differently, but the first step is to determine objectively which of these three trends defines the market at a given time. While this sounds relatively simple, it's surprising how few investors even make the attempt.

Additionally, three different phases occur within every stock market cycle. The first and most important is the primary trend, which is the longer-term trend that can last from six months to over a decade. The primary bull market in stocks that characterized the 1990–1999 bull run is a perfect example of a primary trend, as are the primary bear markets that characterized the 2000s (January 2000 through March 2003, October 2007 through March 2009), and the 1930s (1929–1932).

---

[1] Mebane Faber, "A Quantitative Approach to Tactical Asset Allocation," *Journal of Wealth Management*, February 2009.

The second phase in the market cycle is the secondary trend, which is a shorter-term swing that typically lasts one to three months and works to correct intermediate-term excesses that build up. Secondary trends are necessary in allowing bull and bear markets to correct, catch their breath, and ultimately resume their primary trend, and they tend to be more fast-moving. During a primary bull market, a secondary corrective trend serves to shake out the weak holders, check unbridled optimism, and allow more savvy investors to add or readjust market positions. In bear markets, secondary trends function in a similar though more erratic fashion. A secondary corrective trend in a bear market tends to be more violent and explosive, with heavy volume characteristic of the initial thrust as nervous shorts and eager longs combine their buying demand in a market lacking eager sellers. Many investors mistake secondary corrections for the beginning of a new primary trend, as their time horizons and patience levels are short and anchored to the prior investment cycle.

The third phase of the stock market is the swing trend, which consists of the day-to-day, week-to-week fluctuations in the stock market. Each day the market digests and discounts news, new buying or selling pressures, and myriad miscellaneous factors. This process results in intraday and day-to-day volatility and price swings that can be profitably traded by short-term professionals. This daily action provides innumerable clues to the health or sickness of the stock market. Through daily price swings, a savvy trader can determine which markets are in focus and how the market is handling good or bad news.

The key for a trader is to know in which direction the market is trending and to position himself to best take advantage of that knowledge. It is most important to identify the primary and secondary trends of a market cycle, as this is half the battle for stock market survival and profitability. It is amazing how many investors are either ignorant of or ambivalent about the big-picture trends. They justify their indifference by focusing on "fundamental bottom-up work" or saying that they are "investing" and not trading. Whether your outlook is short term or encompasses a two- to three-year view, it is critical to at least determine the existing primary trend of a market and act accordingly. Would you drive a car without checking the gauges? Then why not spend the time to determine the primary and secondary trends of the market each week?

You can use several possible measures to determine objectively the trend of any given market. The first is traditional technical analysis, which you can use to see plainly if the market is making higher highs and higher lows by drawing a trend line to show the current trend. Another way to determine the trend of the market is to use Dow theory, which, while it works with a lag, does a good job of showing the big-picture trend. Other mechanical measures, such as whether the market is trading over a rising 200-day moving average line or is on a weekly Moving Average Convergence-Divergence (MACD) buy signal, can also be used as objective trend-spotting tools. In short, there are numerous ways to determine the trend of a market, but the point is that each trader should develop his toolkit so that he can answer the basic question, "Are we in an uptrend or downtrend?" in an objective manner.

After you identify the primary trend of the market, there are certain trading tactics you should use, depending on which type of market you are dealing with. Table 2-2 highlights the correct tactics to employ in each market environment.

Table 2-2. Trading Tactics Appropriate for Each Type of Market

Trend	Trading Tactic
Uptrend	Buy breakouts in leading stocks and leading markets. Trade longs while avoiding the short side.
Downtrend	Raise cash and short markets showing relative weakness. Exercise patience if you are long only.
Sideways	Hold 20-50% cash. Trade the leading stocks and markets only. Buy pullbacks and sell rallies.

This may sound simple, but your mind will tend to get in the way. People tend to trade their wishes more than the reality that is in front of them. You must maintain flexibility, as change is the one constant in the markets. One month you will find yourself in a downtrend, but then the character of the market will change, bad news will be bought, and before you are mentally ready, an uptrend is in full bloom. It is imperative to remain open, flexible, and willing to continue to flow with reality and not with your hopes and wishes. Keep an eye on the big picture, and remember that when you start to lose money, the odds are good that something has changed, so your strategy and tactics will need to adjust accordingly.

Market Stats

Knowing the landscape and understanding the opportunities and risks is at the heart of any worthwhile endeavor. So let's dive right into the historical risk/reward profile of the stock market. Stocks are a terrific longer-term investment and historically have outperformed all other major asset classes.

Cash, gold, commodities, bonds, art, jewelry, and real estate all deserve consideration for a properly allocated portfolio, but stocks are the best place to be. Why? Well, as the famous bank robber Willie Sutton said when asked why he robbed banks, "Because that's where the money is!" Since 1900, the stock market has averaged a 9.3% return per year. While there is no such thing as an average year in the stock market, this figure highlights the investment opportunity available.

Since 1950, there have been ten bear markets, together averaging a 34.2% decline in overall stock prices. They happen about once every six years, and given that each of the three most recent bear markets have resulted in declines greater than 40%, it's safe to say that they can be particularly violent. Bear markets hurt investors in two ways. First, obviously, they cause investors to lose capital. The second and more sinister way they hurt investors is by discouraging investment in the stock market and triggering the fear that causes long-term investors to sell low and buy back only when the markets are significantly higher and investment sentiment is brighter. This is a trap that dooms the long-term investor to dramatic underperformance. The fear of bear market losses also keeps countless millions of investors in misallocated portfolios that do not factor in the long-term risks of rising inflation and erosion in purchasing power. For the trader, these problems are much less severe, assuming she has correctly identified the prevailing market trend and adjusted her holdings accordingly.

There is no reason to invest against the prevailing trends! It is as foolish as fighting the current of a mighty river or the gusting of the wind. Trends will not change to accommodate you; you must adjust to the investment landscape. Suppose that a large ship is moving through the sea at a brisk pace, with its lights shining into the distance. Ahead another light shines back, highlighting the reality that the two are on a collision course. The captain of the ship picks up the radio and communicates with the second light: "Advise that you shift course, as we are on a collision course!" The second replies quickly, "Advise that you shift course 20 degrees to port." Enraged, the captain of the large vessel shouts back, "Demand that you shift course at once! This is a Navy destroyer and we are staying on course!" In an even tone, the second light responds again, "We are a lighthouse, your call." The market is the lighthouse, so it is you, the ocean-going vessel, riding the primary and secondary investment tides, who must analyze, accept, and flow with the investment reality before you. If you don't, the market will break you and your portfolio over its sharp rocks without a second thought, let alone remorse. Flow with the trends. Doing so is not only more profitable; it is also more enjoyable to be in sync with the stock market. It will put your profits, energy, and mindset in the right place.

Corrections Are Common

Even in a bull market, corrections, or secondary market moves, happen with great regularity and can hit different groups of stocks at different times. Since 1900, there has been an average of three corrections of 5% or more per year. These secondary market moves are less important for longer-term holders, who should remain almost exclusively focused on the primary trend. For traders and those focused on the intermediate trend, however, they are very important. While a 5–10% loss doesn't sound particularly onerous, corrections can hurt traders in a few other ways. First, while the market may correct by only 5–10%, individual stocks can decline 20–30% without any change in fundamentals, as momentum investors and traders rush to the exits. This is why corrections are so important and should not be ignored. Further, corrections happen without any dramatic change in the fundamental investing landscape. In addition, since sectors correct at different times within an uptrend, a savvy trader must be prepared to rotate to the strongest areas as trends change.

An interesting study done by Lowry Research showed what percentage of stocks are actually trading at or within new highs as the stock market is making a new high.[2] The research, highlighted in Table 2-3, covers the period from 1929 to 2000. You can see that 32.5% of stocks are already in a bear market when the stock market is making a new high. This again highlights the importance of being in the right sectors and stocks, along with the right market.

Table 2-3. Stocks Trading at Highs as Market Makes a New High (Source: Lowry's Research)

Trading % Off New High	% of Stocks
0% (new high)	6.0%
within 2%	16.9%
>20%	22.0%
>30%	10.5%

---

[2] Paul Desmond, *An Exploration of the Nature of Bull Market Tops* (New York: Lowry Research, 2006).

I advocate several tools and tactics for both identifying and profiting from market corrections. For example, sentiment data are a good tool to use to identify the possibility of an upcoming correction. Anecdotally you will begin to hear the creeping rise of confidence in the media among pundits and pros alike. During a bear market, "permabears" will be trotted out, boasting of gains in their portfolios and warning of further losses to come, while during bull phases bursts of euphoria can be readily registered in market data like equity put-call ratios, which will often signal extreme bullish or bearish sentiment. When you see these extreme readings, they should set off a mental alert. The Arms Index (or TRIN) may also register extremes, signaling that buying or selling exhaustion may be nearing. Additionally, the market will very often become overbought or oversold and possibly show lagging internal strength as fewer and fewer stocks advance, even though the stock market as a whole continues its rally. If you are interested in analyzing any of the aforementioned data sources at any point in time, you can simply turn to investing websites and technical services on the internet, where information has become more democratic than in any political system.

The above tools are all useful in identifying potential divergences as the market heads one way while the indicators signal a potential impending shift. The trader should use these warning indicators in the following fashion: raise as much cash as you can, staying only with your strongest stocks and sectors. Do not trade against the prevailing trend, and wait until the short-term trend indicators tell you that a secondary trend change is upon you. I use the standard Moving Average Convergence-Divergence (MACD) as my main indicator of the secondary trend. I also use the short stochastic oscillators, the Coppock curve, the weekly parabolic, the McClellan Summation Index, advance-decline statistics, moving average crossovers, and technical patterns to determine the trend. If the above sentiment indicators are negative *and* the trend changes, I will then trade against the primary trend and with the secondary trend—or at the very least I will move to the sidelines in a defensive position and wait for a better opportunity before entering new positions.

The main point is to trade with the prevailing trends and to know your time horizons and plan of attack. You should approach trading with the idea of minimizing your risks while maximizing your returns, and trading with the prevailing primary and secondary trends is the best way to meet this objective.

Market, Sector, then Stock

Notice the order of the heading above: market is first, sector is second, and stock is third. This is the order you should follow as you should begin your campaign for investment profits. Sadly, most people do this in reverse order or completely omit steps one and two. Don't be one of those people. The

Capital Asset Pricing Model (CAPM) explains that 70% of the movement of any stock can be accounted for by the overall stock market and the sector the stock belongs to. That leaves only 30% of a stock's movement that is attributable to stock-specific factors like management, earnings growth, competitive factors, market capitalization, and so forth. In a classic case of misallocation of resources, the vast majority of business schools, as well as buy-side and sell-side Wall Street research and individual investors, focus ninety percent or more of their efforts on the bottom-up individual stock fundamentals and ten percent or less on stock market and sector work, which is more important. Their loss can be your gain.

If you think about it, the relationship of a stock to its sector is readily observable for most stocks. The majority of stock groups essentially consistent of homogeneous companies or are in industries that are subject to similar supply and demand characteristics. There are plenty of exceptions, but large groups like banks, oil majors, oil services stocks, utilities, transports, consumer staples, and large consumer cyclicals are each homogeneous to varying degrees. A company caught in the exciting rapid growth and early adoption of its products is the exception. Recent examples here include Apple, with the Mac/iPod/ iPhone/iPad growth cycle, Blackberry, with the smartphone acceleration, and Google, with its early domination of the exploding internet search market. In the 1990s, there was Dell, with low-cost PCs, Cisco, with the explosion in networking, and Microsoft, with its Windows growth. The 1980s were about mass-market retailers like Gap and Limited erupting onto the scene. These are the true leaders that buck industry and market trends. They are the kind of stocks you want to own during their growth cycle, but they are the exception to the rule. In Chapter 3, I will focus more on how to find these rockets of powerful growth, as they are the key to dramatic alpha-generating outperformance.

For now, focus on the real thing in your work—first the stock market, then industry groups, and then individual stocks. Most stocks will come apart during bear markets, whereas great stocks will tend to tread water or pull back slightly as investors adopt more defensive positioning during stock market corrections.. There is no use fighting an uphill battle every day. Put yourself on the path of least resistance, flowing and not fighting.

Groups, Groups, Groups: The Prevailing Fashion

While our process starts with a big-picture view of the stock market, stock groups are the real key to generating alpha. Along with the stock market, a stock's group accounts for 70% of its moves, so groups are the single biggest factor in determining whether a certain stock will rise or fall. Think of stock groups as the prevailing fashion. For any number of reasons a certain group will catch the investing imagination of pros and individuals alike. They are the leaders in any rally and in some markets can simply pull the flow of assets like a magnet. Technology in 1999 is a prime example. If you didn't invest in technology in that year, you badly lagged, as it pulled in virtually all the capital flows coming into the stock market.

While the 1999 tech boom is an extreme example, in any given year three to four groups will account for the bulk of the upside action in any market. The rest will either mark time or drift lower. Any number of factors can account for this heightened investor attention. I've seen reasons as diverse as war with Iraq (oil), Chinese growth (metals), the credit crisis (financials), booming foreign trade (emerging markets), benign inflation and oil prices (retail), and dollar devaluation (gold). The reasons aren't as important as spotting the action and identifying the sectors that benefit.

Table 2-4 shows a list of three sectors and the companies that are their top components. Actively monitoring these groups will provide continuous market clues and will keep the trader focused on the top trading vehicles for the current market cycle. The expansion of exchange traded funds (ETFs) has dramatically increased the range of sector vehicles available for traders to profitably execute trend trading strategies across a full sector menu.

Table 2-4. Examples of three sectors and the stocks that are their top components

Oil Services	Technology	Banks
Schlumberger	Apple	Wells Fargo
National Oilwell Varco	Microsoft	JPMorgan Chase
Halliburton	IBM	Citibank
Baker Hughes	Google	Bank of America
Cameron International	Oracle	US Bancorp

You can find the leading groups trading most strongly on up days and pulling back only slightly during down days. They will generally be on the new high list, and they are often, but not always, the engines driving whatever growth cycle that defines the current economy. The key is to spot the leading groups and buy the leaders within those groups. Trading in the leading groups allows you to generate enormous returns relative to the market as a whole. During a growth cycle, you should concentrate your investment dollars in these groups and avoid other stocks, unless those other stocks are engaged in their own stock-specific growth phase. It is simply much easier to make serious returns in the leaders. Do not try to buy the "safe" or "chicken" stocks to play along. Trade to win and commit to buying the leading stocks in the leading groups. Action speaks louder than words, and their action is telling you they are the place for your capital.

Investors as a group behave much like a startled herd of cattle. Once you get the lead bulls moving, the rest stampede without any other reason than the instinct to follow the crowd, even though they will try to justify their position by reciting the latest financial meme and consider themselves rational and informed investors. Normally, groups will stay in favor for 6–18 months, but some will have a longer run if they reach the mania stage. You can spot this stage when popular magazines, your local news, and your dentist start to share their acumen about the popular group.

It is important to understand the fickle nature of groups because the focus of investor attention will change, and when it does, it is time to move on to the next thing. The worst strategy is holding on to a fading group that moves from a growth sector to a value sector. That is a painful adjustment process that you want no part of. The first sign that a group is losing its luster is fading relative strength. The group will fail to make new highs and lack the ability to power ahead as it used to. Other groups will take its place, or the market as a whole may be due for a rest. Either way, it is time to move on and forget the story everyone will still be telling you about why the group is declining. It's now discounted in the group, and the scales are weighted against invested longs as an overcrowded sector meets ever-greater distribution at the margin and rotates back out of fashion.

It's All Cyclical

For students of the stock market, it is will find it important to realize that the market functions as a discounting mechanism. The market tends to discount events as far out as three to nine months into the future, and its ability to predict economic and business cycles is uncanny. It is, in fact, a component of the leading economic indicator readings released each month by the US government. To understand why this is so, you simply have to remember that the millions of investors who enter the market each day bring their own experience and economic information to bear on the market, and their outlooks register as buys or sells. People from every industry and background use their unique insights to drive their investment decisions. The brightest minds— the smart money, as it were—buy and sell each day and leave visible tracks.

That is why, when a market begins to sell off and react poorly to good news, you should become more cautious and examine possible scenarios that could lead to lower prices in the future. The market is telling you something, if you will only listen. The same is true at bear market bottoms. A stock market that begins to bottom and hold or rally in the face of continued bad news is telling you, as plainly as it possibly can, that it has anticipated and already discounted this information and is looking forward to positive changes in the future. Listen to it, and endeavor to figure out where these improvements might come from. If you free your mind of fixed viewpoints, you can recognize the price action and put it to good use.

The stock market also functions as a barometer of the health of the general economy, and the cascade of economic data released almost every day is closely scrutinized by the largest investment funds in the world. It's little wonder that these releases are of such great interest to the world's best and brightest investment funds. After all, the business cycle (notice my use of the word cycle, not one-way trend) is as old as the modern economy, and many of its indicators and economic releases have early predictive value for the stock market and ultimately for the economy. As a result, the business cycle as it pertains to the market and the economy is a subject that serious investors should keep in tight focus.

The business cycle's bigger-picture indicators should be in the back of your mind at all times so that you can reasonably gauge where the economy falls in the scheme of the current expansionary or contracting cycle. The first thing to consider is the current Federal Reserve interest rate policy. The Federal Reserve wields vast power to raise or cut interest rates. In normal cycles, the prevailing interest rate will ultimately have a large effect on the willingness of banks and other financial institutions to lend and extend credit. When the Fed is tightening, especially if it is already three cuts into its rate-hike cycle, you should be especially cautious and on the lookout for a probable market top. You can still invest in leading groups, but monitor the situation and sell longer-term holdings. The reverse is also true. After a recession has taken hold and the Fed is into its interest rate–cutting cycle, it is time to watch for a potential stock market bottom. You already know that nothing is foolproof, but Fed policy is significant, as the Fed has the ability to expand and contract credit and the cost of borrowing, and this is the lifeblood of a modern credit-based economy.

The yield curve, which measures the difference between short-term interest rates and longer-dated interest rates, is another important barometer to watch. One reason the yield curve is so important is that there is nothing with a better record of forecasting recessions than an inverted yield curve. While it may work with a lag of 6-12 months, an inverted yield curve is telling you that a recession is very likely to occur. Therefore, when you see an inverted yield curve, be on the lookout for a potential top, as the market may soon begin to discount a recession. The reason is that banks borrow on the short end of the curve and lend on the long end. An inverted yield curve takes away banks' incentive to lend and leads to a contraction in credit. This will ultimately slow business activity and usually portends a contraction or deeper recession.

The role and importance of credit in a levered, finance-based economy cannot be overstated. Ours is a highly unstable and vulnerable financial system built on high debt levels at the banking, sovereign, and consumer level. Stable cash flows and growth are required in regular doses in order to sustain the system. The best analogy is comparing our financial system to a great white shark. Our system is large and impressively strong, but if it stops moving it dies from sheer inertia. Cut credit for any reasonable period, or curtail growth levels, and the system collapses upon itself. This need for credit and economic growth is a serious vulnerability in the current system of credit leverage, and it only increases the likelihood of larger boom/bust episodes in the future. Central bank and political solutions have only served to feed the beast and have made the system more, not less, vulnerable and turbulent.

Figure 2-1, courtesy of SentimenTrader, highlights the profound impact the yield curve has on the stock market and business cycle. You can see the S&P 500 at the top of the graph and the difference in yield between two-year notes and ten-year government bonds. When this yield spread is tight or even negative, liquidity and lending activity are likely to slow, and a recession is probable. You can see that a negative yield curve presaged recessions in 1990, 2001, and 2008. Conversely, when the yield curve becomes very positive, with ten-year rates exceeding two-year notes by 2.0% or greater, the economy is likely to reaccelerate. Stocks will begin to rally in advance of an improving economy, as they discount the recovery three to nine months in advance.

Other important economic releases to monitor include the employment report, jobless claims, consumer and producer price indexes, manufacturing surveys, and gross domestic product releases, among others. In short, you should monitor the big picture, keeping an especially close eye on the credit and interest rate cycles, as they tend to lead the others in predicting the business cycle. Figure 2-2 highlights the spread between corporate bonds and 30-year Treasury bonds. You can see that the yield spread between corporate bonds and Treasuries will tend to spike during recessionary periods as corporate default risks rise. During such periods, bond investors sell these riskier securities and seek the safety of government bonds. The markets are constantly giving valuable feedback to those investors astute and open-minded enough to listen and take advantage of it.

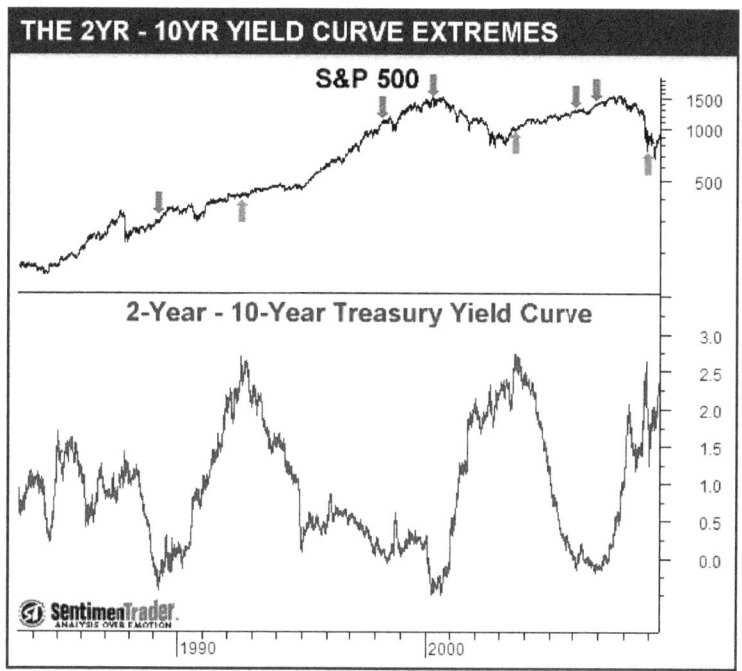

Figure 2-1. The yield curve has a major impact on the business cycle. (Source: SentimenTrader)

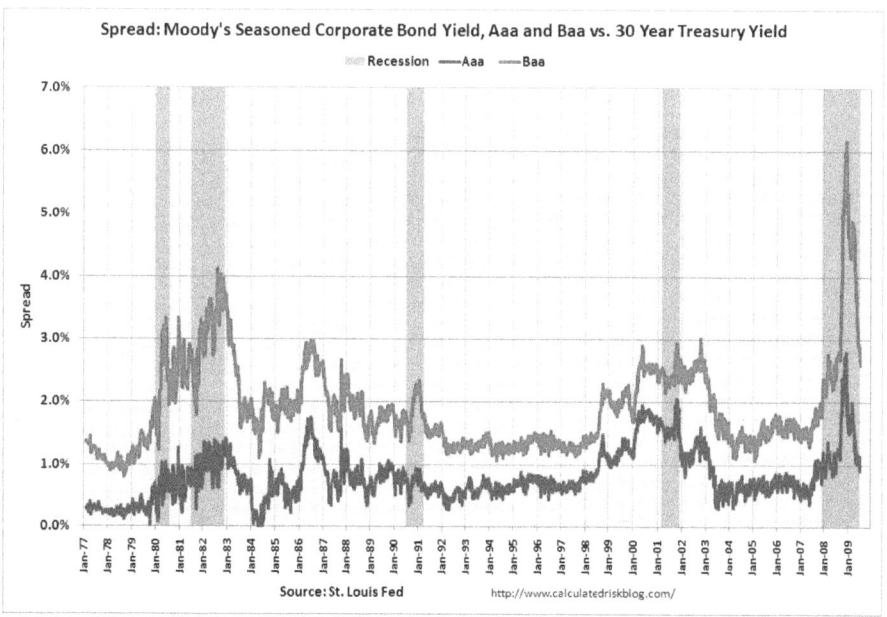

Figure 2-2. Credit and interest rate cycles have great predictive value. (Source: St. Louis Fed)

Chapter 2 | The Market Backdrop

If I impart nothing else in this chapter, I want to drive home the point that change in the markets is constant, and your mind and methodology should be in a position to profit from and account for this fact. Mental flexibility guided by a disciplined investment approach is the key to long-term success and survival as a trend trader. If you prefer things to stay the same and are uncomfortable with change, you will have to do some work on your mindset. The market, sectors, and individual stocks are always changing, and that is the only constant. No one can tell you what the next change will be, but the market will tell us in its own time. I can only predict that it will all change tomorrow and accept that fact.

There is an upside to all this change. If you can adapt to the uncertainty and have a disciplined system in place, you can both protect yourself when you are wrong and profit handsomely when you are right. Look at Figure 2-3, which depicts the emotional cycle that plays out over the course of a typical bull and bear market cycle. As a bull market builds in price and extends in time, investor sentiment becomes increasingly optimistic. At the peak of the mania, the crowd throws caution aside and fully commits itself to the narrative fallacy of the day. Oil, gold, internet stocks, emerging markets, biotech, gaming, real estate, and the nifty fifty all have undergone boom/bust cycles and have taken many investors on this emotional ride. As a trend trader, you must take advantage of these cycles by profiting on the upswing and avoiding or shorting the down cycle.

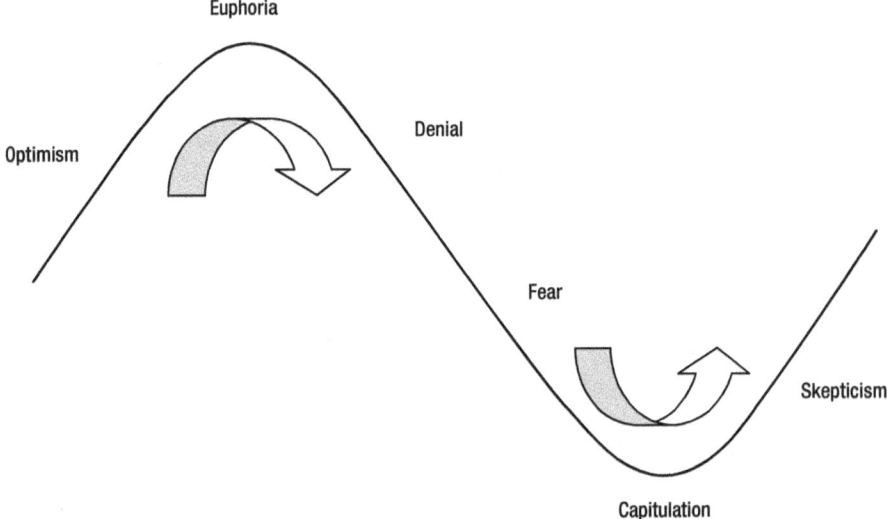

Figure 2-3. On an emotional ride, take advantage of the cycles.

Seeing the emotional stages of an investment cycle unfold is an invaluable tool in positioning yourself correctly to pull in profits. At the top of a cycle, you will hear experts extol the virtues of a given investment and tell you why it is different this time. It is never different this time! Success ultimately sows the seeds of the down cycle, as any given opportunity is exploited to capacity. The same is true at bottoms. Once investors and the public become despondent and give up all hope on an asset class, the stage is usually set for some type of recovery period. The more broadly defined the asset class, the more likely this is to be true.

My mantra is to accept and flow with reality, so as reality changes, so does my positioning. While the trading environment is constantly changing, with different stock groups and individual stocks coming into focus and the market alternating between bull and bear trends, there are enough similarities from one cycle to the next to make sense of it all. Over time, your experience will greatly enhance your ability to recognize that while no two cycles are the same, they do follow the same patterns.

Checklists, Indicators, and Signals

Now that I've mentioned some of the leading economic indicators to monitor, it's time to unveil the technical toolkit for the professional trader. Just as I have constructed both a long-term and an intermediate-term proprietary measuring tool that I update every week, each trader should have her own checklist of important indicators that experience has told her hold value. In this section I will highlight the more important technical factors that should guide the serious student of the markets, but before I do that, keep in mind something William Hamilton wrote many years ago: "The Dow Jones averages have a discretion not shared by all prophets. They are not talking all the time."[3] It's the same thing with these indicators. They will often go silent for months at a time before emerging with an important message for the astute observer.

Sentiment indicators do a good job of measuring the temperature of amateur and professional investors alike. Put-call ratios, which are released daily by the CBOE, are very good at measuring sentiment extremes at turning points. By charting these readings, you can get a very good look at when the long or short side becomes crowded. Figure 2-4 shows the equity put-call readings versus the stock market during the period from 2004 to 2006. Put-call ratios are read in a contrary fashion, meaning that excessive call buying is bearish, while excessive put buying is bullish. These readings are an excellent short-term barometer of investor psychology.

---

[3] William Hamilton, "A Study in the Price Movement," Wall Street Journal, December 17, 1925.

Chapter 2 | The Market Backdrop

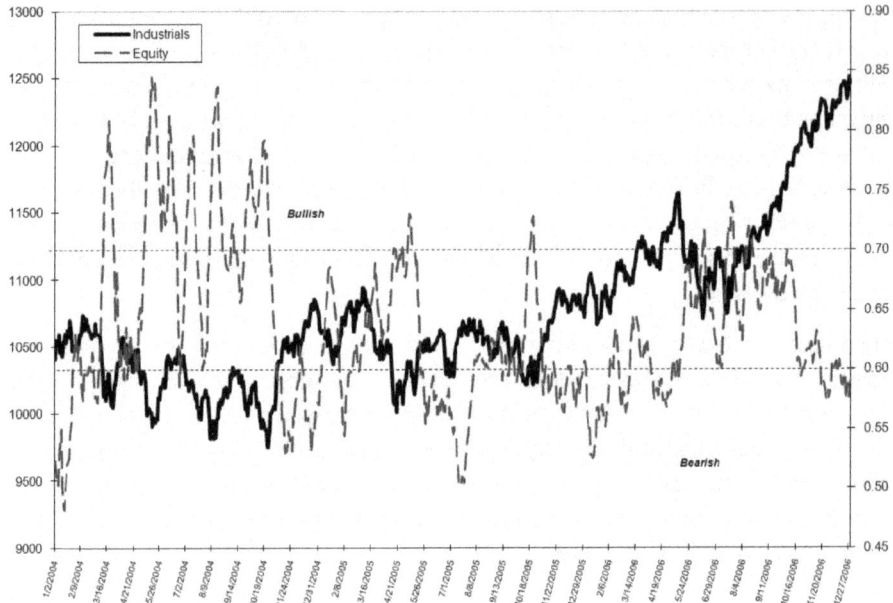

Figure 2-4. Sentiment indicators take the temperature of investors.[1]

The crowd is very often wrong, especially at extremes and significant turning points. A rising put-call ratio indicates excessive put buying as investors brace for a stock market correction. It is an indication of fear and usually occurs in concert with some news that is expected to exact damage on the markets. Remember: we love a good story, and the power of the latest narrative is excuse enough to buy puts and protect oneself. You can see that when put activity spikes relative to call activity, the market is typically at a turning point and may be ready to begin an advance. There were four meaningful put-call spikes in 2004 alone, and each led to a tradable reflex rally.

Likewise, excessive call buying is a meaningful clue that the crowd is becoming too bullish and too comfortable in their positions. Excessive call buying spikes can be seen in early 2005 and again in 2006 and led to a meaningful correction each time. I would caution that while sentiment indicators are excellent tools, they should be used in concert with price action. The trend should be your main tool, but sentiment indicators can alert you to potential turning points and times when it pays to be more cautious in your positioning.

Figures 2-5 and 2-6 display proprietary technical composite indicators that I developed to aid my analysis of the stock market and the investment cycle.

---

[1] The sources for all figures, unless otherwise stated, are from everTrend Global, LLC and the Chicago Board of Options Exchange (CBOE).

Tactical Trend Trading

The first, shown in Figure 2-5, is a short-term indicator that is intended to operate in a contrarian fashion and spot potential inflection points, and I use it as a barometer of short-term risk. Readings of greater than +30 are bullish, while readings under −35 are bearish. Figure 2-5 covers the period from 2002 to 2004, and you can see how well this indicator worked in identifying the 2002–03 bear market bottom, as the indicator reached +100 during the weeks of the ultimate stock market lows. It also clearly delineated the risks in early 2004, with a reading of −95. I use these indicators in my work and update the readings weekly. They serve to alert me to short-term risk and reward, and the exercise of updating the readings weekly makes me aware of potential shifts in the investment climate.

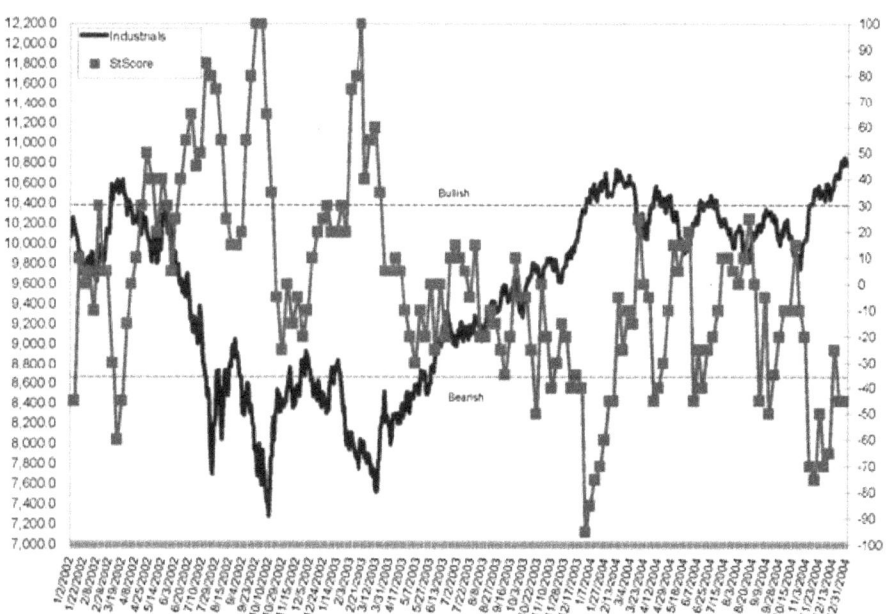

Figure 2-5. A short-term indicator to spot potential inflection points

The chart shown in Figure 2-6 is another proprietary tool that I developed, but this one is an intermediate-term timing tool. It incorporates technical, economic, credit, and sentiment indicators, all of which have a good record of forecasting future prices. Figure 2-6 covers the period from 1996 to 1998, and readings of +20 or greater are very bullish, while readings of −20 or lower are bearish. You can see that this indicator correctly identified the market risks in 1997 and 1998 well before the markets turned lower. In fact, it scored one of its most bullish readings in the fall of 1998, well before the market bottomed. I update this composite indicator weekly, and it is an invaluable tool in

Chapter 2 | The Market Backdrop

highlighting the risk/reward opportunity that is present in current market conditions.

The power of these indicators is that they allow me to spot potential short-term and intermediate-term opportunities well before any trend changes. I then use this information to reduce exposure as a market run is ending or pick up exposure once the trend turns higher off a defined low. I don't use this information to fight a trend, but it may cause me to hedge more as the indicators reach more extreme readings.

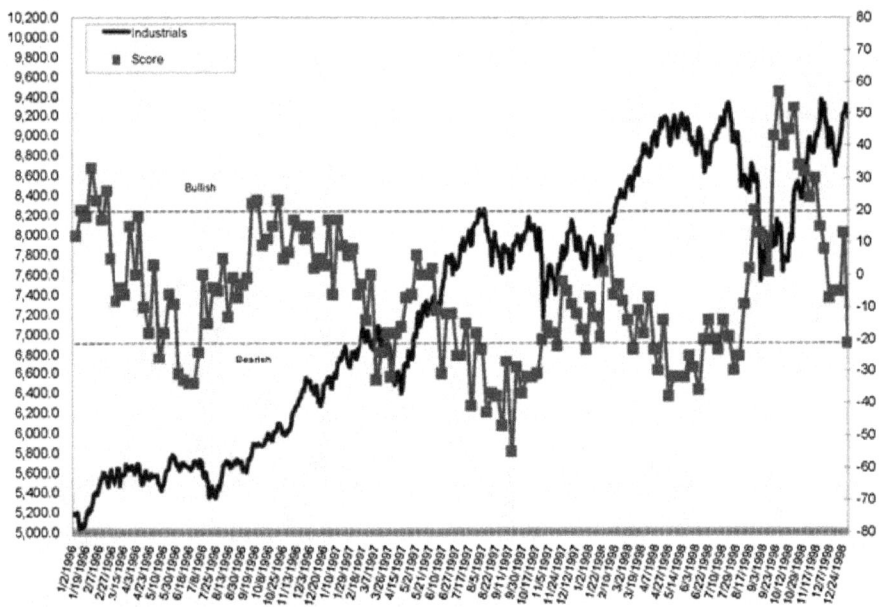

Figure 2-6. Intermediate-term timing tool incorporates a number of indicators.

Another useful set of sentiment indicators includes readings from the American Association of Individual Investors (AAII) and Investors Intelligence (II). These are to be used as contrary investment opinions as well, with ebullient bullish readings serving as a potential sign of a correction and vice versa. In addition to these indicators, I monitor insider buying and selling, which is to be followed, not faded (i.e., to go against the price move). Especially after a more protracted sell-off, it is a good rule to look for a large pickup in buying by corporate insiders. Its absence would be a large negative, as it would indicate that insiders don't view declining prices as an opportunity to add to holdings, signaling that the downside probably has further to run. I also use mutual fund inflows, put-call ratios, Rydex fund data, and many other indicators in my work, but here I wanted to touch on the more pertinent pieces of the technical puzzle. If you monitor these indicators over a number of cycles, they will become even more useful and almost second nature in their application.

As with all indicators, remember that these are only tools to be used to check excessive optimism or despondency and are secondary to the prevailing trend. They are extremely useful but should be used with this caveat in mind: think of these technical readings much as a pilot would look at his instrument panel. They are the warning signs that tell you that even though the plane is still flying high, bright lights are flashing red warning signs, telling you that not all is well and defensive action is called for. Buckle up!

Futures

The first modern organized futures exchange began in 1710 when Japan began trading rice futures. Chicago followed in the early 19th century with futures for corn and other agricultural commodities. They were created to allow producers and consumers of foodstuffs to lock in prices and mitigate the risk of adverse price swings. In the early 1970s, financial futures started with interest rate futures and currency futures. In the last twenty years futures have become far more global and liquid with active twenty-four hour electronic participation by producers, hedgers, and speculators.

Macro Trading

Macro trading is investing across the global range of asset classes and markets. It is big-picture, opportunistic trading, where the trader is looking to identify the most favorable risk/reward markets and position himself accordingly. Traditionally bonds, currencies, equities, and commodities form the backbone of the macro trader's toolkit. These markets are analyzed in a global framework to identify big-picture trends and opportunities for future change. Macro trading also involves constant reading and analysis to identify potential global themes and changes. For example, the growth of many large countries, such as China, India, Brazil, and Indonesia, has profound implications for global food and energy needs, consumption patterns, and infrastructure building. This growth trend and its various investment implications emerged in the 2000s and reached a short-term zenith in early 2008, buoying stock markets in India and China, increasing global grain prices, and leading to a bubble in crude oil prices. And what provided the backdrop and tied these seemingly unrelated moves together? That's right: macro analysis did.

Macro trading is about taking an assortment of big-picture developments and weaving them into a series of trading positions. These larger investment themes tend to last for two to three years on average and offer numerous ways to express the trading viewpoint. Housing, for example, offered long homebuilders, long lumber futures, long credit default swaps, long government bonds, long investment property, and short banks at different points of its macro cycle. The first Iraq war offered short stocks, long oil, long defense stocks, and short industrial commodities as instruments to express a macro view.

Macro traders tend to have a global viewpoint and are adept at taking disparate data and using it to form an investment thesis. They invest in many of the largest markets in the globe, and they tend to closely follow central bank action, interest rates, and traditional macro markets like oil, copper, and stocks for clues in the investment landscape. In addition, they analyze the economy to identify where the current environment lies along the expansion/contraction cycle. Macro trading involves the ability to see the investment markets and fundamental data within the larger system-wide context. The data and technical action then begin to draw a picture that may highlight profitable investment opportunities.

Intermarket Analysis

Each chart of the markets is a picture that portrays the outcome of the daily battle for investment profits. On its own, this picture is a snapshot of the current state of the market as well as a history of its ever-evolving character and trends. Accurately reading this picture can put you in sync with the underlying market and reveal its peculiarities. But if you want to gain an even greater understanding of the investment landscape, you must read the pictures of over 40 futures markets, distill the common messages and investment themes among the individual markets, and then weave them together into one overriding investment thesis in a process called intermarket analysis. Understanding the action of any one market and its underlying supply/demand characteristics allows a trader to profit from that action. Taking it one step further and applying intermarket analysis, however, makes for an even more effective investment process, as the trader can then trade in sync with both the individual market trend and the big-picture investment landscape.

Intermarket analysis is a three-step process:

1. Analyzing the charts of the constituents of the four major futures sectors: stocks, bonds, currencies, and commodities.

2. Writing down and mentally noting the picture that is revealed by market consistencies as well as outliers. This will involve looking at the underlying trends as well as understanding the nature of each market and its characteristics in the investment cycle.

3. Questioning, probing, and remaining curious as to the relationships and trends you observe and the implications of your analysis.

The first step of intermarket analysis involves going through the charts of the relevant markets within each of the four sectors mentioned above. Within stocks, you should look at daily and weekly charts for each of the major regional stock indices, starting with the stock markets of the United States, Europe, and Asia. You should then drill down into the regions, so within Asia, you would analyze the charts of markets in Japan, Korea, China, and Hong Kong, among others. You should also include global emerging markets, including India, Brazil, Mexico, Russia, Eastern Europe, Indonesia, the Middle East, and Africa.

To expand your intermarket analysis further, you should analyze the sectors within a major market to determine which areas are showing relative strength and which are showing relative weakness. For the United States, this sector focus should start with larger sector markets, such as the S&P 500, the NASDAQ, the Russell 2000, and the Dow Jones Transportation Average. You can then narrow your focus and go down to the level of the major stock sectors to include the financials, technology, utilities, retail, metals, oil, consumer goods, industrials, and health. This continuing analysis begins to paint a picture that will reveal broad trends, which leads to the second step of intermarket analysis.

Let's say that the theme of strength develops in the emerging markets, with relatively trendless activity occurring in developed markets. If we look back at 2007 and early 2008, this exact picture emerged, and leadership pointed the way to profitable investment positioning. In this case, intermarket analysis favored positions in markets benefiting from this investment cycle. Translating this picture into an investment thesis would have led you to put trading capital in emerging market futures or ETFs and into commodity-related markets, including oil futures and metals and mining stocks and futures. Within currencies, your intermarket analysis would have favored long-side positioning in currencies that had exposure to economically sensitive commodities, such as the Australian dollar, Canadian dollar, Norwegian krone, and Brazilian real at the expense of the U.S. dollar. It also would have pointed to short positions in the Dow Transports, as higher input costs combined with tepid economic growth argued for reduced earning power.

Another major theme emerged in the aftermath of the 2001–02 bear market. In order to reinvigorate the economy, the Federal Reserve aggressively lowered interest rates. This investment theme showed itself powerfully in the global bond markets as they rallied strongly during this bear market in stocks. Recessionary environments tend to be extremely bullish for bonds and bearish for economically sensitive commodities and currencies as well as equities. Seeing these broad trends in place paints an economic picture of recession.

You can also get more granular on the intermarket picture as it relates to one country. For instance, in the early part of 2012, Japan provided an interesting picture of intermarket analysis, with several potential trend developments. Japan's economic strength comes from a high-value-added export-driven economy. While the country has been in economic decline relative to the rest of Asia, it still had run a trade surplus for 30 straight years. All of this ended when, in 2011, the country reported its first trade deficit since 1980. Faced with a loss of competitiveness, poor demographics, and a looming and ever-growing budget deficit, the country could not afford to add a trade deficit to the mix without serious consequences over the longer term. The yen had been strengthening in steady fashion since 2007 and, by several measures, was overvalued by 25%. But the strength of the yen served only to make Japan's economic engine more prone to disruption, as it made her exports more uncompetitive.

That, then, was the backdrop: the yen was strong and potentially overvalued, Japanese bonds were incredibly strong and resilient, with ten-year yields at the 1% level, and equities were weak but trying to find a bottom. The Bank of Japan was under pressure from business and politicians to take action to further ease monetary policy and reverse the yen's strength in order to restore Japanese competitiveness. This intermarket picture suggested that a move to ease policy was likely and would lead to yen weakness and potentially significant equity strength, with bonds remaining well supported. As of this writing, this is what has happened. So, as the Japan example makes clear, intermarket analysis can aid in framing a fundamental view and allow the trader to wait for the technicals to confirm this development.

There are many ways to apply the picture provided by intermarket analysis in adopting an investment posture. The key is to continue to analyze the macro markets and allow them to reveal the inherent message behind the intermarket trends that you see. This is the third step, and it involves continued analysis with an open mind. No trend lasts forever. No cycle runs forever. Change is the normal condition. A good trader will remain curious and on the lookout for changes in existing trends and the development of new trends. He will continue to probe, to analyze, and to ask questions that reveal the meaning behind the ever-evolving tapestry of the investment landscape. He will participate in trends while remaining on the alert for changes in market tone. Flowing with these trends and remaining curious can aid in keeping your investment posture a strong one.

Sector and Market Selection

Once you're in sync with the prevailing trends and intermarket thinking, how do you best position yourself to take advantage of them? What markets best maximize the risk/reward equation? The key is to seek those markets showing both the greatest relative strength and the best ability to benefit thematically from the macro environment. Several examples will serve to highlight the importance of market selection. In the Japan example described in the previous section, it eventually became clear that the yen was likely to weaken, while equities strengthened and bonds were confined to a narrow range environment. Therefore, the investment stance the savvy trader would have taken would have been to short the yen and go long on equities, or both. In this case, assuming both trades had similar risk/reward metrics, it could have come down to how a trader's current portfolio was already positioned. If a trader was already long other equity markets, it might have made sense to take only the short yen position. This would also have been the case if equities globally were in bear markets because of a recessionary environment. However, if a trader was extremely bullish on equities generally and his current equity exposure was too low, he might have been better off overweighting the Nikkei position while avoiding or only marginally shorting yen futures.

Another way to select the market to best express a macro view is to go with technical strength. If a trader is bullish on equities and, particularly emerging equities, then it is time to drill down to the top emerging equity markets to identify their relative positions. It may be the case that out of the top ten emerging markets, seven are in emerging uptrends, while three are lagging and either in trading ranges or in downtrends. Of the seven in uptrends, there may be a picture emerging in which the strongest emerging markets are resource rich. For example, emerging markets in Indonesia, Brazil, Chile, Russia, and Africa could be showing strength relative to emerging markets lacking critical commodities, like India and China. In this case, trend identification has narrowed the list of markets from ten to seven, and the resource theme has further narrowed the list to five markets. This would then give the trader a more focused list of markets to choose from as well as further benefit her macro positioning. Given the above, she would also likely be more bullish on coal and copper markets than she would on retail or service markets. As you can see, combining relative strength with joint macro and intermarket views results in a powerful tool for letting the market narrative position the trader most effectively.

Within a sector such as metals, you can also use macro work, intermarket analysis, and relative strength to identify the most well-positioned target markets for investment. For example, if the economy is vibrant, unemployment rates are low and falling, and financing is readily available, a trader would likely consider positions in copper, platinum, and palladium versus gold or silver. If copper futures, the Chilean market, and copper stocks were all trading poorly while global auto stocks were in a leadership position, then a trader might target platinum and palladium while dropping copper from the list of markets. Similar work could be done within grain markets, where subsidies on corn and sugar for biofuel combined with relative strength could lead the trader to focus on these markets at the expense of soybeans and wheat. Again, using macro work, intermarket analysis, relative strength, and technical work should paint a picture and highlight the best areas for probable investment success.

Commitment of Trader (COT) Data

Commitment of Trader (COT) data are released each Friday, reporting the positions of three main groups of traders for each US futures market, including commercials, large speculative traders, and small speculative traders. Commercials are the large end users and producers of the underlying market. In corn, for example, commercials include companies like Archer Daniels Midland and Kellogg, while in oil, commercials include the refiners and exploration companies. Commercials are looking to secure physical delivery of the underlying commodity or to hedge price risk and lock in future selling prices today. They are smart and savvy in their underlying area of expertise, but instead of looking to maximize price, they are trying to ensure the stability of their supply/demand situation at good prices and hedge out price risk. They are sellers of risk. Large speculative traders, on the other hand, are funds and large traders in each market. Most are trend followers of some variety, and they are looking to buy risk and assume pricing exposure. Finally, small speculative traders are individual traders that buy risk to assume pricing exposure. You can see that commercials and speculators make for a natural market, as one group is looking to sell risk exposure while the other is a natural buyer.

COT data can be useful in identifying potential market turning points, particularly at multiyear extremes. The key is to look at the position of each group on a relative basis as well as focus on the action at extremes in positioning. Keep in mind that you should only use COT data as an additional tool and not as a primary indicator. It can be very useful at these major turning points in identifying potentially meaningful changes to the macro outlook as well as highlighting special investment situations. Figure 2-7 shows a price chart for copper along with graphing the positioning of commercials and speculators. Notice that commercials, marked by the solid black line, were early buyers at multimonth lows in 2011. They were also sellers or hedgers on price strength throughout 2011.

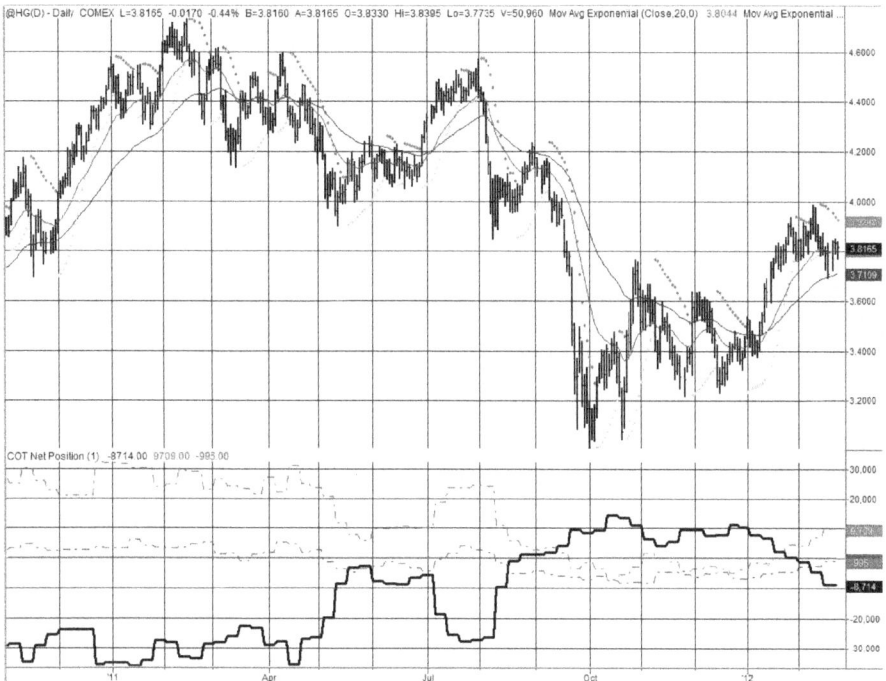

Figure 2-7. Copper buyers and sellers

You can witness similar action in the US 30-year bond chart from 2011 and 2012. As shown in Figure 2-8, commercials were heavy buyers at the bond market lows in March and April of 2011 and continued to buy through July before a large upward move in bond prices. They then scaled out of positions into strength in September and October, booking healthy profits in the process.

The key to using COT data lies in viewing the data in relation to historical activity. Each market is different. In addition, keep in mind that the data should not be used as a timing tool but rather as another indicator to confirm a possible trend change.

Patience and Discipline Are Key

Patience is not passive; on the contrary, it is active; it is concentrated strength.

—Edward Bulwer-Lytton

Patience is a position of strength in the markets. There are so many paradoxes in trading, and here is yet another: most professionals who are drawn to the trading field are hardworking, energetic, and bring a can-do attitude to their

Chapter 2 | The Market Backdrop

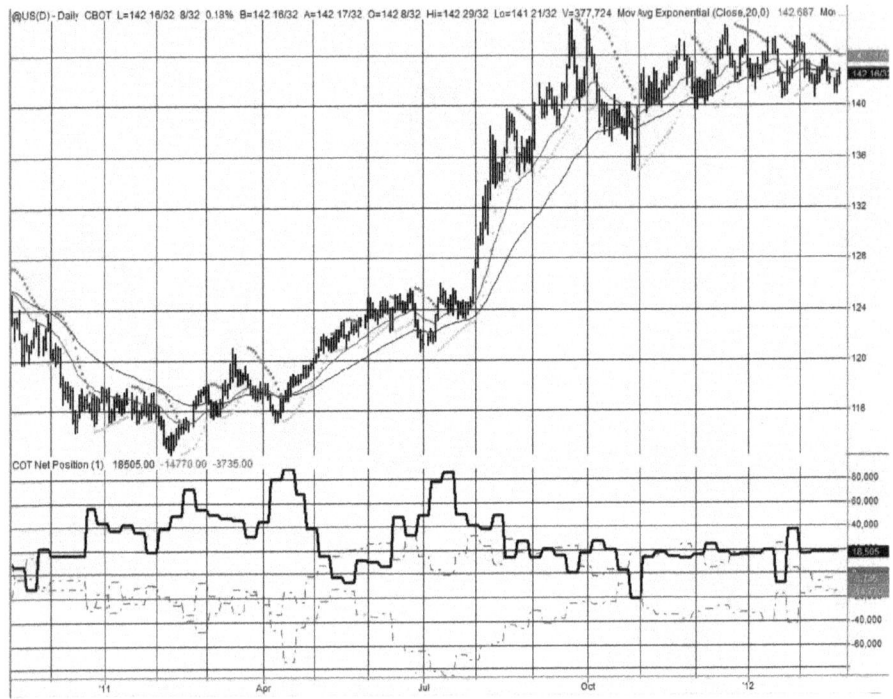

Figure 2-8. Commercial traders' bond action in 2011

profession. They also tend to come from backgrounds where putting your nose to the grindstone and working 12-hour days is to be expected. It is therefore emotionally tough for these people to do nothing, or to do no harm, as I prefer, for large stretches of time. A trader has an edge and a workable market two or three times a year, each lasting four to eight weeks, to make his year. The rest of the time he would be better off strolling through the neighborhood, spending time with his children, and doing stock market research. There is a trading rule that states you must trade what you see, not what you desire. Accept and flow with the reality before you. If the trade you want is not there, don't take something else instead. If it is, then go for it, and put your capital to work.

This takes a rare kind of patience and mental discipline to carry out. If you've watched top predators like lions hunting, the approach is similar. They don't run around aimlessly, needlessly wasting energy. Instead, they lie in wait until a worthwhile opportunity presents itself, and then they strike with maximum force. In trading it is necessary to operate in a similar manner, as trading is a very demanding and stressful profession, and we all need the mental break a few days away provides. Besides this benefit, your P&L will improve greatly.

Like most traders, I am prone to impatience and I dislike sitting on the sidelines. It's not easy to take a break, but it must be done occasionally. Trade when your method tells you the time is ripe for gains and your edge is clear, and remain on the sidelines in cash when it is not.

Discipline isn't something you see too often in modern life. Pop culture and business advertising bombard you with the constant message that if you want it, get it now! Now! Now! No money, put it on credit, but get it now! In trading, however, a lack of discipline comes with a very real and heavy cost. You must use the tools in your arsenal, do your work, and stay true to your risk discipline. When your method tells you it's time to buy—buy; when your stock hits your target or sell-stop—sell. Having the discipline to successfully execute a trading strategy is even more important than having a great strategy. You can adjust your method over time and should remain flexible in order to improve, but you must at all costs stay true to your discipline. In fact, there is no more important rule than staying with your sell discipline at all times. It will ensure your survival when times are tough and all those about you are seeing their portfolios come apart at the seams. Having this discipline will see you through, but it is something that must be developed over time. Stay with it and exercise both patience and discipline in your work. Paradoxically, if you keep your long-term picture in place, you will be more able to exercise patience and steadiness in your daily operations.

CHAPTER 3

Setups and Chart Patterns

I'm always looking, like a child, for the wonders I know I'm going to find.

—Richard Feynman

This chapter is all about generating returns, finding alpha, and big game hunting. It's about the offense in your football team's playbook. Just as with any good offense, you need a balanced attack led by playmakers who know how to put points on the board.

What Are We Looking For?

I've already established that market conditions should be in your favor before you take on trading exposure. When trading stocks, the broad stock market, as defined by the S&P 500, should be in one of two phases in order to support long positions—in either an uptrend or a sideways trend. With these criteria satisfied, you should establish which handful of stock sectors is showing relative strength. This display of strength and leadership is the most important driver of individual stock outperformance. Many times, only two to three sectors will be enjoying bull markets while the better part of the stock market is either trending sideways or grinding slowly lower, so sector leadership is paramount. In fact, most large stock winners will be found within these leading sectors.

Additionally, your futures trading should be in sync with your position in the macro cycle. Once you identify the macro themes that you wish to exploit, you should use further chart work and intermarket analysis to identify the top markets to trade from both the long and short side. These are the markets that are benefiting from favorable supply/demand dynamics and are trading in sync with your bigger-picture investment outlook. A good market will have three things going for it: technicals, market tone, and fundamentals. Your technical work should suggest that a market is trading within a trend, and you should be able to identify points within the trend where you can initiate or add to positions. Market tone should be favorable, such that a market is able to shake off bad news and rally strongly through good news. There also should be a fundamental story behind the market's movements, and supportive supply/demand dynamics should be in place. As I will reiterate numerous times throughout this book, it is far easier to flow with the market as opposed to fighting it and hoping to correctly identify turning points.

Once you've identified the leading futures markets and sectors within the market, your search becomes easier. You should always keep a few general principles in mind when you're on the hunt for a good stock. Relative strength is the key, telling you that a certain market is enjoying increased demand. There can be any number of reasons why institutional and smart traders are buying. Perhaps the future prospects for a company are solid and improving, or there may be company-specific changes at play. A company may have a new product that captures market share, as was the case with Apple's release of the iPod, iPhone, and iPad. A company may also be in an industry seeing favorable secular shifts. Examples here include Visa and MasterCard, which benefit from increased credit and debit card usage as a percentage of purchases globally; biotechnology stocks benefiting from the aging of the population; oil service stocks, which benefited from high and rising crude oil and exploration budgets from 2005 to 2008, or housing stocks, which enjoyed robust secular demand from 2003 through 2006. At any given time, there will typically be two to three groups enjoying important secular shifts that may last several years. In the end, though, it matters not *why* traders are buying a particular stock; the very fact of their buying is all that's important. Tastes in demand change much like fashion, and entire industries are subject to the whims of the marketplace.

The key takeaway is to concentrate your efforts and your trading capital on healthy, growing companies, and the best way to do this is to maintain your focus on the situations and sectors that are most in demand in the economy in which you're trading. Focus on growth, not decay; focus on leaders, not laggards; focus on healthy balance sheets and operating margins, not highly leveraged, undifferentiated companies. Ask yourself, "Do people really want and need this company's current offering, or can they easily and quickly go somewhere else to find a replacement?" If consumers can easily move on, odds are high that margins and growth will be tough to achieve. On the other hand, if the product or service is highly coveted and has some stickiness to its usage, and if the company can continue growing its revenues for the foreseeable future, then you have a candidate for trading and your investment dollars.

The Ruling Reason

For everything there is a season, and for every trade you must have a reason. Why are you buying the market you're buying? Why are you looking at this trade? Why do you expect this sector to advance? What is your ruling reason? You should have one core reason to enter every trade in a market, industry group, or stock. It should be simple enough to convey to a ten-year-old. If you can't convey it simply or if you feel the need to engage in convoluted circular logic, then you don't have a ruling reason for being in the trade. So why are you there? If you crave action over profitability, you will find it.

In trading, you must probe your reasoning, especially when you are in a slump or find yourself stopping out of too many trades. Is your reasoning faulty, or are you just in a tougher period that calls for cutting back on trading in general? George Soros said it best when he commented that he's not a security analyst, but rather an insecurity analyst. You should never be stale or comfortable in your investment outlook. Keep asking, keep probing, but make sure that you have a ruling reason when you enter a trade. The reason you must do this is so you can easily see when your trade is going to work or if it may be in trouble. If your working investment assumption, your ruling reason, is proved invalid, you should immediately sell the position and move to the sidelines. If you have this ruling reason in place, you will have a barometer to check whether your rationale for entering a trade is still valid. If you don't have a thesis, a ruling reason, how do you know whether you are right or wrong? Traders are lucky in the sense that their theories can be carried out in real time with an objective measuring stick—price.

Setting Up Risk vs. Reward

On each trade you make, keep the big picture in mind. Remember: the goal is not necessarily to profit right now, from this market, but rather to understand how each trade fits into the bigger picture of your trading plan. With this viewpoint in mind, it becomes easier to take your small losses or pass on marginal trades, where the potential reward is not large enough to compensate for the potential loss. An example of a marginal trade, then, would be if your hypothetical gain is $2 per share as you anticipate a stock moving from $20 per share to $22 per share, while your potential risk is also $2 per share if your stop is placed at $18. Such a trade has a reward/risk ratio of 1:1. This type of trading leaves little margin for error over the longer run. You should only take trades where you have at least a theoretical 1:2 ratio, and I recommend 1:3 or higher for the bulk of your trading. Now, let's say that the stock you are looking at has run from $16 to $20 and is in a tight flag pattern, trading between $19 and $20, thereby allowing you to size up an attractive trade. The target price would be $24, while your stop could be placed at just under $19. In this case, your risk/reward ratio would be almost 1:4, yielding you large profits even if you are right only 50% of the time.

The latter theoretical trading situation is yet another reason you should trade liquid, leadership stocks. They make it easy to get out of the market, so that once your stop is hit, you see little slippage. On an illiquid name, on the other hand, if there is market slippage, your $1 stop could turn into $1.50 or more if you trade with any size. Also, a slow moving name probably won't give you the necessary theoretical upside to justify tying up your capital. If you are targeting a $1 profit, it isn't worth the time and risk in the long run. Experiment with a risk/reward ratio that works for your style, and you will put the odds in your favor over the long haul.

Swing Trading

The type of trade that is most likely to maximize the risk/reward equation is the swing trade. Swing trading is defined as trading with a time horizon that is roughly 1-12 weeks in length, and it essentially means trading markets over a shorter time period as they emerge from technical patterns that highlight the possibility of explosive short-term gains. The benefits of this style of trading are as follows: significant moves of 10-30% or more are possible in individual markets, and the style is such that ideas either emerge and show profits quickly or hit your stop-loss points and minimize any damage to your trading account. What's more, the trader employing this style keep herself, by definition, in tune with the markets' leaders at any given time and out of markets that don't show any ability to lead.

During bull markets, the potential for very explosive gains is noticeable, while in quiet markets the trader either is not engaged or is focused only on the few markets that are showing strength. The technical patterns I mention are such that the trader can readily recognize mistakes so that he can move safely back to cash when markets do not fulfill their technical implications. Swing trading allocates your capital very effectively by committing new cash only to situations that have the potential to generate very solid returns with well-defined risk. The balance works for those with the discipline to carry it out. Patience is the most underappreciated and undervalued commodity among amateur and seasoned traders alike—especially when it comes to swing trading.

The Best Patterns

Now to the heart of the matter! I have provided you with the framework and outlined the thought process you need in order to correctly approach trading so that you maximize the risk/reward equation. Now you'll learn about the patterns that provide the setups and opportunities traders prize. Technical analysis is the study of supply and demand in the marketplace. The core goal of technical analysis is to identify, via charts and indicators, whether buying or selling power is in control of the market at any given moment. The technician is not concerned with *why* buyers or sellers are in control, but with *who* is in control. As such, technical analysis deals with the supply/demand–based reality of the marketplace, not fundamentals or economic inputs. A chart is nothing more than the graphic snapshot of a multitude of investors stamping their buying or selling decisions upon the marketplace, and it is this snapshot that the technician analyzes. The great thing about charts is that patterns that worked in 1900 are just as likely to work in 2100. While the tools of the trade and the instruments traded may change, human psychology and supply and demand dynamics continue to work in much the same way. Trends will always be around in the markets, just as they always have been in fashion, art, and politics.

For the sake of clarity, I have divided this chapter into discussion of two main classes of chart patterns. The first is bases, or patterns that are characterized by longer periods of accumulation, distribution, or consolidation, where neither the buying nor selling interests are in control. Bases appear during sideways trends and in periods when a market is undergoing a state of change from an uptrend to a downtrend or a downtrend to an uptrend. Why is this so? Because it is during these periods that buyers and sellers slug it out in often long-drawn-out and dramatic battles. Some of these patterns mark bottoms and tops, while others are a pause within an existing primary uptrend or downtrend.

The second type of charts I will discuss is continuation patterns. Most of the patterns you will see in the continuation pattern section of this chapter use bullish examples, but these same patterns also occur in bear markets. The charts can be used for individual stocks, sectors, and the stock market as a whole. They also apply to commodities and financial futures, as well as any other publicly traded instrument. Depending on what additional resources you are reading or have read, you may see the same patterns I refer to in this book by one name given a different name in another resource. Where possible I have used the classic book *Technical Analysis of Stock Trends* by Robert D. Edwards, John Magee, and W.H.C. Bassetti (BN Publishing, 2008) as the basis for this book's terminology. For each pattern, I will define and describe its market dynamics, discuss the relevant trading tactics, and provide at least one example.

Bases and Bottoming/Topping Patterns

Bases and bottoming/topping patterns include the following: rectangle, double bottom/top, head and shoulders bottom/top, and rounding/bottom top. I describe each below, with examples.

Rectangle

Pattern: This pattern represents a period of indecision between buyers and sellers and typically occurs with lower volume and less violent swings than other bases. It is usually, but not always, preceded by a continuation pattern that marks a lengthy pause after an extended advance or decline. Volume will tend to taper off as a market extends throughout the pattern. Rectangles show a discernible range, where buying comes in at the lower end of the range and selling develops toward the upper end. Most rectangles last for four to eight weeks and occur after a strong prevailing move has run its course. In some cases, the rectangle can represent a bottom or top, although this is more prevalent with individual stocks than it is with futures markets.

Tactics: There are several ways to take advantage of a rectangle pattern. I should note that the trading moves that are most effective in concert with rectangles are not explosive and involve more of a hit-and-run style than other patterns. One method involves buying the market toward the bottom of the range and using a stop-loss just beneath the lower end of the range. This can be done more precisely if the trader waits for upside volume to appear after the market begins a bounce from the lower end of the range. The trader would then sell toward the top end of the range. Another tactic is simply to wait for the pattern to resolve itself on either the upside or downside of the range with a defined breakout. This is the better way to use these patterns. To confirm an upside breakout, the market should clear the range by at least 2%, and the move should be accompanied by a pickup in volume.

In Figure 3-1, you can see that following a dramatic selloff from $4.00 to $1.30, copper began a two-month rectangle consolidation pattern. Prices oscillated in a relatively tight $0.20 range from $1.40 to $1.60 before decisively breaking through this pattern in early March 2009. As with most bases, once the new trend was established, prices went on an extended, longer-lasting move. The initial gains were robust, with a 35% gain seen within six weeks of the breakout. The initial minimum technical target was $1.80, which is derived by taking the amount of the range of movement from high to low within the rectangle and adding this amount to the top end of the pattern. In this case

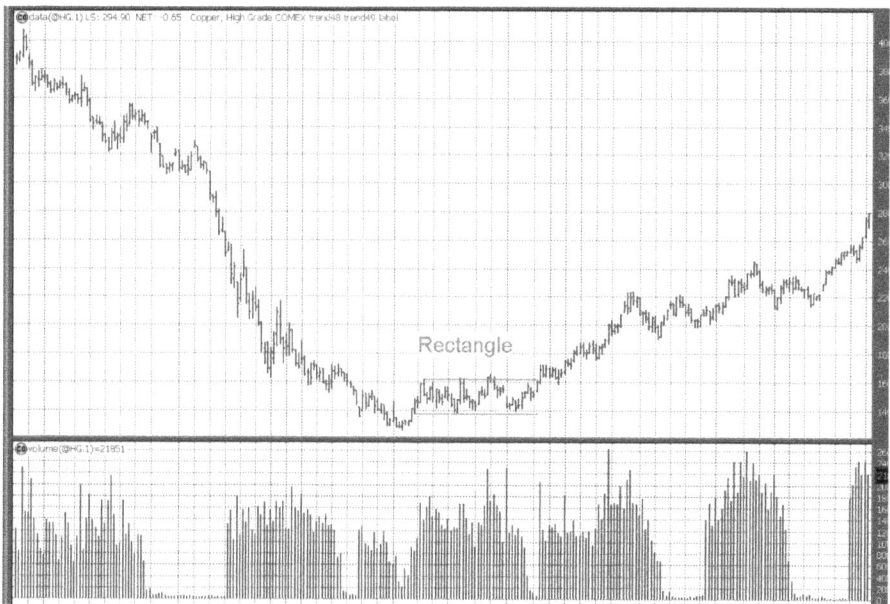

Figure 3-1. Copper showed a two-month rectangle consolidation pattern in 2008–09.

the amount was $1.60-$1.40 = $0.20, so the minimal target was $1.60+$0.20 = $1.80.

As you can see in Figure 3-2, crude oil witnessed many of the same dynamics as copper during this same period, as it is also an economically sensitive commodity. In the case of crude oil, the rectangle's base was longer and encompassed a three-and-a-half-month span. The range was $34 to $50, so the initial target upon completion of the pattern was $66 (50-34 = 16, and 50+16 = 66), and this level was reached rather quickly. Unlike the copper example in Figure 3-1, crude oil underwent a longer consolidation pattern once it broke through the range. You can see the month-long wedge and five-day flag pattern that followed the breakout from the rectangle's bottom. This is a typical example of a market's movement from the bottom of a rectangle, as buyers gain greater certainty once a trend is more firmly established in both time and price. Consolidation patterns like flags, triangles, and wedges are typically seen following the initial move from a bottom or top. Buyers and sellers typically pause and wait for confirmation of their views as an early bull or bear market gathers steam.

Double Bottom/Top

Pattern: A double bottom is a more emotional and violent pattern than the rectangle. These patterns typically take 4–12 weeks to resolve themselves

Chapter 3 | Setups and Chart Patterns

Figure 3-2. Crude oil showed a longer rectangle and longer consolidation pattern in 2008–09.

and usually involve an explosive expansion in volume, especially at the low points of the pattern. There is a large turnover in holders as fear takes hold of selling interests, and the market is accumulated by smart money into weakness. (Smart money is defined as those who are ultimately proved right!) Volume will tend to run at least 50% above the prevailing three-month average, and typically some headline news issue drives the day-to-day trading movements and provides the rationale for panicked selling. The left side of the double bottom will typically exhibit the greatest volume, and then a rally will develop that emboldens some sloppy buying. The market will then sell off again to probe the area of the prior low. It is not important whether this retest results in slightly lower or higher prices—and I actually prefer token new lows, as they induce more panic selling. The market then re-rallies on higher-quality internals and solid volume. Once the market or stock surpasses the highest point of the pattern, it completes the lows. The inverse happens with a top; simply reverse the emotional pull from fear to greed. You will see these patterns mark the ends of both primary and secondary market swings. There are also triple bottoms that form from time to time, but they are not nearly as common.

Tactics: You can employ various tactics when confronted with a double bottom, depending on your time frame. For the more intermediate-term player, I recommend accumulation on both the retest of the prior lows and again on the completion of the pattern. The swing trader should be on the lookout for the stocks that decline the least and show relative strength on the retest. These stocks should then be purchased and added to on breakouts. You should exercise patience to wait for the pattern to run its course. Extremely high volatility on both an intraday and day-to-day basis is to be expected, making the use of stop-loss orders costly. It is for this reason that I advocate waiting for the retest and trading the strongest markets. For double tops, the opposite would apply.

The double bottom shown in Figure 3-3 marked the end of a short but vicious bear market decline in the fall of 1998. The decline from the peak in July to the first low occurred in less than two months but took the S&P 500 down over 22%. Fear was palpable during this decline, and rumors of financial instability at major brokerage houses were rampant. A solid rally from the low at point (A) ensued. This rally carried the index back to the August resistance at 1,060 before it failed and the markets rolled over. You can see that volume at point (a) was dramatically higher. After the market decline, buyers returned near prior levels, but you'll see that the second low undercut the initial lows. Volume was materially less at point (b) than it was at point (a). Prices on the second low modestly undercut the initial low, although some double bottoms see the second low hold at higher levels.

In my experience, it is preferable to have modest new lows put in, as this shakes out the weaker holders and paves the way for stronger gains. The key

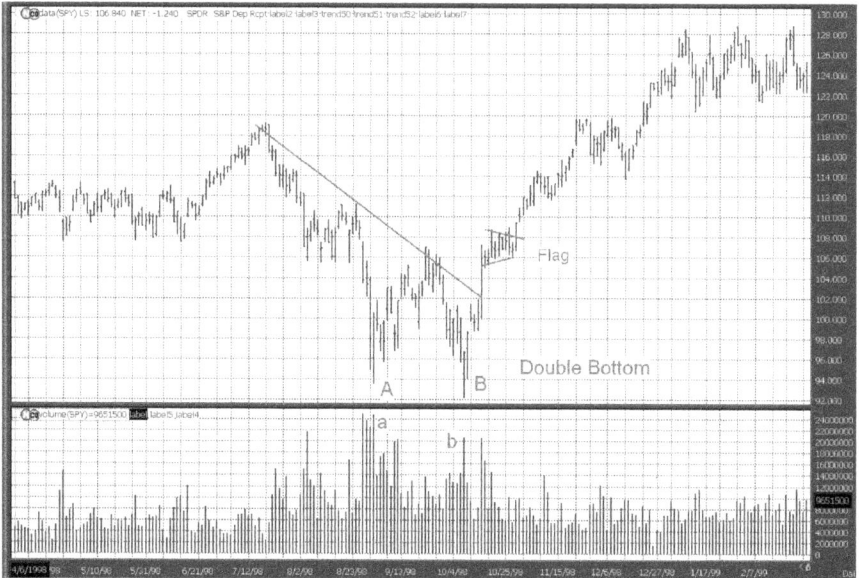

Figure 3-3. Double bottom in S&P 500 marked the end of a short but vicious bear market decline in 1998.

is that volume should be less on the retest—and that is the case in this example. The double-bottom pattern is complete once the rally peak after the first low has been exceeded. You can see that this was accomplished by October 1998 and occurred on sharply higher volume—a real plus. A flag pattern then developed, and its tightness indicated a lack of further selling pressure. You can see that prices promptly rallied extremely sharply, with the stock market making new all-time highs by the end of the year. Bottoms that occur in this fashion tend to be news-dominated and carry high emotional swings. It is best not to trade these patterns until they are coming off the second low so that the most violent moves are behind you. If you trade before this occurs, it is likely that any stop you use will be taken out as the market spasms from one extreme to the next. Patience during this formation is important, as the risks are typically highest with this type of pattern.

The double top shown in Figure 3-4 marked the end of the largest investment mania of modern times—the dot-com craze of 1999-2000. The gains and losses during this time period were simply spectacular. From October 1999 to the peak of the mania in January 2000, the HHH (Merrill Lynch Internet HOLDRS Trust), or Internet ETF, rallied 85%! The index then engaged in a 30% pullback before it led a final assault to token new highs at the $187 level. You can see that volume at point (a) is much higher than the lackluster volume at point (b). This was a clear sign that true demand was lacking on this second

Figure 3-4. Double top in 2000 marked the end of the dot-com craze.

high. Volume accelerated dramatically once the internet stocks began to sell off from this peak as panic selling ensued. Prices gave up their entire 85% rally in one of the more dramatic rises and falls that the markets may ever see.

The market gyrations caused by the dot-com craze showed a perfect display of weak volume forming on the second peak and were a clear indication that buying power was waning. Once a double top is completed, a move that has taken years to build can unravel in weeks—which is exactly why it is so important to monitor volume configuration as the double-top pattern is forming.

The double top in the Euro STOXX 50, shown in Figure 3-5, formed from January to May 2011 and presaged the European bank and sovereign liquidity crisis, which erupted in the fall of that year. The market peaked in February, underwent a 10% correction, and then rallied back to its prior high, failing to exceed the first high marked at point (A). The market then slowly rolled back down, and a large top formed. This top was broken with violence in August, and the measured move was down to 2,100. This target, which was taken by measuring the top from the neckline of support, was quickly reached, as the market simply crashed.

Figure 3-5. Double top in the Euro STOXX 50 presaged the European bank and sovereign liquidity crisis in 2011.

Chapter 3 | Setups and Chart Patterns

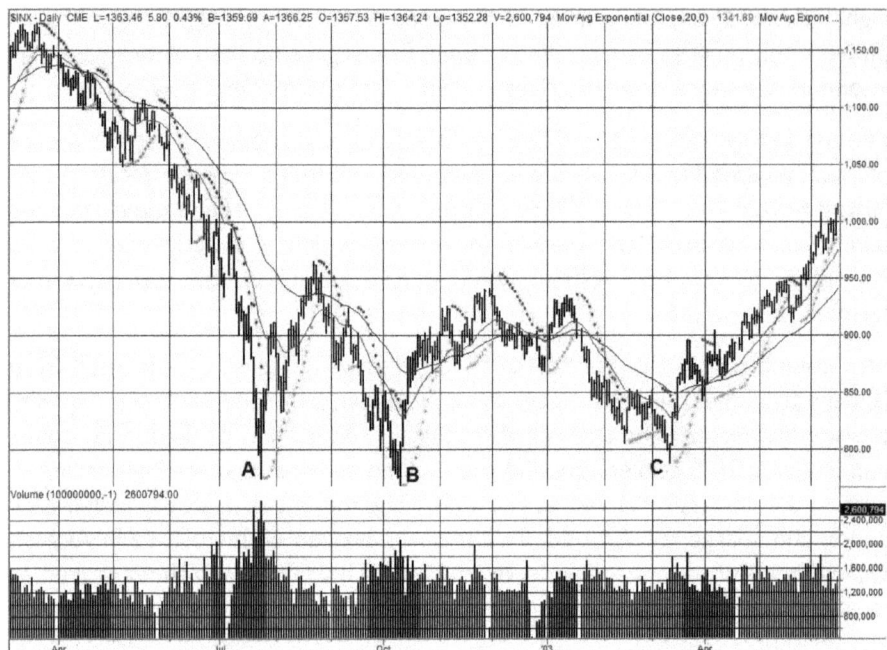

Figure 3-6. Triple bottom marked the bear market of the S&P 500 -2002-2003.

The lengthy and volatile triple bottom you see in Figure 3-6 marked the longest bear market since the 1973 to 1974 period. There is symmetry to market movements, and the reason this bottom lasted so long and endured such chaotic swings was because of the length and depth of the bear market that preceded it. Investors who had piled their life savings into stocks and mutual funds in the late 1990s had never witnessed a protracted bear market. The two-year, 40% decline led to record mutual fund outflows. Assurances and promises made to investors that the bear market would end in 2000, 2001, and early 2002 were thoroughly dismissed by March of 2003, and pessimism ruled the investment world. Fear was running rampant, and the Federal Reserve was desperate to kick-start the economy and stock market.

The great bear finally bottomed out in July 2008 at point (A), but it would be another eight long months before the third and final bottom was in place at point (C). Typical of panic environments, you can see that the rally from the first low at point (A) was impressive, with a rise of over 20% in just one month. Hopes were quickly dashed, though, as the markets retested the original lows, and another 20% rally ensued over the next two months. Finally, with war in Iraq looming, the markets headed lower again into point (C). This would prove to be the lowest low, with the market simply exploding higher over the next five months.

Head and Shoulders Bottom/Top

Pattern: The head and shoulders bottom is a complex and lengthy technical pattern. Typically lasting for 4–12 weeks but extending longer on occasion, this pattern is marked by three rally peaks and looks like a person's left and right shoulders, with a head in the middle. The left shoulder will typically exhibit the highest volume on its rally. A pullback will ensue but will be checked by more buying interest coming in. This buying interest will then show signs of deterioration, even though the rally will carry the market to new highs. Volume will be lighter and the internal strength (or advance-decline line, in the case of the stock market) will usually show negative divergences. This occurs because the bulk of the market is already deteriorating. The market thus moves higher under a false guise of strength only to later pull back and hold near the previous sell–off point. Buying interests once again come in, and another rally ensues.

It is this rally that is important to watch, as another low-quality rally is a sign that it's time to become strongly defensive. Volume will be poor, typically the lowest of the three tops. Internals will be noticeably worse than before and in some cases will show outright retreat under the surface. Selling pressure will come in again and will show a notable uptick in downside volume. This is a sure sign of more weakness to come. A brief pause at the now-formed neckline will sometimes, but not always, appear. A high-volume break confirms the pattern, and a measured count can be taken to propose a minimal downside target. The measured move is taken by using the distance from the neckline to the head and extending this number under the neckline.

Tactics: As the pattern implies, the weakness in the head and shoulders pattern begins to show during the formation of the head. On this weakness the prior leaders will tend to lag and break down, which is the first signal to lighten up. Traders should reduce their exposure throughout the pattern and exit completely or short on a break in the neckline.

Head and shoulders bottoms are just as common as tops, and the volume patterns and characteristics are very similar. Since these patterns mark the beginning and end of bull markets, the first moves upon completion of the pattern can be very explosive and profitable. The key is to wait for the pattern to near its end and to exhibit the patience to hold through the first stage of the advance. The volatility will lessen toward the end of the pattern, which provides excellent opportunities to initiate new positions. The target for the move upon completion is taken by measuring the distance between the tip of the head and the neckline of the pattern and then adding this to the neckline. As an example, if a market makes a low of 40 and the neckline is 50, then 50-40 = 10 points. These 10 points are then added to the neckline to get 50+10, or a target of 60 for the ensuing advance.

Chapter 3 | Setups and Chart Patterns

The classic head and shoulders bottom pictured in Figure 3-7 marked the end of a vicious bear market in the bond market in 1994. Prices formed their ultimate lows at 75, with a well-defined neckline at 79, implying a minimal measured upside target of 83 once the pattern was completed. This initial target was reached in less than two months. A perfect triangle formed after the completion of the bottom, and once this triangle ran its course, prices simply exploded to the upside in one of the more dramatic bond moves in recent memory. This rally helped fuel a broad stock market advance that lasted over five years.

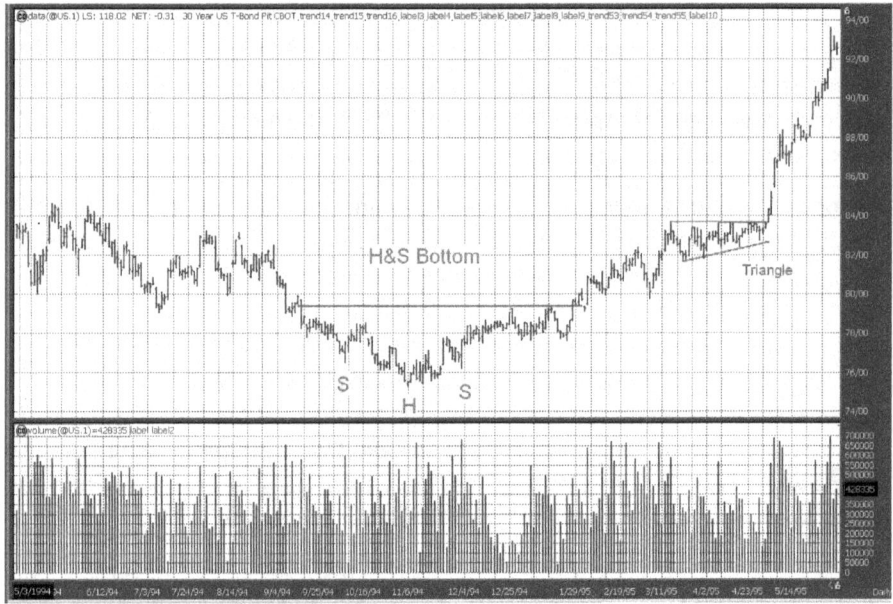

Figure 3-7. Head and shoulders bottom marked the end of a large bond bear market in 1994.

The bottoming formation in Figure 3-7 took four months to complete and came at the end of a large bond bear market, which makes sense, since head and shoulders patterns tend to come at the end of long rallies or declines and typically mark the beginning of a longer-term move. The patterns also tend to occur over many months as the necessary shift in sentiment and turnover in holder base become long-drawn-out affairs.

From 2003 to 2007, a bubble in credit- and housing-related activity took the United States by storm. The factors that fed the ravenous lending activity were myriad and included overly accommodative monetary policy, regulatory failings, governmental incentives, and ultimately the greed of consumers, bankers, and politicians. When the bubble burst in 2008, the carnage in credit ravaged global markets. Banks and a host of pseudo-financial firms that were spawned to feed the hunger for easy credit suffered far in advance of the underlying economy and other sectors in the market.

Figure 3-8 shows the head and shoulders top in Citigroup, which took almost four months to complete. You can see that once the neckline at $50 was undercut on heavier volume, the highs were in. The stock then formed a three-month-long rectangle pattern as buyers and sellers again waged war to determine the next trend. This time, as prices broke the rectangle to the downside, the selling pressure burst like water through a broken dam to the downside. Again, you can see that as prices get further away from the ultimate highs of the consolidation pattern, the price movements accelerate in both direction and timing. This happens because the level of conviction in the new trend gathers force and acceptance among market participants.

Figure 3-8. Head and shoulders top appeared in Citigroup before housing bubble burst.

The chart of the Dow Jones Industrial Transport Average shown in Figure 3-9 is one of the most classic head and shoulders patterns you will ever see. The neckline at 2,600 is clearly delineated, marking numerous trading lows over the six-month span of the top. The top of the pattern is 3,050, so the measured move for the minimal downside target was 2,150 (3,050-2,600 = 450; 2,600-450 = 2,150). This initial target was quickly met in a few short weeks.

As Figures 3-8 and 3-9 demonstrate, head and shoulders patterns, as well as the others, can play out in a number of different ways. Some patterns take

Chapter 3 | Setups and Chart Patterns

Figure 3-9. The DJIA showed a classic head and shoulders pattern from January 2002 to June 2002.

many months to play out, while others offer instant gratification to those who heed their messages.

Rounding Bottom/Top

Pattern: This pattern is also relatively lengthy, running 4–12 weeks or longer. A rounding bottom is generally marked by lighter volume throughout the pattern, with more volume coming on the initial sell-off and toward the end as the market rallies. A market will typically pause and consolidate toward the end of the pattern before it breaks out and completes the rounding bottom. Rounding bottoms and tops have been popularized by William O'Neil and many other traders, who refer to it as a cup-and-handle pattern. The pattern can mark either a bottom or a top or function as a consolidation phase, particularly in explosive markets. Supply and demand in this pattern are generally more in balance, with less volatility than in head and shoulders patterns or double bottoms/tops, but that is not always the case.

Tactics: This is a very profitable pattern to trade, as the risk/reward characteristics are extremely attractive. In the early and middle stages of a bull market, traders can see these patterns in abundance, and they should take full advantage of them. The most profitable setups occur when the pattern is nearing its completion and consolidates just before breaking out.

The volume that carries the market to its breakout point will typically confirm the movement with a surge in interest. As the market consolidates, volume will taper off. It is at this point that the trader should be ready, willing, and able to fire at will on the next high-volume breakout. Once the base is cleared, volume will tend to accelerate. These patterns are typically seen in growth stock leaders and momentum markets and can carry the market to significant gains.

Like most major bottoms, the rounding bottom for Whole Foods shown in Figure 3-10 took considerable time to run its course. From the dramatic decline from $20 in October 2008 to the bottom in November at $7, to the upside resolution in March, this pattern represented a six-month duel between buying and selling interests. Within this pattern, you can observe several nuances as demand began to slowly take control of supply. The first was the higher high of $13 per share set with the rally in January. From there, prices fell back into the area of the former lows, near $9 per share. The most definitive sign that the bull market in the shares was set to resume was the large 20% upside gap in February that occurred on the second highest volume of the year. Prices then held firm in a wedge pattern—an impressive show of strength, given the bear market that was still raging in the broad stock market. Upon completion of the pattern with the move through $13, the initial technical target could be arrived at by adding the width of the pattern to the top end of the range. In this case, that target was $19 ($13-$7 = $6; $13+6 = $19), which was quickly met by late April.

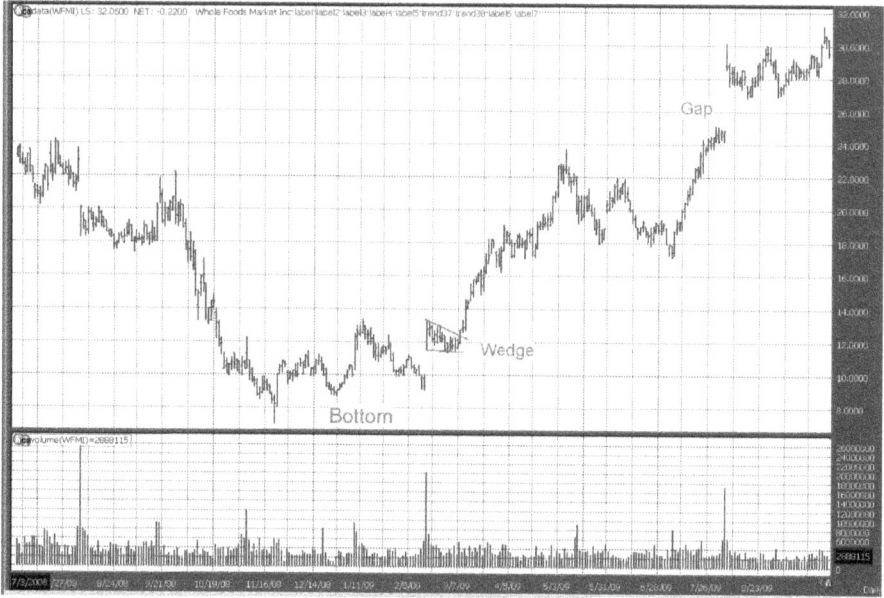

Figure 3-10. Whole Foods rounding bottom in 2008–09 took a long time to run its course.

Chapter 3 | Setups and Chart Patterns

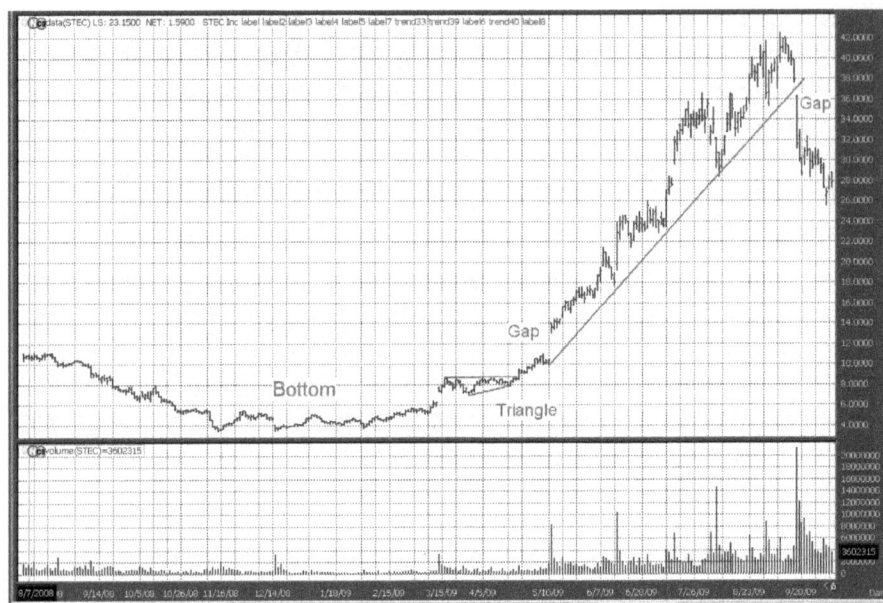

Figure 3-11. STEC, Inc. rounding bottom in 2008–09

Figure 3-11, showing activity in the shares of STEC, Inc., is another typical example of a rounding bottom, with prices trading in a rounded pattern for five months. The stock then emerged on an impressive burst of volume in an upside gap, marking the end of the bottom and the beginning of a new trend. In this case, that trend was quite strong, as prices simply exploded from $8 to $40 in five short months. Upside gaps played a large role in this upswing, as a continuation gap in March quickly accelerated the bull move.

The rounding bottom shown in Figure 3-11 bears out the premise that good trading comes from waiting for patterns to resolve themselves, as gains from consolidation patterns can accrue rapidly for those with the patience to wait for a pattern's completion. Traders who enter the market in the midst of one of these patterns are more likely to be shaken out or, worse, trapped in a market that doesn't complete this pattern in a positive manner. In your trading, focus on relative strength and clear patterns for your capital.

Figure 3-12 shows a rounding bottom in Research In Motion that is typical of a growth stock. In this case, the rounding bottom marked the end of a correction that took the stock back to a support area. The duration of the bottom was therefore shorter and well defined, lasting four months and marked by lows near $20 and the top at $26. At the end of the pattern, a flag marked a pause in the action before the rounding bottom resolved itself to the upside on a good burst of volume. Note also that the downtrend was broken in June as the stock gasped higher on another uptick in trading activity.

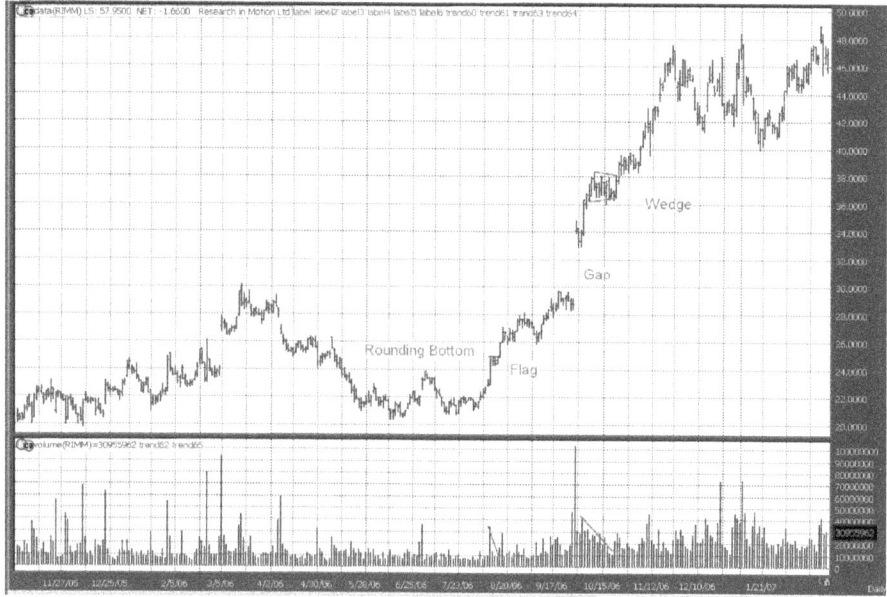

Figure 3-12. Research In Motion rounding bottom in 2005–07.

After the stock broke through to complete the bottom, it accelerated higher in a dramatic upside gap that was accompanied by the largest volume day of the year. This breakaway gap began a lengthy bull market in the stock. It is common to see this type of rounding bottom in the middle of bull markets, as different stocks and sectors undergo normal midcycle corrections.

Continuation Patterns

The three types of continuation patterns are flag, wedge, and triangle patterns.

Flag

Pattern: This pattern, which looks like a flag fluttering in the wind, represents a brief pause in a strongly trending market, usually occurring as a bull or bear market is more advanced and moving along with either buyers or sellers in control. A bull flag is a consolidation pattern typically marking the halfway point of a swing trade. Flags are great short-term trading patterns and carry solid risk/reward profiles. In a typical flag, a stock will have advanced into the pattern on a solid amount of volume. Buyers are in control of the market, and fast moves in leading stocks are the rule. Volume will then taper off as the stock consolidates for a short time. These patterns are the shortest in duration, typically occupying two to seven days of trading activity, and since they pattern the midpoint of a stock's move, a technical trader can set a profit objective equal to the point move coming into the flag. When volume accelerates to the top end of the flag and the price hits a new high, the pattern is complete, and the stock should be on its way.

Tactics: Flag patterns are easy to spot, very profitable, and sport excellent risk/reward characteristics because they occur in well-defined bull and bear moves, where either buyers or sellers are in control. There should be little doubt about what type of market you're in when you see flag patterns. Risk/reward is excellent because the stop point is well defined at the low end of the flag, while the upside moves are explosive, with the potential for very profitable trades. The volume characteristics are well defined, with volume high on the move preceding the flag, low within the flag, and accelerating again on the breakout from the flag. In a healthy market, these patterns should be traded aggressively, with long entry on a move through the flag accompanied by high volume. Stops are set at the low end of the flag.

The move should happen quickly or not at all, so selling out is straightforward. The targeted profit should be set so that the flag is at the halfway point of the move. As an example, if a stock moves strongly from $40 to $45 on high volume and then pauses for three to four days between $44 and $45, the measured target would be $50 ($45-$40 = $5, $45+$5 = $50). Keep in mind that flags work well in bear markets as well.

Those who traded during the late 1990s will remember what a unique environment it was for aggressive trading. Flag patterns are the patterns of momentum moves in stocks, and in Figure 3-13, which tracks the period between late 1999 and early 2000, you can see two clearly marked flags. The first flag appeared in November and carried Yahoo! to new highs on a move to $50. This was a $5 move, so the short-term target was $55, which was calculated by adding the preceding move of $5 (from $45 to $50) to $50 in order to arrive at the $55 target. Yahoo!'s target was met quickly—as must be the case if the flag pattern is valid.

Flags are great short-term patterns for a few reasons: the target is clear, the stop is well defined, and the pattern works either quickly or not at all. For Yahoo! the next flag was more dramatic and was defined by the consolidation pattern at $85, which occurred after a monster move from $55 to $85. This implied a measured move to $115 ($85-$55 = $30; $85+$30 = $115). In the end, the target was met in only nine trading days, again highlighting the value of flag patterns for the short-term trader. Note that volume was relatively poor on the move to $115, an early warning sign to the technical analyst.

In major uptrends, it is common to see multiple continuation patterns as a stock experiences its most explosive price gains. As you can see in Figure

Tactical Trend Trading

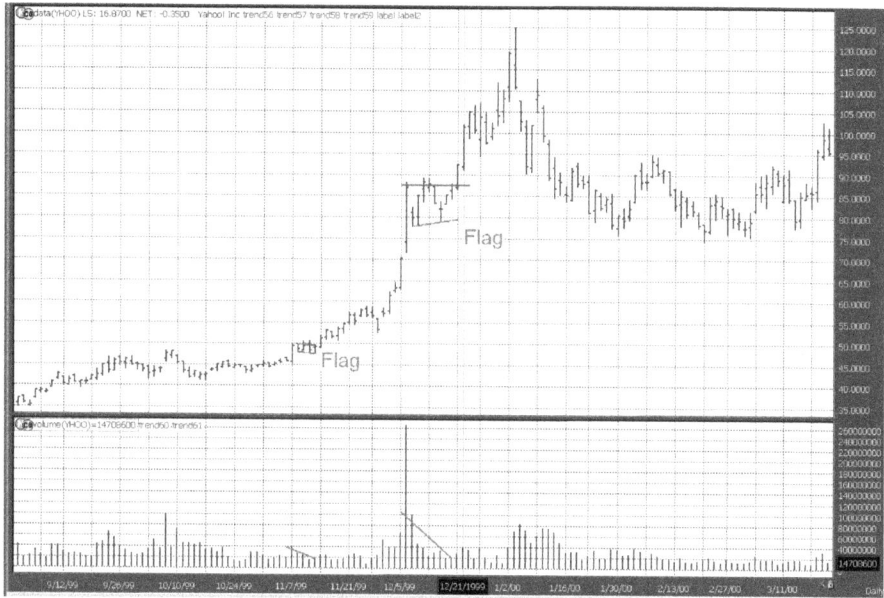

Figure 3-13. Yahoo! stock showed two flags between September 1999 and March 2000.

3-14, this was the case with Google as it moved from $100 in August 2004 to $200 by early November! The first flag came at the $120 level, as the stock paused for a few days before accelerating anew. The measured target for this first flag was $140, which was met in six trading sessions. The next flag consolidated this move at $140 and carried a minimum measurement of $160, a target that, again, was met in less than ten trading days. The stock then underwent a more lengthy consolidation with a failed breakout attempt along the way in January 2005. The final flag occurred in April 2005 as the stock posted a continuation gap on massive volume. This last flag consolidated the gain from $180 to $220, so the minimum measured target was $260. The behavior of Google shares shown in Figure 3-14 is typical of the movements seen in explosive growth stocks.

For the next example, turn your attention to the flag patterns in Figure 3-15. As you can see, after breaking out of a three-month consolidation on impressive volume, Cisco consolidated its gains in a three-day flag pattern at the $42 level. The move into the flag carried the stock price from $36 to $42, so the measured target was $48, which was met in seven days. The price movement in Figure 3-15 shows why flag patterns are the perfect technical pattern to trade for explosive short-term moves. They can provide enormous short-term percentage gains and carry excellent risk/reward characteristics, and, as shown in Figure 3-15, even volume considerations were ideal in the initial flag. A few months later, in February 2000, another flag developed. This

Chapter 3 | Setups and Chart Patterns

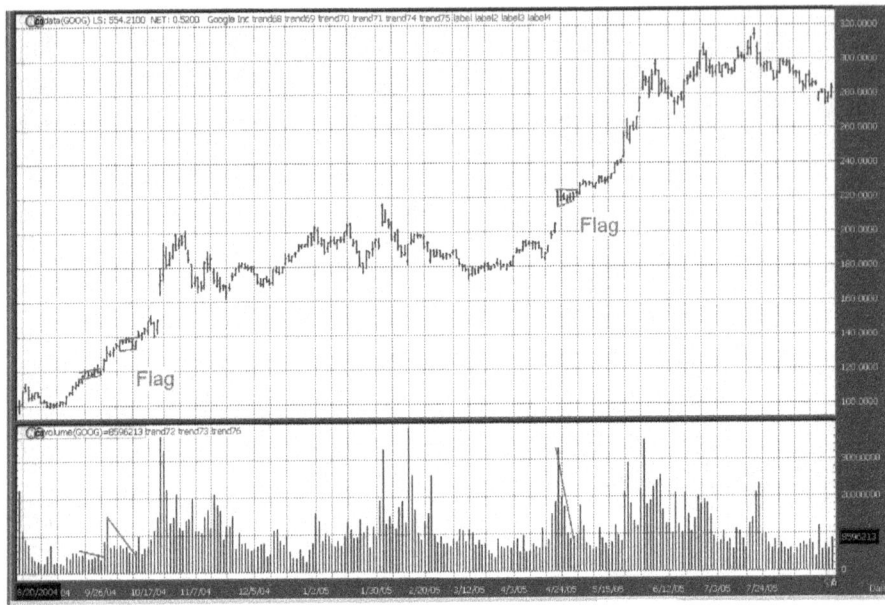

Figure 3-14. Google showed multiple continuation patterns as it posted huge gains in 2004–05.

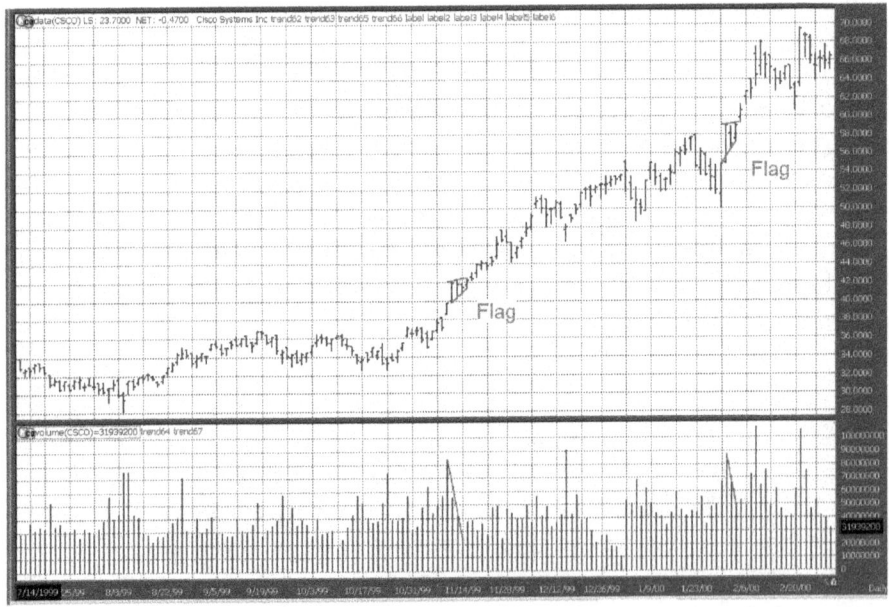

Figure 3-15. Cisco movement in 1999–2000 demonstrates why flag patterns are ideal for explosive short-term moves.

flag marked the halfway point in the stock's move from $50 to $68, and volume was again ideal in confirming the validity of the pattern.

Explosive technical patterns can be witnessed in cyclical stocks as well. As shown in Figure 3-16, U.S. Steel experienced two consecutive flag patterns after the stock emerged from a multimonth base in mid-2007. The second of the two patterns occurred after U.S. Steel moved from $125 to $145 in a few short days. The stock flagged and volume characteristics were ideal, with large volume on the move higher and light volume within the flag pattern. The measured target was $165, which was met one month later. While it took longer for the second flag in Figure 3-16 to meet its measured target than it takes most flag patterns, it is important to realize that each situation is moderately different. In this example, the low end of the flag was $140, and this would have served as the stop point once a long position was taken. Another thing to note is how quickly the stock began to decline through the $170 level in July 2008, a circumstance that highlights the necessity of protecting gains with a selling discipline once a trend reverses course.

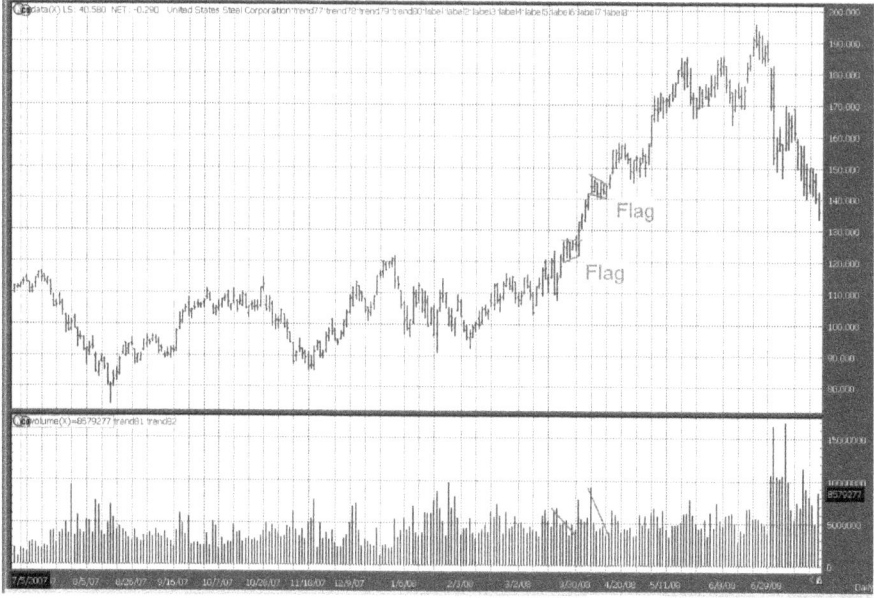

Figure 3-16. U.S. Steel showed explosive gains through two flag patterns.

Wedge

Pattern: A wedge is similar to a flag but has some notable differences. First, a wedge is longer in duration than a flag and will typically show more of a pullback in price. The usual duration of a wedge is one to three weeks, and it

Chapter 3 | Setups and Chart Patterns

is marked by a channel and decreasing volume throughout. As the stock emerges from the pattern, volume will again accelerate. Declining wedges are typical in bull markets and rising wedges are common in bear markets.

Tactics: Like flags, wedges are great patterns for the technical trader. Their setup gives you a good risk/reward ratio, and their consolidation leaves a well-defined entry point. This buy point should be just over the upper channel formed by the wedge and should be accompanied by a sharp increase in volume as the stock emerges from its downward-sloping channel.

Wedges are useful in trading growth stocks and can lead to sharp moves in a good market. The stop should be set at the low point of the breakout day; otherwise, a percentage stop can be used. Normally stops should not be placed at the low end of the pattern unless the pattern is very tight. As a market rotates among leaders, different sectors will pause at different times, so as one group emerges from a wedge, another group may enter a wedge pattern. It is during such times that a trader can allocate capital very effectively.

Wedge patterns are just as beneficial as flags for the tactical trend trader. They are similar technical configurations, with the same outstanding risk/reward characteristics. The two wedge patterns in Amazon, as shown in Figure 3-17, are representative of this type of setup. The first wedge occurred on the back of a large breakaway gap that broke the stock's prior downtrend and carried Amazon to $65 per share in early 2009. The wedge pattern lasted

Figure 3-17. Amazon's wedge patterns in 2008–09 were ideal for the tactical trend trader.

several weeks, with volume tapering off within this wedge. Prices then leapt through the top end of the wedge on expanding volume.

This setup was an ideal pattern for the tactical trend trader. The measured target was $80, which was determined by the calculating the height of the move coming into the wedge ($65-$50 = $15) and then adding that amount to the breakout from the wedge pattern. In this case, that target was $65+$15 = $80, a level that was quickly met before the stock went into another wedge pattern in April. This second wedge was more steeply sloped on the downside, indicating more selling pressure coming into the stock. Again, prices quickly rallied once they broke through the declining wedge.

Now let's take a look at our next wedge example. Coal stocks were market leaders in 2004, and as you can see in Figure 3-18, Peabody Energy played right along with the group. The stock entered into a wedge pattern in November 2004 and then consolidated the strong move from $13 per share. You can see that volume was ideal, with strong turnover into the new high and much more subdued activity once it was within this consolidation pattern. Once the stock price broke through the wedge to the upside, it accelerated to $20 before undergoing another pause.

The trade setup in Figure 3-18 would have given you an excellent risk/reward ratio. Once you were long at $16, you could then have placed a trailing stop at $15, and with a minimum target of $19 ($16-$13 = $3; $16+$3 = $19),

Figure 3-18. Peabody Energy offered an excellent risk/reward ratio in 2004–05.

your reward/risk would have been at least 3:1. This type of setup is what makes wedges such profitable trading patterns. In Figure 3-18, you can see the development of multiple flag patterns as the stock continued its uptrend throughout the year.

Figure 3-19 shows the price action for natural gas in 2011–12. After making a top in the $4.50 area, natural gas went sideways for six weeks before it resumed its downside move. The commodity made a couple of wedge patterns during the ensuing decline, with the first occurring in October 2011. The downside target for this first wedge was $3.50, as the wedge at $4.00 had formed after a decline from $4.50. The second wedge at $3.50 also carried a $0.50 downside target, in this case to the $3.00 area, which was met only one month later. Figure 3-19 shows that the price of natural gas was clear in its technical patterns and stayed in a tight downtrend channel during its six-month decline. At no point was there any bottoming action that would have suggested from a technical basis that traders should take a bullish stance.

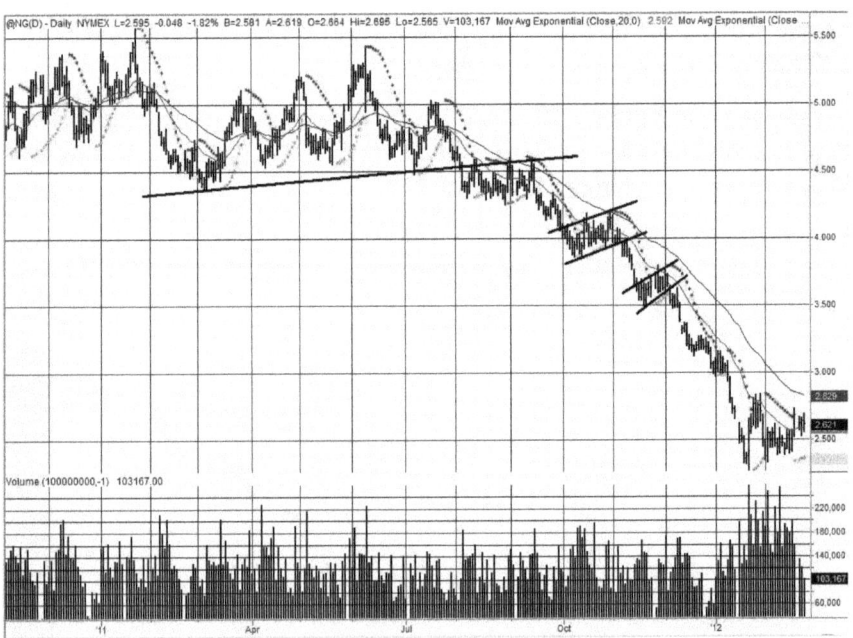

Figure 3-19. Natural gas price decline in 2011–12 showed clear wedge patterns.

Just as you saw in Figure 3-18 that coal stocks were market leaders during 2004 and 2005, the housing sector was also a leadership group during that period, as can be seen in the chart of Toll Brothers in Figure 3-20. Toll Brothers formed its first wedge in November 2004 as it broke out to new highs on a breakaway gap accompanied by extremely high volume that exploded to the

Figure 3-20. Toll Brothers showed very bullish wedge formations in 2004–05.

highest levels of the year. This action was incredibly bullish, and such actions should always merit a second look from astute growth traders. The measured target was $32, which was met only five days after Toll Brothers broke out of its first wedge pattern. As a general rule, the more quickly and perfectly technical targets are reached, the more bullish the stock is for traders. After meeting the first target, the stock then made a rising wedge pattern, which is both an unusual and an extremely bullish formation, as it indicates buying interests are in complete control. The minimum target for this second wedge pattern was $41 ($34-$27 = $7; $34+$7 = $41), and once again this target was met quickly. As Figure 3-20 demonstrates, wedges, much like flag patterns, are the most prevalent patterns within strongly trending growth and momentum stocks.

Triangle

Pattern: In trend trading, triangle patterns look like a geometric triangle, and come in one of three forms: symmetrical, ascending, or descending. Triangles are normally continuation patterns but may, on occasion, act as reversal patterns and signal a short-term change in trend. They are normally two to four weeks long and exhibit volume patterns similar to a wedge, with volume tapering off throughout the pattern only to accelerate as the stock emerges on either side.

Chapter 3 | Setups and Chart Patterns

A symmetrical triangle moves to a perpendicular point with narrower and narrower price swings. For the symmetrical triangle pattern to be valid, the stock or commodity will normally emerge about two-thirds to three-quarters of the way through the triangle on a burst of volume. An ascending triangle, on the other hand, will be marked by a horizontal line at the top end of the pattern and a rising line at the low end. Finally, a descending triangle will show a horizontal line at the low end of the pattern and a falling line at the top end. In all three, volume and trading characteristics are otherwise similar. Normally, in the case of ascending and descending triangles, the triangle will resolve in the direction of the horizontal line.

Tactics: In order to successfully trade a triangle pattern, you must wait for the triangle to advance toward its apex. You need to check volume to make sure it is generally quiet as the pattern is forming. Unlike with flags and wedges, you should also be careful to avoid assumptions about the direction of the breakout. For ascending and descending triangles, your trading bias should be to buy the breakout of the horizontal line, while with symmetrical triangles your general trading bias should be to look for a continuation of the ongoing trend. You should wait for both an increase in volume and a breakout of the triangle pattern before committing capital in the direction of the price movement.

In Figure 3-21 you can see two perfect bearish triangle patterns form in the S&P 500 during the credit crunch of 2008. The first was a three-month-long

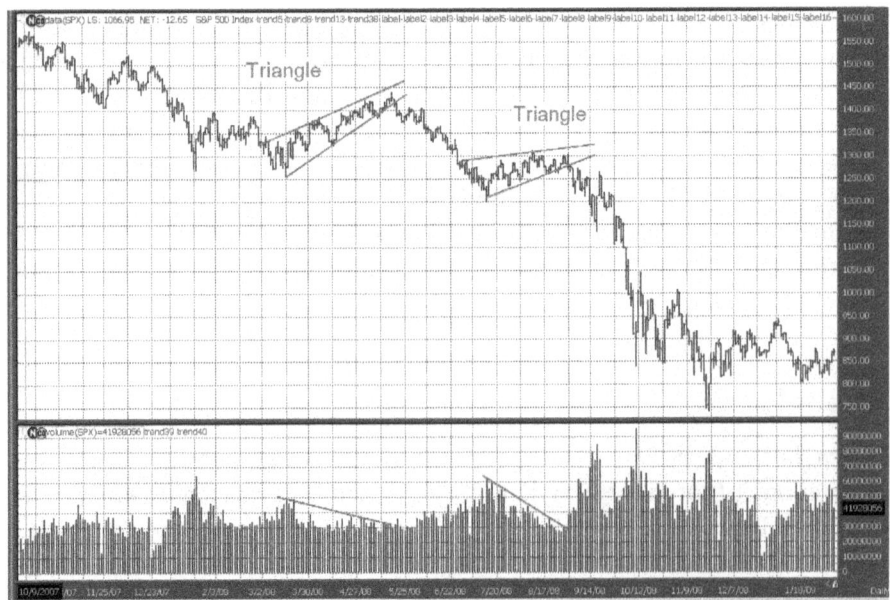

Figure 3-21. The S&P 500 showed two perfect bearish triangle patterns during the 2008 credit crunch.

rising triangle pattern, and you can see that the range of movement within that pattern was more compressed as the triangle evolved. Several reversal days were also evident during the last month of the pattern as the market tested the top end of the triangle, and these reversals were further evidence of distribution under the guise of strength. Once prices broke through on the downside, the resumption of the downward trend in stock prices gathered force.

The second triangle was two months long, and you can see that the volume pattern was ideal as activity dried up into the triangle. Once prices broke through the triangle on the downside, volume accelerated sharply, and soon thereafter the market crashed into October. Note that the downtrend line of the stock market coincided with the end of both triangle patterns.

Next turn your attention to Figure 3-22, which shows a textbook case of a reversal triangle pattern in copper. After suffering a 31% decline from July to October 2011, copper began a three-month triangle pattern characterized by lower highs and higher lows. The chart pattern also showed a few positive developments that supported a bullish resolution to this pattern. First, the Commitments of Traders (COT) commercial data were very bullish, showing a large increase in positions during this several-month-long decline in price. Second, you'll notice that downside momentum was lessening while MACD

Figure 3-22. Copper in 2012–12 was a textbook case of a reversal triangle pattern.

Chapter 3 | Setups and Chart Patterns

averages were bottoming, with the short-term average signaling a buy in copper by January. Triangle patterns typically resolve themselves two-thirds of the way through the pattern, so this triangle was overdue for a move in one direction or the other. The decisive break through $3.55 was the buy signal, and the measured target to $3.95 was met within six short weeks.

In Figure 3-23, silver shows what a star performer it was in 2010. After a good run from its lows in 2009, silver spent many months moving sideways in spite of a very bullish fundamental backdrop. From May to August 2010, it consolidated in a four-month triangle pattern just under the prior high of $20. In August it broke out, and in September it posted new highs—and there is nothing more bullish than new highs for a market. Once you see new highs, patience should be your mantra in holding a long position. Silver's August breakout measured a target of $22, which was quickly met. You can see that there were no notable corrections until November, which saw a pullback from $29 to $25.50. By April 2011, silver traded to $50 for an impressive gain of 150% from the initial breakout at $20.

Figure 3-23. Silver was a star performer in 2010 with a four-month triangle pattern, followed by a breakout.

My next example features Apple, which was one of the leaders in the great NASDAQ move of 2009. As shown in Figure 3-24, the stock exhibited excellent relative strength versus the broad market in March, as it held above

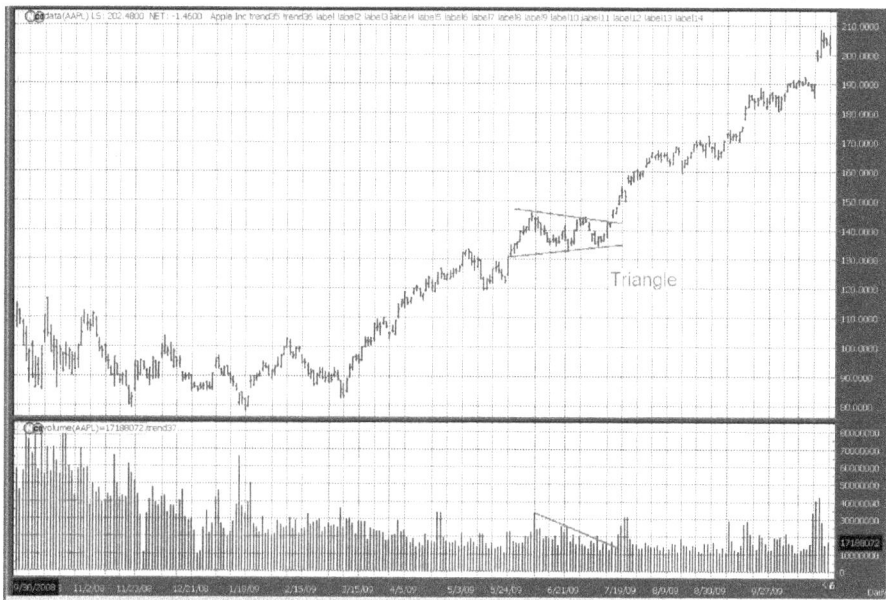

Figure 3-24. Apple showed numerous flag and wedge patterns in 2009.

its fall lows while the S&P was down 25% at the same point! This is extremely bullish activity. Once it crossed the $100 mark in March, the stock then broke its downtrend and began a new bullish trend. In June the stock entered a symmetrical triangle pattern, and volume was ideal during the consolidation. As prices broke out of the triangle, volume picked up and prices resumed their uptrend. The measured target for this move was $170, which was quickly met. As is typical in strongly trending stocks, there were numerous flag and wedge patterns that marked the path of this bull move.

Baidu was another technology leader during the bull market of 2009. This stock was a triangle machine during its run, churning out more triangles than a sadistic geometry teacher. It displayed characteristics similar to Apple in that it showed excellent relative strength in March and was even quicker to resume its uptrend.

Figure 3-25 highlights the fact that stocks exhibit their own unique trading characteristics. When you trade a certain stock frequently, you will get a feel for how it acts. In the case of Baidu, which sports higher volatility and therefore experiences erratic price movements within its triangle patterns, each of its triangle patterns quickly met its technical targets. You can see that the trading ranges in Figure 3-25 are wider than those seen in the preceding chart for Apple, which is a larger and more established stock.

Chapter 3 | Setups and Chart Patterns

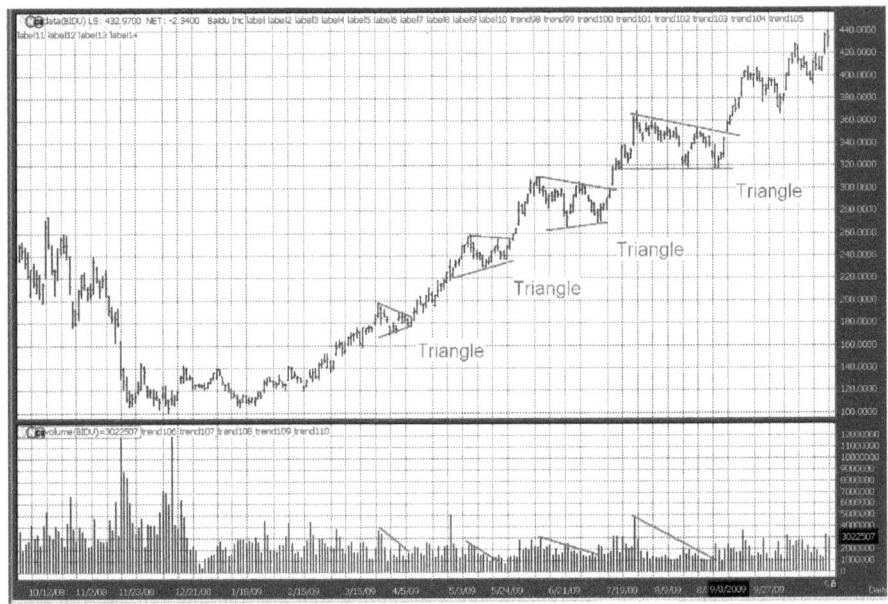

Figure 3-25. Baidu—the triangle machine!—showed wider trading ranges than Apple during its bull run.

In this chapter, I've highlighted many of the key technical patterns and outlined the best way to trade them. In Chapter 4, I'll go further and explore more advanced technical and trend-following concepts. I'm a big believer in using all of the tools at your disposal to flesh out your trading approach and take full advantage of the synergy this analysis provides.

CHAPTER 4

Technical Tactics

There are numerous technical charting styles and minor technical patterns, along with some important technical considerations, that every trader should be familiar with. I would stress knowing and mastering the basics before delving into more complex styles and tactics, but as you gain experience and develop your own trading style and favored indicators, you can more readily determine whether additional indicators will be a good fit or will detract from your unique approach to the markets. Until then, mastering the basics while continuing to learn your craft is a good strategy. What follows is an overview of several of the more basic technical indicators you will encounter in your day-to-day trading activity.

Gaps

A gap in a chart occurs when a given day's trading range is completely outside of the range of the previous day. Generally caused by dramatic news, gaps in stocks are typically the result of a stunning earnings surprise or other fundamental bombshell that has an unusual impact on the perceived value of the stock. In futures markets, gaps are typically caused by the announcement of a supply shock or a significant macro event, such as war in the Middle East.

You should be aware of three types of gaps: runaway gaps, continuation gaps, and exhaustion gaps. A runaway gap is the most useful of the three and has the greatest intermediate-term implications. It occurs when a stock has been trading in a defined range and then suddenly bursts into new high or low territory on a material change in the investment outlook. These types of gaps normally lead to follow-through in the same direction for the next several

Chapter 4 | Technical Tactics

months at a minimum, and the growth trader can exploit them for solid gains. A runaway gap in the opposite direction of the trend or channel can also signify an immediate trend change. The second type, continuation gaps, occur as a stock is already running within a defined trend and then gaps up or down in the same direction as the existing trend. Pay close attention to these gaps, as they confirm the underlying trend. Finally, exhaustion gaps and island gaps can be part of the same pattern and imply that the stock is moving up or down in a final spurt of capitulation before the existing trend reverses. These moves can be quite powerful, and in up trends they can represent a combination of massive short covering and ill-conceived momentum buying by excitable investors.

Gaps: Examples

In Figure 4-1 you can see a couple of significant technical patterns at work. In 2009, Peet's Coffee & Tea was in a well-defined ascending triangle pattern with highs marked at $30, which was also a retest of the September highs. This level acted as resistance for four months as the pattern drew closer to the apex of the triangle until, in dramatic fashion, the stock scored a runaway gap on tremendous volume. With this move, the stock broke out to new yearly highs and through the triangle in one dramatic thrust. The initial target was $34, but the bullish configuration argued for patience as the stock broke

Figure 4-1. In 2009, Peet's Coffee and Tea scored a runaway gap on tremendous volume.

out further to new highs. The other constructive aspect of this chart is the length of the base. Because it worked sideways for four months, the stock had room to run once it finally overcame this key resistance level.

Like Peet's Coffee & Tea, in the spring of 2009 Green Mountain Coffee scored a massive runaway gap—perhaps one of the largest you will ever see—and gained over 40% in one day! As you can see in Figure 4-2, leading up to this gap the stock had broken through the top end of a lengthy base and scored new yearly highs. There is a myth that all gaps need to be filled, but this is both erroneous and irrelevant, as the trader is not concerned with whether a particular gap will be filled at some very distant point in the future. She is concerned with the price action today, and a runaway gap typically marks the start of a meaningful move higher.

Figure 4-2. In 2009, Green Mountain Coffee scored a massive runaway gap, gaining over 40% in one day.

Runaway gaps are typically sparked by some extremely bullish piece of information that changes the outlook for a given stock in a material way. Since positive fundamentals take time to work their way into a stock price, this type of gap will tend to understate the longer-term implications of this change in outlook. Even though some of the initial percentage gains can be very impressive, a trader should hold on, as runaway gaps typically signal that much more upside is forthcoming.

Trendlines

The purpose of trendlines is to highlight the current trend of a stock or market so that traders can trade in the direction of the existing trend until the uptrend or downtrend is violated. Trendlines are constructed in such a way as to connect the lows in an uptrend or the highs in a downtrend. Examples of each are given below. Trendlines also aid the trader by identifying reasonable areas where a stock can be bought on pullbacks and pinpointing when the ongoing trend is in danger of losing steam. As with physics, an object in motion will tend to stay in motion until it meets an opposing force. In the market, that opposing force is a noticeable shift in the supply and demand dynamic. When a stock that has been in an uptrend for three to four months breaks the uptrend line, a trader should cut commitments and move out of the stock. A broken uptrend line indicates that supply has taken control—or at least has checked the strength of current demand. If the stock later regroups after a few weeks of consolidation, a trader can make new commitments.

Trendlines: Examples

Before you can rise, you have to stop falling. Just as a ball needs to hit the ground before it can be expected to bounce back, a stock needs to break its downtrend line before it can be expected to begin rising. As you can see in Figure 4-3, JPMorgan Chase suffered in the credit downturn of 2008, although it held up better than most banks. In March 2009, it finally broke its downtrend and bolted quickly higher. A wedge pattern developed after the stock was turned back from the fall resistance level of $36-38, and once it emerged from this pattern, it quickly resumed its uptrend. This rise began first and foremost with the break of the downtrend line.

In Figure 4-4, you can see that cotton participated in the great agriculture bull market of 2010, running from 20 to 160 cents per pound in a span of eight months. It made a double top in February and April, and this peak formed part of a triangle pattern, which turned out to be a reversal pattern. The break under 150 confirmed the top. The lengthy uptrend line was broken at 125, and the market came back up to test the breakdown area with a rally back to 140. This trendline break put an end to the cotton bull market and a great upside move.

The chart of STEC in Figure 4-5 highlights the importance of seeing multiple technical signals converge at a single point. The stock had been on a fabulous run during 2009, moving from $5 per share to a high of $42. There were a few tests of the trend along the way, and the action in July was sloppy, but the

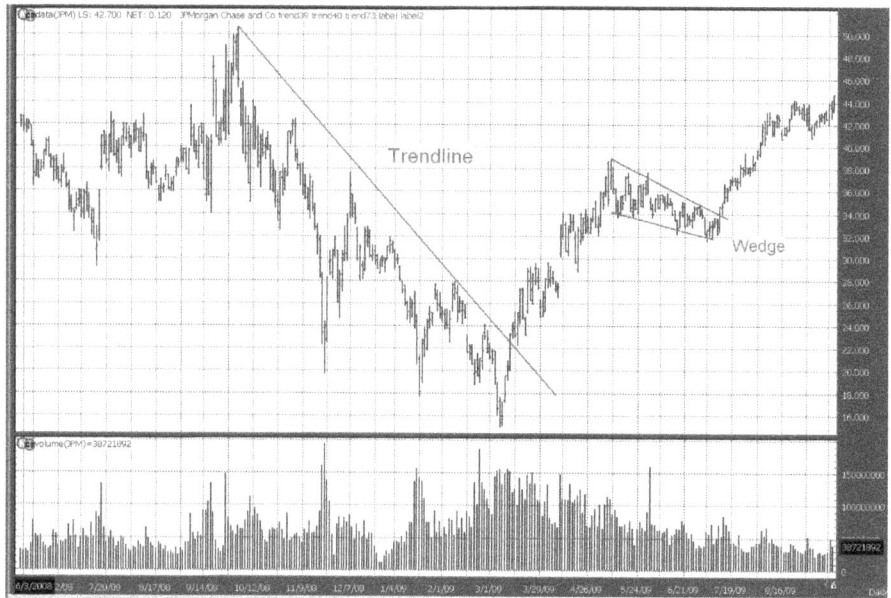

Figure 4-3. JPMorgan Chase's rise in 2009 began with the break of the downtrend line.

Figure 4-4. Cotton's move in 2010 was an excellent example of trendline breaks.

Chapter 4 | Technical Tactics

warning signs grew clearer in September. There were several key reversal days on heavier volume as the stock attempted new highs above $40, and the last rise occurred on weaker volume. Suddenly, in late September, the stock broke in such a way as to indicate that the run was over:

- Volume on the break from $38 to $32 was the heaviest of the year.
- The stock broke its five-month-long uptrend line.
- STEC scored a runaway gap that signaled a trend change.

Figure 4-5. In 2009, STEC showed multiple technical signals converging at a single point.

This confluence of factors meant that in one day, the story had changed, and the bears were now in control. Any time this happens, your first sale is your best sale. Immediately sell out of any position that sees this sort of development, and don't worry about the quality of your execution. Worry about the quality of your discipline, and take a loss or your trailing profit, whatever the case may be. Invariably there will be fundamental opinions that justify the drop and extol the virtues of holding on for higher prices. Ignore them. Runaway gaps that accompany a trendline break indicate that the story is over, and the trend has changed.

Financial stocks were severely battered during the bear market of 2008–09, as you can see in Figure 4-6, showing the trendline for the Financial Select Sector

SPDR (known as the XLF Financial Sector ETF). In early 2009, the short-term downtrend line carried the index from $24 to $6 in March alone, a dramatic decline that threatened the solvency of the entire financial system. Without government intervention, the entire money center, banking, and brokerage complex would have collapsed upon itself in a self-fulfilling cycle of destruction. We were mere days away from utter collapse. In the heart of the storm, the XLF broke its downtrend line and moved higher on a solid increase in turnover, marking the end of the carnage and signaling the beginning of the recovery. Once the downtrend was broken, prices rallied from $6 to $13 in two months. The XLF then based before it gradually worked its way higher. The beginning of the bull market began with the break in the downtrend line.

Figure 4-6. In March 2009, the Financial Select Sector SPDR (AMEX: XLF) broke its downtrend line, signaling the beginning of the recovery.

Reversals

Reversals occur when a market starts the day trending in one direction and then turns sharply in the opposite direction. Considered more valid indicators when volume is running at least 200% of normal, reversals are categorized as either upside reversals or downside reversals. An upside reversal or series of reversals will tend to occur late in a market's intermediate-term downtrend, as a market is beginning to undergo accumulation and a potential trend change. As a market is bottoming, you will see these patterns across many different stocks simultaneously. The greater the volume, the more significant these days can become. A series of downside reversals works in much the same way, indicating that supply is meeting demand, with selling arriving each time the market displays early-day strength. The presence of a downside reversal is a sign that eager sellers are taking profits and exiting their positions. The trend-following trader should heed this type of distribution by selling off his holdings.

Reversals: Examples

Within technical patterns, the day-to-day action can signal potential profit opportunities as well as potential troubles. Especially important is the action around the high-volume days, as this activity signals the true position of buyers and sellers and reveals which faction is in control at any given time. In the Apollo Group chart in Figure 4-7, you can observe myriad negative reversal days and see that they gave ample warning of impending drops and the end of the initial uptrend at important turning points. You should note that these days were also marked by a notable increase in volume, which signified the importance of these reversal days in foreshadowing the downside that was to come.

Figure 4-7. Apollo Group's chart in 2009 had numerous negative reversal days.

Support/Resistance

Support and resistance are two sides of the supply and demand coin. Support levels work with a market that is in an uptrend, and a support area is an area where the market has spent a significant amount of time trading prior to its breakout from that area. For instance, if a market is now trading at 100, having spent the previous three months trading between 85 and 90, then 100 represents support for the market. Support is also an area where any declines should be checked by buying interests that look to accumulate on weakness. Lower-volume pullbacks into support can be used as reliable indicators for buying, and these signals are even more compelling when accompanied by a high-volume reversal that briefly touches the area of support and then closes strongly, indicating very eager buying interest. In this case, the reward/risk ratio is extremely attractive, as you can buy the market with stops just under the low of the reversal day.

For a market in a downtrend, resistance functions in the same way. The resistance area will tend to act as an indicator of supply, as previous longs look to sell positions close to their breakeven levels, and new shorts look to set up attractive new short positions. Low-volume rallies in a market that is trending down into resistance areas make for solid risk/reward trades. Another tactic a trader can use when nearing resistance is to start a partial position into resistance and then add to a short on weakness as volume accelerates to the downside.

Support/Resistance: Examples

In the chart for Intel in Figure 4-8, you can see a line that represents the significance of the $20 level, which functioned as resistance in November 2002 and again in April 2003. Once this level was overcome on a dramatic increase in volume in May 2003, the stock carried higher to the $22 level and then pulled back to the $20 level. This time, the $20 level served as support, as buyers who initially missed the move bought the stock on this pullback. The trend had now changed to a bullish configuration, and the same $20 level that earlier had served as resistance now served to halt a decline. As this example should make clear, support and resistance levels serve as fulcrum points around which you should watch a stock closely. The ability to break through resistance serves as a solid buying point, while the failure of support to hold serves as a shorting or sell point.

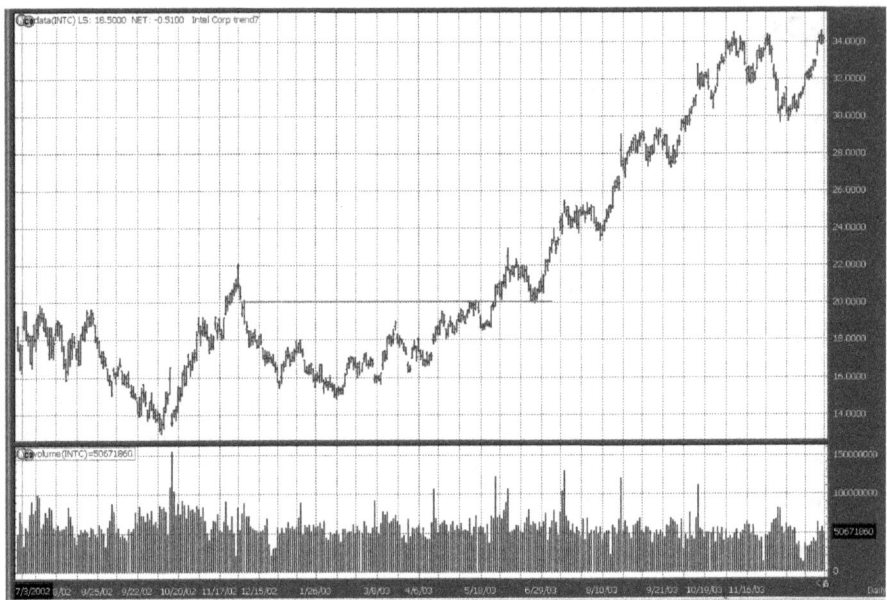

Figure 4-8. For Intel in 2002–03, the $20 level served first as resistance, then as support.

In the chart for sugar in Figure 4-9, you can see that in 2008–09, the $14 level served as resistance, while the $11 level served as support. This held true for almost a year before prices surged to new highs on increased volume. For an asset to break intermediate-term resistance, while setting new yearly highs in the process, is extremely bullish and can lead to rather large moves. In this case, sugar shot up from $14 to $24 in just three months. As a general rule—and as Figure 4-9 so clearly demonstrates—having a lengthy resistance area in place provides a solid foundation for future gains once resistance is overcome. Figure 4-9 also highlights how the bulk of an asset's gains occur in very short spurts of activity. The rest of the chart is marked by inaction as the forces of supply and demand battle for control in a range-bound environment. Given this pattern, patience in the setup and action on the breakout will greatly improve your trading results.

Moving Averages

Moving averages come in as many styles and cover as many time periods as there are trading methodologies, but there is no one "right" or "wrong" moving average that you should or shouldn't be using. Rather, the important thing is to use moving averages that correspond to your trading style. So, what *is* a moving average? It is simply the average price for a market over a given time period, so (for example) a 50-day moving average is the average

Tactical Trend Trading

Figure 4-9. The chart for sugar in 2008–09 shows how the bulk of an asset's gains occur in very short spurts of activity.

price for the previous 50 days of trading activity. For intermediate work, I prefer the 50- and 200-day moving averages, but I also use the 10- and 30-day averages for shorter-term charts. In addition to simple moving averages, I use the Moving Average Convergence Divergence, or MACD, as both a crossover and divergence tool in my work. The MACD is a set of exponential moving averages that applies more weight to recent trading activity.

Moving averages are excellent tools to add to your trading arsenal, and there are numerous ways to use them in your work. In this section, we'll consider three of those ways. First, you can use them much as you would a trendline. With this method, a market is considered positive if it is trading above the moving average and negative if it is trading below. Second, moving averages are helpful in crossover analysis, which is where I use them most extensively. A positive crossover occurs when the shorter-term moving average crosses over the longer-run moving average, a situation that often unfolds near turning points and when the primary or secondary trend is just changing course. The third way to use moving averages is as a divergence measurement. If a market is making new highs or lows and yet the moving averages are not moving to equivalent extremes, then you are staring at a divergence. A negative divergence occurs when the market makes a new intermediate-term high while the moving averages fail to best their previous rally peaks. Negative divergences are red flags indicating a loss of upside momentum.

Chapter 4 | Technical Tactics

As with most indicators, you should consider moving averages as secondary to the overall trend and be sure to confirm them with other indicators.

Moving Averages: Examples

The examples that follow highlight the different ways I use moving averages in my own tactical trend trading.

The MACD

In Figure 4-10, the S&P 500 is plotted in the left-hand scale of the chart, and the MACD can be seen in the right-hand scale. When the MACD fast line crosses above the slow line, the moving averages are on a buy signal, and when the fast line crosses below the slow line, they are on a sell signal. In the chart, the S&P is shaded lightly when it is on a buy signal, while the dark shadings show when it is on a sell signal. You can see that the MACD caught virtually the entire downward move of the S&P 500 into the early part of 2009, so this tool could have helped you avoid the S&P 500's precipitous 25% drop. Then, when the MACD turned positive again on the first upside day of March, you would have been ready to catch the move just off the low. Finally, if you had been using the MACD, you would have known to get into the market in early July before things got choppier in August.

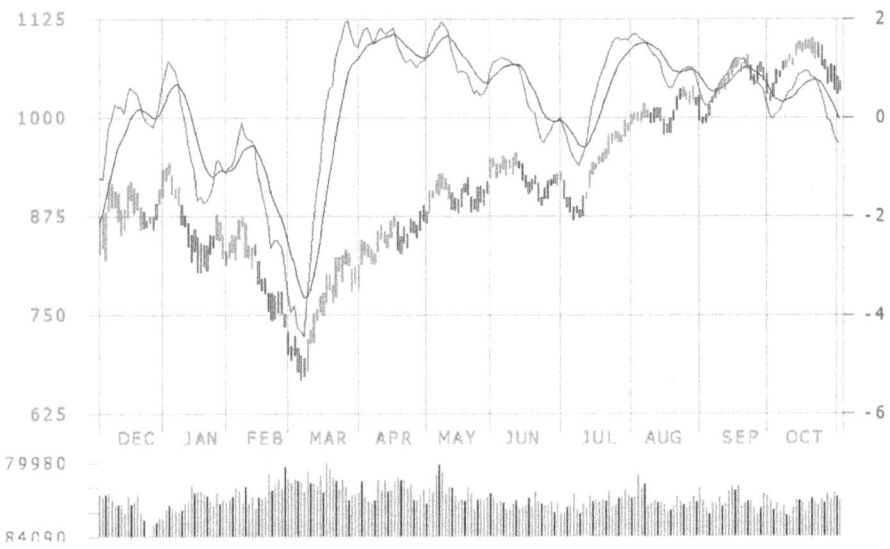

Figure 4-10. The MACD caught most of the downward move in the S&P 500 into 2009 and then signaled positive movement.

Tactical Trend Trading

The MACD is one of a large number of trend tools I use to tell me objectively whether the market is in an uptrend or a downtrend. The advantage of the MACD is that it will often warn of trend changes ahead of price weakness or strength. It's good to have in your arsenal, but it is a shorter-term tool, so remember that you should use it only in concert with other technical indicators.

Another way to use the MACD is to confirm the momentum of market moves against the averages. In Figure 4-11, I've highlighted several positive and negative divergences between the S&P 500 and the MACD. The first divergence occurred in the fall of 2008 as the stock market crashed in October. You can see that downside momentum peaked in October at point (a) as the stock market sold off to the 850 level, which is marked by point (A). The stock market then bounced and declined again to point (B) at the 750 level, which was a new low for the move. Meanwhile, the MACD made a higher high at point (b), which was a positive divergence. At point (C), the market made its ultimate low at 666, while the MACD again scored a higher high at point (c). Clearly, this was another positive divergence and a bullish indicator, despite the fact that the market was bottoming. You can see a negative divergence develop between points (D) and (E) as the market moved from 900 to 950 at each respective point. The MACD scored a lower high at point (e) than at point (d), and this signaled a weakening in the upward momentum of the

Figure 4-11. In 2008–09, the MACD confirmed the momentum of market moves against the averages, as shown in this chart of the S&P 500.

stock market. After a 5% correction, you can again see a positive divergence at points (F) and (G). The stock market made a lower low at point (G) versus point (F), while the MACD made a higher low. The MACD also quickly crossed into a buy signal off the lows at (g), indicating that the uptrend was ready to resume.

The DMI

Figure 4-12 introduces another trend identification tool used for swing trading. This indicator, the Directional Movement Indicator, or DMI, is a moving average of range expansion over a given period. A positive DMI (or +DMI) measures how strongly prices are moving upward, while a negative DMI (or –DMI) measures how strongly prices are moving downward. As such, the two lines that constitute the DMI reflect the respective strength of the buying momentum and the selling momentum. When the +DMI crosses over and above the –DMI, the swing trend is judged to be up, and vice versa.

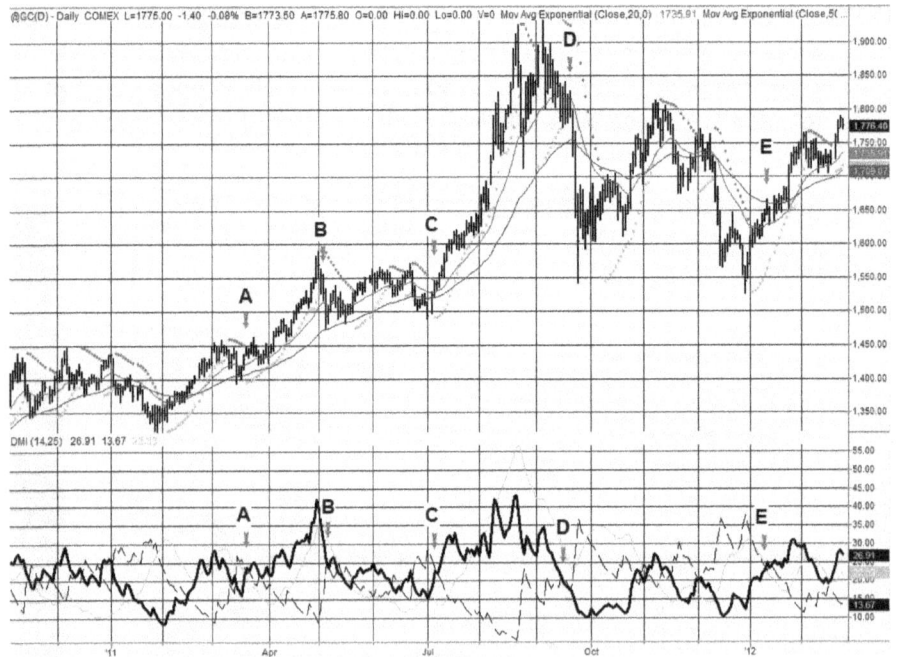

Figure 4-12. The DMI for gold in 2011–12 reflects the respective strength of buying and selling momentum.

In Figure 4-12, the +DMI is represented by the solid black line, and the –DMI is represented by the dashed line. You can see that point (A) marked a positive crossover, indicating the beginning of a potential uptrend. This trade would have been closed out at point (B), when the +DMI dropped back below the −DMI, closing out the buy signal. This trend indicator caught the bigger move at point (C), when gold was trading at $1,550, and would have closed the trade at point (D), when gold was trading at $1,800. A new buy was signaled at point (E), flagging the start of another trend.

Like the MACD, the DMI should be used in conjunction with other trend identification tools. One way to do this is to trade in line with the dominant trend using a longer-term filter so that only long trades are taken when the DMI is on a buy signal, whereas only short trades are taken when the longer-term, dominant trend is on a sell signal.

Simple Moving Averages

Longer-term trendlines are important for both investors and traders. Investors can use them as an extremely effective capital preservation tool, one that performs with robotic consistency, while traders can use them to stay in tune with the long-term trend. Figure 4-13 shows the movement of the S&P 500 from 2005 to 2009 with a 200-day simple moving average. As a trader, you can use this 200-day moving average (200dma) in two important ways. The first is to trade from the bullish side as long as the S&P remains above the 200dma, while trading from the bearish side when it is below the 200dma. The second

Figure 4-13. Simple moving averages like the 200-day moving average (200dma) can help traders keep their capital secure, as shown in this chart of the S&P 500.

Chapter 4 | Technical Tactics

way is to trade from the bull side when the slope of the line is rising, while trading from the bear side when the slope of the line is falling. If you are a long-only trader or investor, you can also set rules for yourself stipulating that upon a break under the 200dma, you will automatically go into capital preservation mode until the trend changes again.

Simple moving averages like the 200dma are, as their name suggests, uncomplicated tools that can keep your capital secure from the large drops that happen on occasion. The downside of simple moving average systems is the occurrence of the occasional whipsaw, and whipsaws are certainly evident in 2005 and 2006 in Figure 4-13. Still, the capital preservation capability of such simple tools is startling and, if they had been widely used in 2008 and 2009, they could have saved global investors trillions of dollars.

Figure 4-14 once again displays the S&P 500 and the 200dma, but this chart covers the period 1998–2005. This tool would have kept you out of the three-year bear market in stocks from 2000–2002, with the exception of a one-month stretch in 2002. It also would have gotten you back into the market in early 2003 as stocks bottomed and were ready to embark on their next bull market. To be sure, there were whipsaws during this stretch as well, with the most notable being in 1998. The plus side, however, is that these whipsaws would have cost an investor less than 100 S&P points. As with any indicator, the 200dma should be used in concert with other tools, but the

Figure 4-14. Use of the 200dma in the period 1998–2005 would have protected traders from the worst effects of whipsaws, as shown in this chart of the S&P 500.

simple, robotic power of this simple moving average to keep a trader on the right side of long-term trends cannot be overstated.

In Figures 4-15 and 4-16, you will find two examples from dshort.com that highlight the effectiveness of a moving average crossover system that uses 10- and 12-month moving averages and generates a buy signal when the faster 10-month moving average crosses over the slower 12-month moving average. Figure 4-15 shows the period 1928–1940, using these moving average crossovers as timing tools. One glance at the chart reveals that an investor using these tools would have been out of the stock market from October 1929 until August 1932. Outside of a six-month period in 1934, the same investor would have captured the five-year bull market that lasted until the next bear market in 1937, at which time he would have stepped out of the market again within 10% of the bull market highs. For such a straightforward tool, the simple moving average is exceptionally powerful as part of a risk control and trend identification strategy.

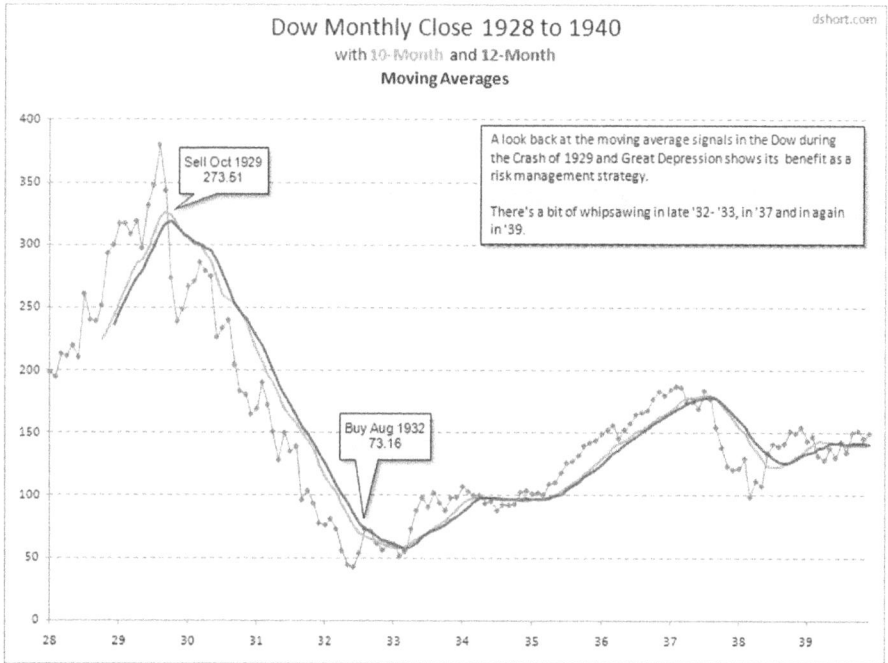

Figure 4-15. An investor using a moving average crossover strategy would have avoided the Crash of 1929 but captured the five-year bull market of 1932–37. (Source: dshort.com)

Figure 4-16, which charts the market in the period 1995–2009, again shows the power of the simple moving average. The chart employs a 10-month simple moving average, and the trader is long when the market is above the line and out, or short, below it. Outside of a two-month whipsaw in 1998, when a savvy trader would have sold low and bought back higher, following the 10-month simple moving average would have allowed a trader to capture the entire end of a decade-long bull market and sold her out of the market within a few percentage points of the top. This 10-month moving average then would have kept the trader out of the bear market until April 2003, only one month from the bear market lows. As stated previously, this tool is simple yet remarkably powerful and offers a better risk-control measure than is employed by the vast majority of the mutual funds in existence. Imagine: a simple line can be a more effective trading tool than reams of statistical data and fundamental analysis could ever be.

Figure 4-16. Using a simple 10-month moving average in the period 1995–2009 would have allowed a trader to capture the entire end of a decade-long bull market. (Source: dshort.com)

The 2003–2009 sequence is no less impressive, with the only issues being the one-month whipsaw in April 2005 and the fact that the 10-month moving average would have caused a trader to miss the dramatic initial rebound off the March 2009 lows. Still, a moving average crossover system is an excellent intermediate- to longer-term tool that can be used effectively to dramatically enhance the risk/reward equation for those trading over a longer time period. Simplicity is powerful.

Another method of moving average analysis for the intermediate- to long-term trader is using the weekly MACD signals to generate buy/sell signals for major asset classes and sectors. The chart in Figure 4-17 highlights the S&P 500 during the worst bear market since the 1930s, in 2008–09. The chart is shaded in grey to show when the MACD was on a buy signal and black when it was on a sell signal. You can see that the weekly MACD would have done an excellent job of keeping investors out of the market, or short, during the market's relentless decline. It captured 90% of the bull market and would have gotten the trader back into stocks only two months from the lows in March 2009. All of these moving average tools speak to the power of longer-term moving averages and the importance of respecting the trend more than personal opinions, economic data, or fundamental guesswork. The trend is your friend, both when it comes to profit generation and when it comes to capital preservation.

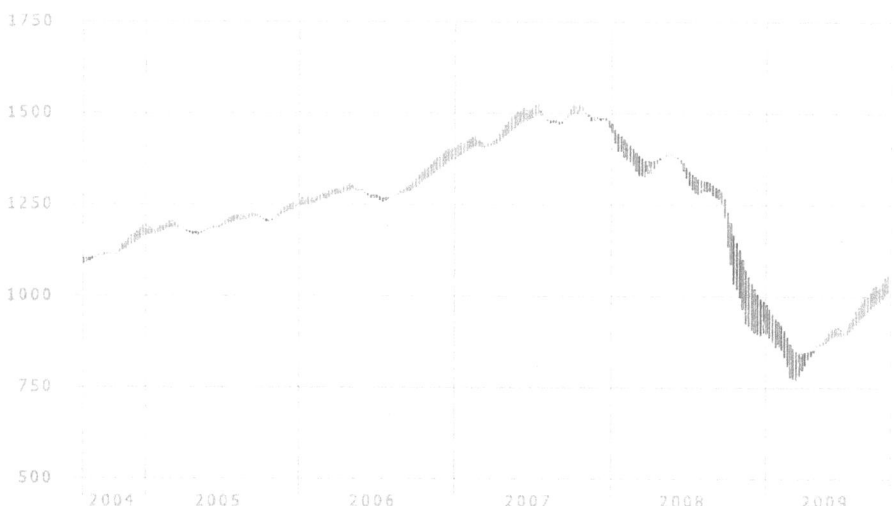

Figure 4-17. Using the weekly MACD would have kept a trader out of the market during the market's relentless decline in 2008 and early 2009, as shown in this chart of the S&P 500.

Overbought/Oversold Indicators

Overbought and oversold indicators attempt to measure when the extremes of buying or selling pressure are likely to exhaust themselves, based on historical precedent. As with moving averages, there is a plethora of indicators to calculate when a market is overbought or oversold, and they are used in a variety of ways, depending on the market environment.

Chapter 4 | Technical Tactics

In my trading work, I use the Relative Strength Index (RSI), the McClellan Oscillator, and a proprietary advance-decline oscillator. For the purposes of this section, however, I'll focus on the RSI, which measures the magnitude of recent gains relative to the magnitude of recent losses to arrive at a ranking ranging from 0 to 100. Readings over 70 are considered overbought, whereas those below 30 are considered oversold. It should be noted that RSI readings differ from market to market, with more volatile markets seeing more extreme readings.

Overbought/oversold indicators like the RSI should be used as secondary indicators, but they can be helpful in spotting potential turning points at the same time that they can act as a check against late buying or selling. As a result, you can use these readings quite effectively in conjunction with support and resistance levels. As an example, if a market trades sharply back into a support area and becomes oversold in conjunction with an RSI reading under 30, the odds of successfully buying into the pullback for a trade have increased. The reverse applies to an overbought stock that runs into overhead resistance, which can make for a good short entry candidate. You can also use the indicator to check for sloppy buying into an uptrend just as a stock is ready to consolidate.

As a rule, when the RSI readings are higher than 80, new buying should be limited. The inverse applies to selling short when the readings drop below 20. These types of situations are prone to quick, sharp snapbacks against the trend and can whipsaw a trader.

Overbought/Oversold Indicators: Examples

In the case of Apple, shown in Figure 4-18, you can see that there were four clearly marked instances in 2007 where the stock was oversold, with a reading of 30 or less on the RSI. Each instance marked a short-term low in the stock. Similarly, there were eight separate occasions marked by readings of greater than 80, and with the exception of the occurrence in September, each marked either a pause or a short-term top. Remember: overbought/oversold indicators are valuable timing tools and should be part of the technical toolkit, but you should rely on them only secondarily to the trend and basic technical patterns.

In the chart for Transocean in Figure 4-19, you see six instances where the RSI dropped to the 30 level, and each one was coincident with a low in the stock price. The most dramatic low was the August correction that took the stock from new highs at $125 to $100 in just one month. With this dramatic drop, the RSI fell to the 15 level and marked the low for the move. Note that this low day at $100 also qualified as a double bottom and a key reversal day,

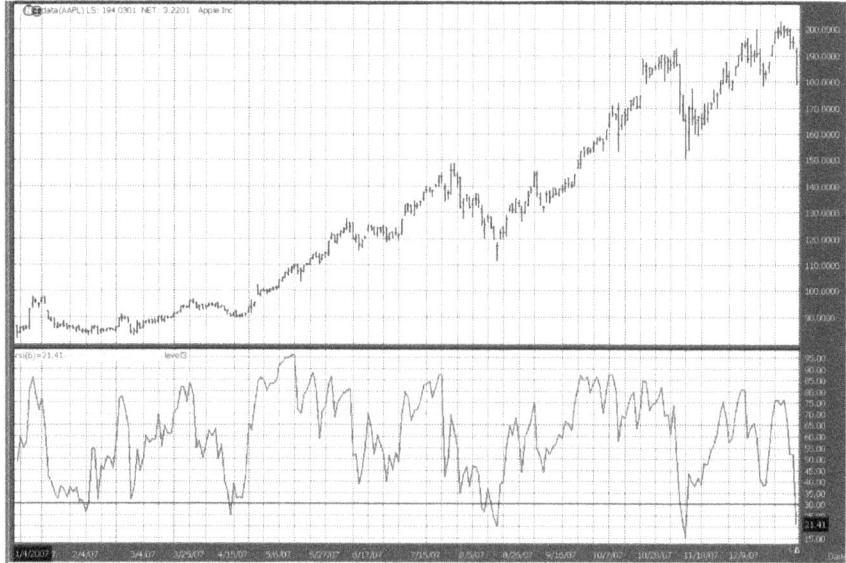

Figure 4-18. For Apple in 2007, oversold indicators marked a short-term low in the stock, while overbought indicators marked a pause or short-term top.

again highlighting the benefit of observing numerous technical signs pointing to the same potential move. In this case, that potential move was a significant bottom, and that turned out to be the right call, as the stock went on to score a move of 40% in the next three months!

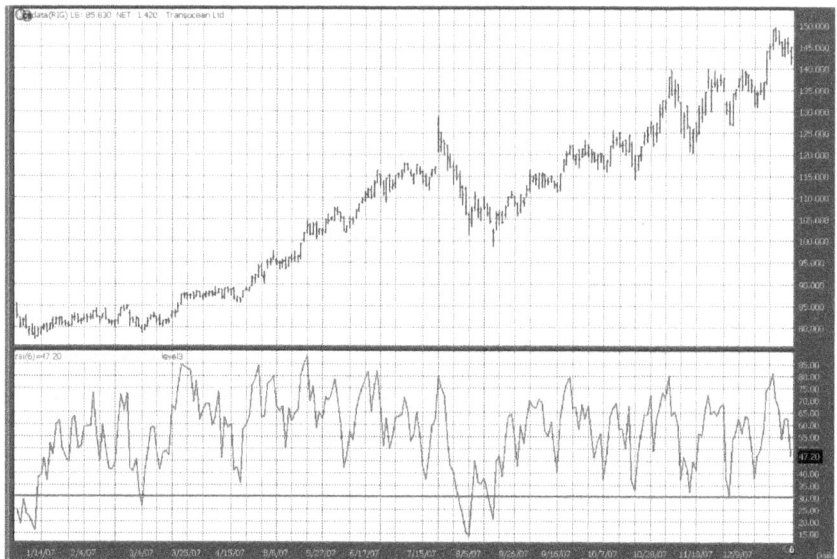

Figure 4-19. For Transocean in 2007, the RSI highlighted potential buy zones

Figure 4-20 highlights another concept that we touched on earlier: market moves often demonstrate symmetry. That is, a lengthy bear market decline will often be followed by a lengthy bull market run, and short, sharp declines like those witnessed in 1998 will often be marked by short, sharp rallies. In Figure 4-20, you can see the symmetry in crude oil prices from 2011 into early 2012. Notice that if you cut the chart in half vertically in September, marked by the dashed line, the two halves of the chart are symmetrical. There is a double bottom on each side of the chart, while the rallies at points (A) and (B) on the right of the split are symmetrical, both in time and price, with the declines at points (A) and (B) on the left side of the split. The symmetrical nature of market moves is something to keep in mind, as the character of rallies and declines will often repeat on the other side of the cycle.

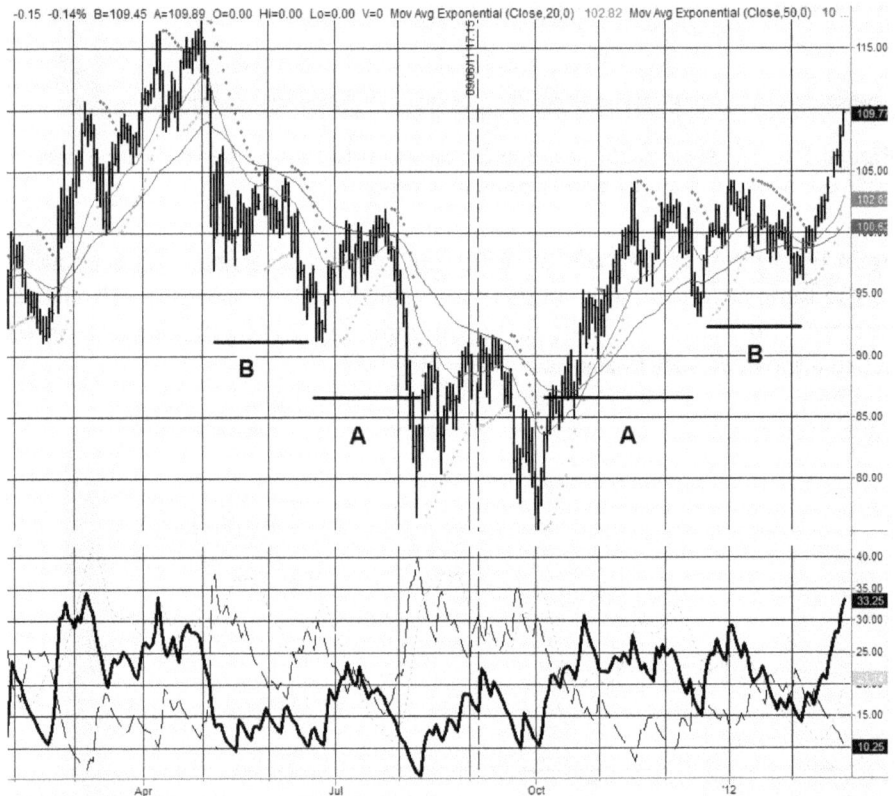

Figure 4-20. Crude oil prices showed symmetry in 2011 into early 2012.

In Figure 4-21, you can see an overbought/oversold gauge that I use for the stock market. The dotted line in the chart represents the overbought/oversold reading, which I update daily in my work, and the dark line represents the Dow Jones Industrial Average (DJIA). Readings of greater than +5 indicate an overbought market, while readings below -5 indicate an oversold market. As a rule, oversold readings are more important than overbought readings in identifying turning points, and in Figure 4-21, you can see how well they can work. The chart covers the period 1996–1997, and the oversold readings identified important lows in July 1996, April 1997, and October 1997.

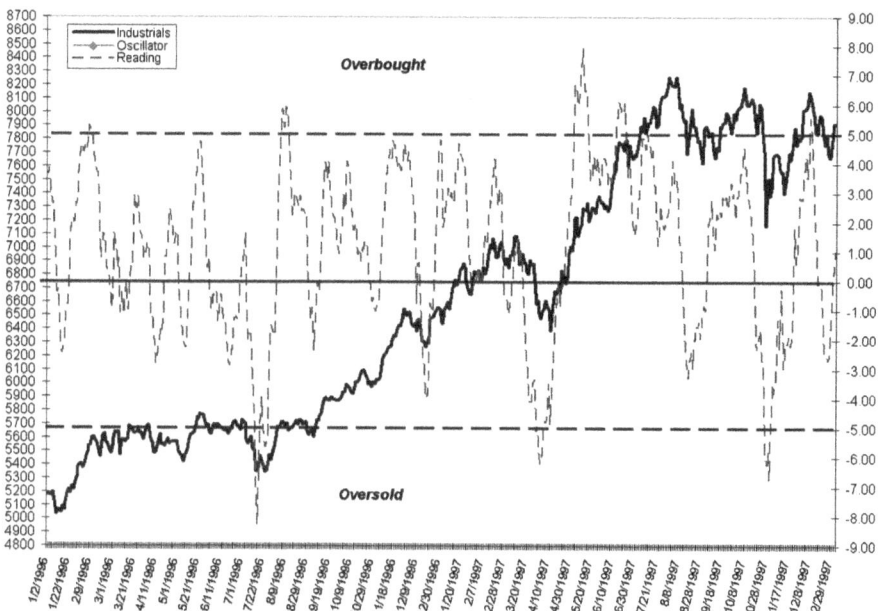

Figure 4-21. Oversold readings identified important lows in the DJIA in July 1996, April 1997, and October 1997.

The overbought/oversold indicator illustrated in Figure 4-21 has been very useful over the years and has helped me catch some major market turning points. I also find it valuable because it doesn't give many signals, and typically the market will become legitimately oversold no more than once or twice a year. But even though my indicator has proven adept at identifying key lows, I would caution you not to treat overbought/oversold readings as though they are absolute confirmations of market turning points. Rather, you should use them as tools in identifying *potential* turning points. Only after short-term trends develop to confirm that the points identified are actual lows should you take any action to go long.

Putting It All Together

You should consider technical patterns in the context of the larger picture and use them so they work together much like a team. For instance, a bullish

Chapter 4 | Technical Tactics

flag pattern that occurs in the context of a downtrend within a narrow stock market advance has a high likelihood of failing and being a losing trade. Putting the technical toolkit together and trading along the line of least resistance makes the signals more powerful and more relevant. Just as you wouldn't read an isolated page from a book and expect to gain much from it, you can't rip an isolated week from a two-year chart and expect to benefit from the pattern. Study the individual pieces that I have outlined, but be prepared to put them together to form the mosaic that leads to profitable trading. Your experience in this exciting field will aid you as you grow more proficient in your trading.

The iShares FTSE China 25 Index Fund (known as the FXI China ETF), illustrated in Figure 4-22, shows the benefits of context in technical analysis. The wedge that formed in May 2007 was potentially explosive for a few reasons. First, the top of the wedge formed at the prior resistance level of $38–39. Second, this area represented new highs if the ETF could overcome resistance. Volume was perfect, with the year's best volume surging on the move to $38. Lastly, the ETF was making higher lows both within this wedge pattern and within the context of the preceding three months. As a result, this wedge was a powerful signal that a strong bull market might be just around the corner.

Figure 4-22. In May 2007, a wedge pattern together with other technical markers in the FXI China ETF signaled that a bull market was just around the corner.

Similarly, the technical picture that developed between August 2007 and November 2007 was noteworthy in many ways. The run from $38 coincided with a key support level and was a dramatic key positive reversal day. In addition, this low came on significant volume and kick-started a quick move from $38 to $50 in eight days' time! The end of the move was also interesting and came with a confluence of negative technical factors. The first of these were the key negative reversal days that marked a double top at $72. The second was the runaway downside gap that broke the rising trendline on a material increase in volume. This day ended the upside trend and began a nasty correction that quickly took prices to the $46 level in two months.

As is clearly shown in the example of the FXI China ETF in mid- to late 2007, if you simply look at technical patterns in context and use them in concert with the trend and other technical considerations, you can greatly enhance your ability to make profitable trades.

The many benefits of context in technical analysis are evident yet again when you look at Figure 4-23, which covers the period 1999–2000 and displays the price action for JDSU Uniphase Corporation (NASDAQ: JDSU), a darling of the 1999-2000 bubble in technology stocks. I remember seeing a slide presentation given by the CEO of JDSU in San Francisco during the height of the Internet mania. He showed the current size of the fiber market on a slide containing an image of a small Jolly Green Giant. Then he turned to the next

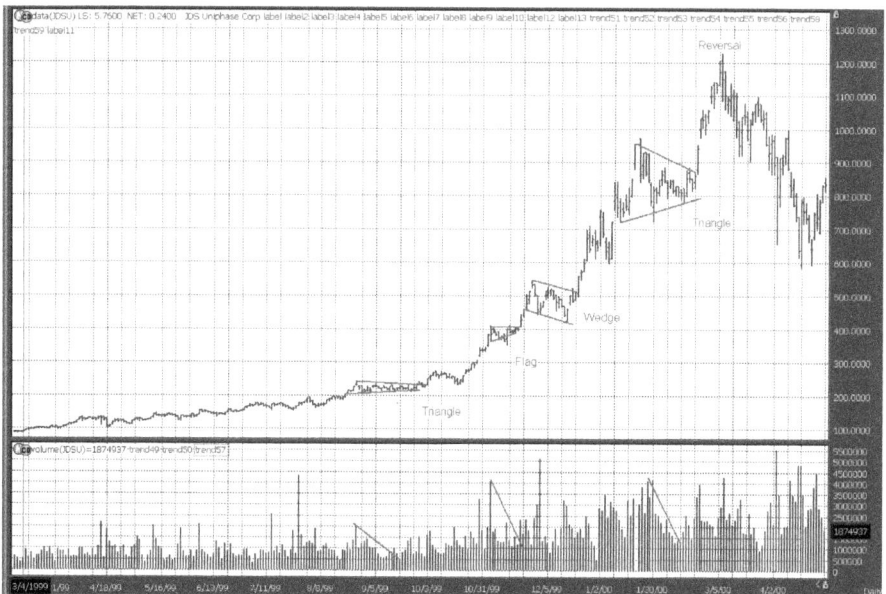

Figure 4-23. JDSU's price action in late 1999 and early 2000 is typical at the tail end of moves in bubbles.

slide, which showed the future potential growth of the fiber market, and this contained one image as well: that of a large Jolly Green Giant. All this while cheerily sporting a black beret! Ah, the days of the technology mania.

Sentiment is yet another tool for the trader, and the JDSU slide show I attended highlighted just how silly things had become—as does the stock's bullish run shown in Figure 4-23. First, the chart shows a large triangle in September 1999. Volume was large on the move to new highs and then tapered off as the stock consolidated. JDSU then traded with more gusto as the move got under way. JDSU flagged at $400, made a wedge at $500, and then developed another triangle at $900—all of this occurring in just two months. We were on Internet time. The chart gets interesting beginning in January 2000, when the first signs of trouble and exhaustion enter the fray. Wild swings are evident, as the stock gyrated from $900 to $700. Next, a key negative reversal day occurred as the stock made its all-time high at $1,200! The uptrend was broken at $1,000, indicating a potential trend change, and this took on added importance given the vertical rise in the stock. Remember that risks rise exponentially at the tail end of growth stock blowoffs. The stock quickly gave up half its gains with a plunge to $600. While the price moves are extreme, the price action for JDSU shown in Figure 4-23 is typical at the tail end of moves in bubbles.

Next, in Figure 4-24 you can see the end of another bubble, as the housing boom eventually went bust and took Toll Brothers with it. We see both the

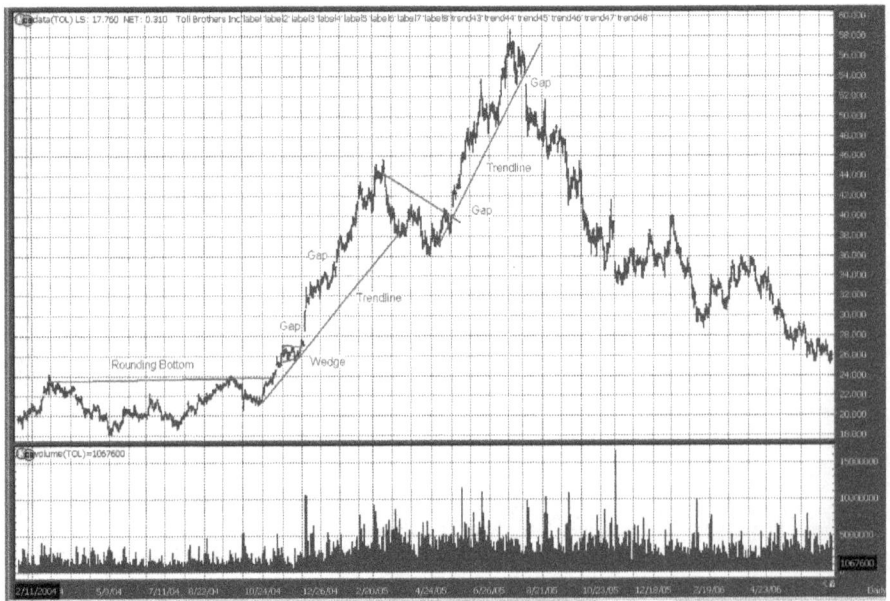

Figure 4-24. Toll Brothers' boom and bust cycle in 2004–06 is seen clearly in this chart.

boom and the bust in this one-year chart, which gives a clear reminder that all things are inherently cyclical in the stock market. After emerging from a nice rounding bottom pattern on a large increase in volume, the stock broke to new yearly highs—a key bullish development—and on the upswing you see combination patterns in October. Then a wedge forms, and the stock breaks through and then forms a bullish runaway gap as it accelerates through the $28 level. Toll Brothers broke the bullish short-term trend line in March, but this proved to be a false signal, as the uptrend resumed on a continuation gap in April. A trader should have sold in March, even though the signal proved false. She could then have reentered the situation on the upside gap at $42 to participate in the next leg of the advance.

The next uptrend line was punctured by a runaway downside gap that formed on massive volume, indicating that the uptrend was over and that downside risk could be large. That was the case here, as the stock sank from $58 to $26 in just a few months. Remember that change is constant, and one cycle's leaders in the bull market can lead the losses in bear markets. Moreover, leadership in the next cycle will typically be different, with new, vibrant sectors leading the charge.

The last example I'll leave you with before moving on to the next chapter can be seen in Figure 4-25—a chart that clearly demonstrates both the power and

Figure 4-25. Crocs, Inc.'s downward spiral in 2007 was atypical but highlights that your first sale is your best sale.

Chapter 4 | Technical Tactics

the danger of momentum trading. The initial breakout of Crocs, Inc. in April 2007 was constructive, as the stock emerged from a lengthy basing pattern with sound volume characteristics. The upside runaway gap in May was dramatic, with the stock running eight points higher on a huge volume burst. The stock then entered a flag pattern, which implied a minimum move to $43, a level that was quickly met. The uptrend continued, but the stock began to see the wild volatility that typically warns of impending trouble (much like our earlier JDSU example). The stock surged from $45 to $60 only to fall back abruptly to the $45 support level. A dramatic one-day reversal sufficed to halt the decline before the stock quickly recaptured the $60 level.

Such wild action is the first sign that a battle between bullish and bearish investors is taking place. In other words, the case for going short is battling the bullish argument for supremacy. In the case of Crocs, the stock continued higher, making its ultimate top at $75. But there was very little warning of what happened next, as the stock plunged to $55 on the open, breaking the uptrend line. This runaway downside gap would mark the end of the bull market for Crocs.

While the downward spiral of Crocs in 2007 was an atypical development, it highlights some key points. The first is that your first sale is your best sale. Selling at $50-55 would have been tough, but it would have been the right thing to do. Once your stops are hit, you should sell first and ask questions later. Crocs sold down to $25 only two months later and would go on to sell for under $5 per share in 2009. As tough as it is to accept, a bull market move can end in one day, and you must steel yourself to this possibility. It is a myth that gaps need to be filled, and this myth is highlighted in Figure 4-25. Stops should be your only fail-safe rule, and this example shows you why.

The discussion in this chapter should highlight the reality that using a disciplined approach, along with several simple tools, can dramatically reduce the potential downside that comes with trading and investing in the market. Simple moving averages, in concert with technical tools, will put you far ahead of most of the investment world in terms of risk-adjusted returns.

CHAPTER 5

Market Considerations

In this chapter, I will discuss other important market factors that you should incorporate into your investment process. The tools and tips presented here are tactics that can give you yet another edge over those who enter this arena ill prepared for the battle before them. At all times, remember that the market is a discounting mechanism as well as a reflection of the supply and demand interplay of millions of investors with differing and conflicting time frames, methods, outlooks, scales of operation, and degrees of investing acumen.

Volume

It may be helpful to think of volume as the fuel behind the price movements you see each trading day. Moves accompanied by robust volume confirm the price actions, while low-volume moves typically have less relevance and impact. Low-volume moves are also more characteristic of countertrend moves, while high-volume movements generally occur in the direction of the trend. This is especially true at inflection points, such as breakouts over technical levels, breakdowns under technical levels, and during the bottoming process. In fact, high volume that breaks through established trading levels is the best indication that the trend is still intact and the forces behind the movement are strong.

There are several ways to use volume to aid your trading. I've already pointed out that high volume seen in tandem with breaks through established technical patterns is a trend-confirming signal, an indication that the trend is still intact and healthy. But you can also use volume to confirm market momentum, given that volume activity will be very different in a market that is bottoming versus one that is topping.

A market that is topping will tend to show lower volumes and lackluster activity over a period of several months, which are signs of ebbing enthusiasm and a weakening market. In addition, rallies that occur in a topping market will show weaker volumes and thus will not confirm the general trend of the market.

Bottoms, on the other hand, are quite different, being quite violent compared with the stealthy nature of most tops. In most bottoms, the market will trade explosively with high-volume turnover as holdings are transferred from weak hands to strong ones in a more emotional atmosphere. In addition, reversal days showing 150-200% of normal volume are typical during the bottoming process and serve as a good sign that strong buying interest is on the receiving end of panicked sellers being flushed out in a spasm of weakness. During bottoms, you will typically also see something called 90% days, which are days where 90% of both trading volume and price movement occur in either the upward or downward direction. The typical sequence in a longer-term bottom begins with a series of 90% down days that unfolds when panicked investors sell en masse. These 90% down days are then followed by at least one 90% up day, the occurrence of which usually serves as confirmation that there will be no further selling pressure and that the trading lows have been seen. From start to finish, longer-term bottoms usually unfurl over the course of 30 to 60 days, although there have been times when the process was spread out over a period of nine months.

Most of the technical patterns I have discussed also have very distinct volume characteristics, where significant price movements occur on bursts of volume, while the consolidation or countertrend movements within a given pattern occur on much lighter volume. This, again, highlights the importance of volume confirmation. Volume shows where the big money is moving, and knowing that is the essence of control in our quest to analyze the balance of power between demand and supply factors in the marketplace.

Breadth

Breadth is the description of how broad-based a market movement is. There are numerous ways to measure breadth, but whatever method you use, the simple aim is to be sure that broad market movements are not confined to an ever-narrowing list of stocks. The advance-decline (A/D) line, one of the oldest tools used to measure the breadth of the market, is useful in spotting an unhealthy situation. In Figure 5-1, which makes use of the A/D line, you can see from the typical yet extreme example of 1999–2000 how the market narrowed, with fewer and fewer stocks powering the upside action. This narrowing was a result of investors feverishly pushing new money exclusively into technology stocks during the late stages of a five-year-old bull market.

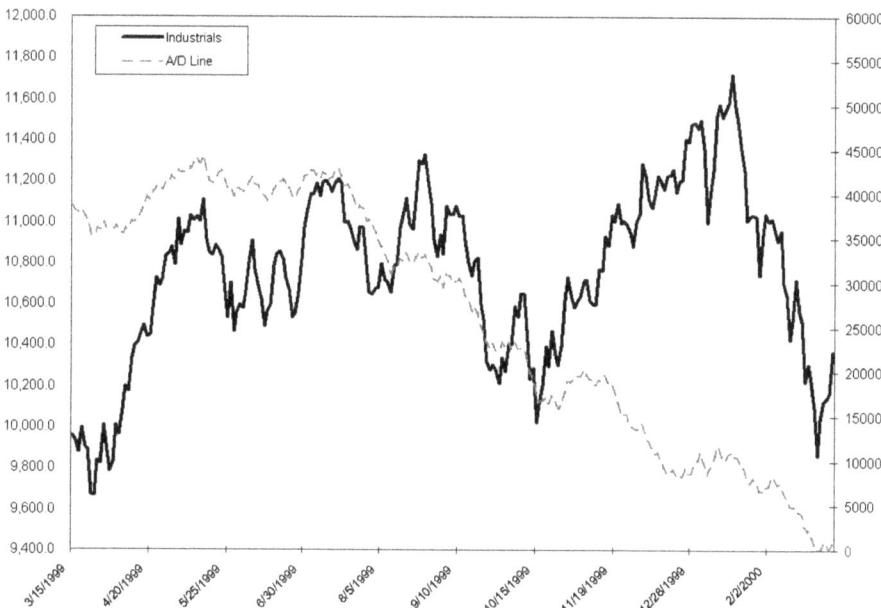

Figure 5-1. In 1999–2000, the A/D line versus the DJIA reflected the narrowing market rally.

In Figure 5-2, which depicts the bull market top of 2007, you see a similar development with respect to the A/D line. Breadth peaked in May 2007, but stocks didn't peak until September of that year in a four-month delay that is typical of the divergences that develop between the broad stock market and the leading indices. The first divergence developed in July, as the market scored a new high while breadth failed to confirm. The second divergence was more sinister, as the market moved in an extremely narrow advance to new highs while the broad market was in the midst of a downtrend. Finally, the advance in December of that year was extremely lackluster, as breadth mounted only a halfhearted attempt to rally.

Figure 5-2 highlights that a top tends to take time to develop—it is a process, not an event. In fact, this entire sequence of forming the top to a four-year bull market that had carried from March 2003 took seven months to unfold. As a rule, major tops and bottoms take four to nine months to form, with ample clues available to the trader along the way.

Chapter 5 | Market Considerations

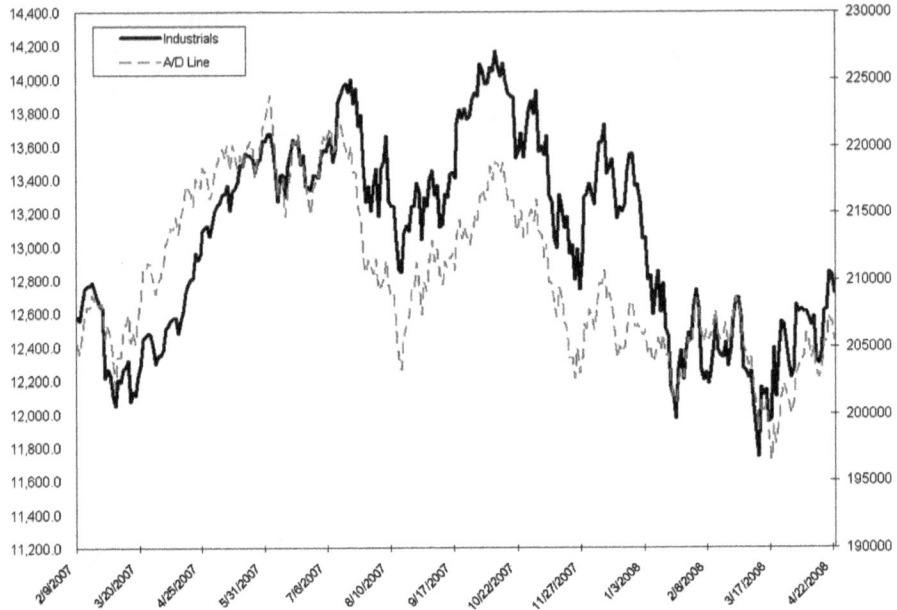

Figure 5-2. The bull market top in 2007, here shown by the A/D line versus the DJIA, took time to develop.

Another way to measure breadth is by the McClellan Oscillator, which is a running oscillator of advancing versus declining stocks. It also happens to be an excellent divergence tool. In Figure 5-3, you can see the notable positive divergences that were evident as early as November 2008 as the McClellan Oscillator made a higher low while the Dow Jones Industrial Average (Dow Industrials, or DJIA) undercut its October low by 1,000 points. Similarly, during what proved to be the ultimate of all bear market lows, the oscillator again made a higher low while the Dow Industrials were 900 points under the November lows and 1,900 points under the October lows. With the oscillator coming off its highest low, you could have made the case that it was in an uptrend, as it had made both a higher high and a higher low. Then, as the market rallied impressively higher from March to May, the oscillator simply exploded to new highs, confirming the underlying market strength and convincingly pointing toward further gains on the horizon.

The example in Figure 5-3 should make it clear that the use of divergence analysis is useful for navigating the course to investment success, because it highlights where you are in the bigger scheme of things. If you don't know where you are, it's a lot harder to get where you want to go.

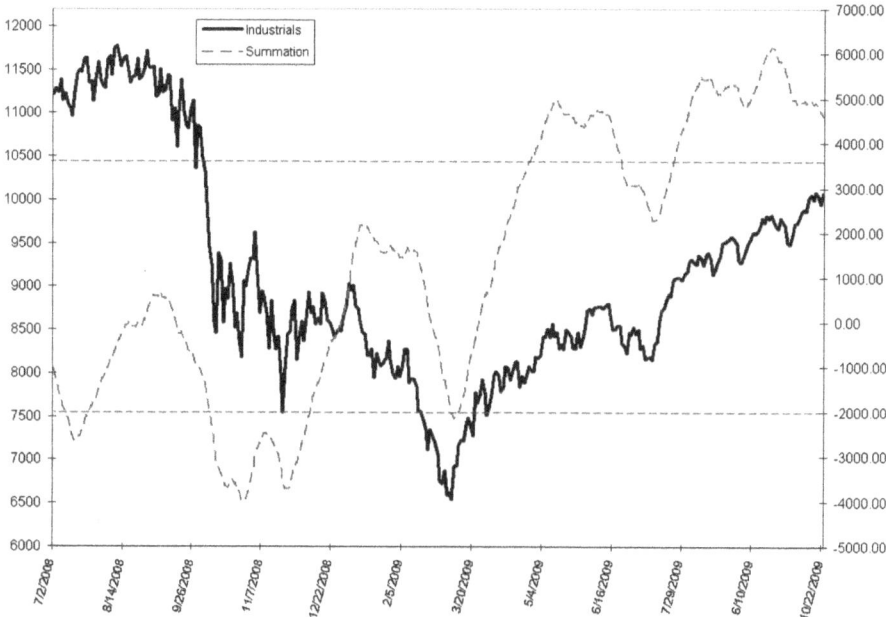

Figure 5-3. The action of the McClellan Oscillator versus the DJIA in late 2008 and early 2009 confirmed underlying market strength and pointed to future gains.

Time

While trend analysis is the most important factor in investing, and price is the final arbiter, time is also a key consideration for the savvy trader. In fact, corrections can occur either in price or over time as a market moves sideways for a certain period, and the marking of time with little upside or downside progress can serve to correct excesses in a bull or bear market just as effectively as a price correction. I have found leveraging time to be an interesting secondary tactic, and I use it frequently in my trading. There are no hard and fast rules concerning how best to leverage time to your advantage, but good guidelines come from Fibonacci numbers. In a bull market, a typical advance will run 20–40 days, with the Fibonacci number 34 serving as a good benchmark to focus on. Conversely, declines, which generally last 15–25 days, are typically shorter and sharper in bull markets, with the Fibonacci number 21 being a good number to watch out for. In a bear market, these rules are often reversed, as selling pressure lasts longer while rallies are shorter. Finally, don't forget the role played by the psychology of buyers and sellers in leveraging these time sequences, since secondary buying and selling cycles run their course gradually as increasing numbers of investors board the train as it moves down the tracks.

Chapter 5 | Market Considerations

News

News inundates the trading landscape and affects the stock market every day. Much of it—in fact, most of it—is simply noise, generating revenue filling airtime the media. But understanding the action of a stock or market in relation to the news can provide profit opportunities. When you can, by all means catch that apple falling from the tree.

For the stock market, news is a less important factor than most assume, but analyzing its impact can be a highly effective test to confirm underlying strength or weakness in the marketplace. As an example, a stock market that is experiencing a string of very positive news items and economic releases and yet fails to make headway on this information is telling you that it has already been discounted. It is also telling you that the incremental demand for stocks is relatively poor. Remember that the stock market is a discounting mechanism that is always peering into its cloudy crystal ball to ascertain the future prospects for business. While most investors are focused on today's news, a market that declines on good news is saying that tomorrow may be worse and current conditions are likely to be unsustainable, so it begins to sell off in anticipation of the headlines yet to be written.

The same thing happens at market bottoms. Larger stock market bottoms—like 1975, 1982, 1990, 2002, and 2009—are not the result of good news but rather are made in the face of bad news and economic recessions. Bottoms occur when the popular press is extremely negative and the investment public is buckling at the knees from one too many uppercuts. They occur when the outlook is bleak, overleveraged companies are going bankrupt, unemployment is still rising, and prospects point to more of the same. In fact, the market typically bottoms three to six months before a recession ends. But just think about the profit potential of "using" the news/reaction sequence. If a market begins to hold up and even rally on horrific news, it is telling you very loudly that this information has already been discounted, and a bottom is probably in the process of forming.

This dichotomy between the news and the reaction to the news is a powerful tool for the trader who has an open mind and is willing to see what is actually happening in the markets. In news-driven market events, the rate of change and the incremental nature of changes may also be factors. For instance, in the 2009 bottom, the rate of change in key economic indicators like Institute for Supply Management (ISM) factory orders, key industrial commodity prices, and consumer retail data began to improve. The chart in Figure 5-4 shows the stock market overlaid with the ISM data from the same time period, and you can see that while the ISM data was still showing year-over-year drops of a stunning magnitude, the rate of change had turned positive as the declines were getting less severe, indicating an improvement at the margin. While the news was still bad, the savvy trader could have deduced that better days might be in the offing and consequently could have used the news to his advantage.

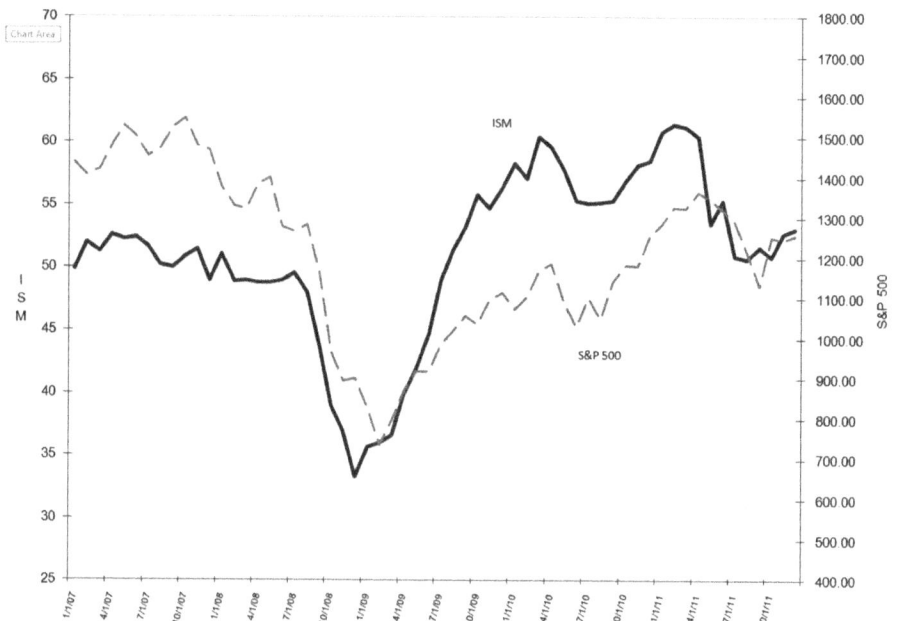

Figure 5-4. In the 2009 bottom, incrementally smaller drops in the ISM data signaled the potential for future improvement in the performance of the S&P 500.

Figure 5-5 depicts the ISM data series going back to the late 1940s. Recessions are shaded, and you'll notice that the ISM manufacturing index is quite consistent in turning down materially before most recessions. This is an important indicator to monitor on a monthly basis, along with the other important economic indicators I mentioned in Chapter 2.

Remember that a market that doesn't do what it's "supposed" to do is telling you something, if you will only listen. This news/action dichotomy expresses itself through the market maxim "fast moves come from failed moves." The fast moves mentioned in the maxim tend to happen at potential inflection points and are typically aided by some fundamental news item, which could be anything from a sell-side analyst downgrade to a negative story about a company in a financial publication to news of insider selling. For a classic example of a fast move coming from a failed move, imagine that a negative news article pushes a stock artificially under an obvious consolidation area. Volume picks up, longs panic out, and shorts begin to pile into the weakness

Chapter 5 | Market Considerations

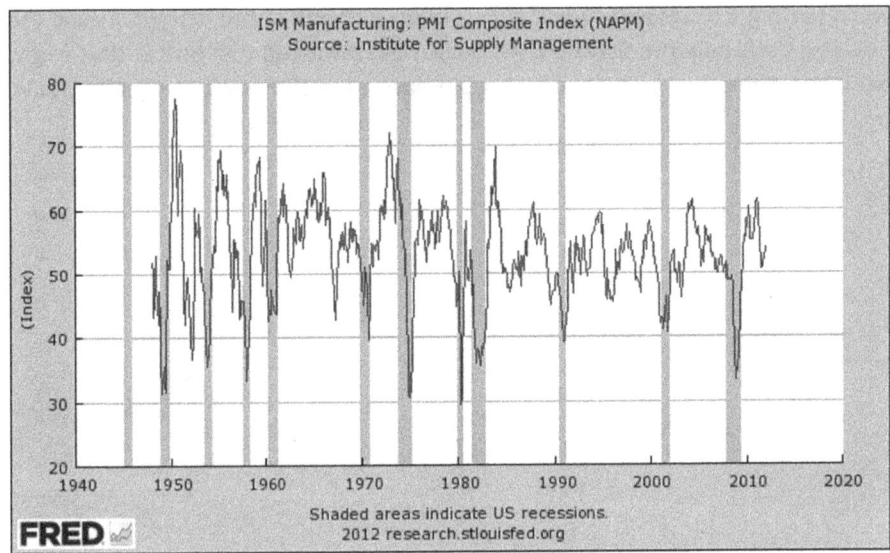

Figure 5-5. ISM data shows consistency in turning down materially before most recessions. (Source: The St. Louis Fed)

as they buy the story. After the break, demand comes in to check the decline, the forces of supply and demand wage a fierce battle, and, with an eruption of buying throughout the rest of the trading day, demand overwhelms the supply, causing an extraordinary upside burst in price. This burst is aided by off-balance shorts, underinvested longs, and new buyers who have found an attractive entry point. Remember that you can put the news to effective use if you correctly gauge the action of a stock or market in relation to the news flow. You should avoid following news in isolation, particularly at turning points.

The Full Stock Market Cycle

Over the course of a full stock market cycle, through both a bull and a bear market, there are three distinct phases. Not all three phases need to be present in each cycle, but it is often the case that all three are fulfilled on the market's way up and way down. Let's start with the beginnings of a bull market and work through the end of a bear market cycle.

In the first stage of a bull market, stocks will discount the extreme pessimism seen previously and return from depressed values to reflect more realistic values. This stage is driven by sentiment and the first glimmers of a budding economic and earnings recovery. It tends to be explosive and is tougher to catch for those waiting for an ideal entry point. Gains occur quickly and explosively as short sellers and underexposed longs work to create a vacuum that is quickly filled to the upside. However, news is still poor, sentiment is negative and skeptical, and fundamentals are at their worst.

The second stage of a typical bull market occurs in sync with improvement in underlying fundamentals, better news, and more positive sentiment. This stage, which is more methodical and measured, is typically the longest of the three phases.

Finally, the market will crest into the third stage, which is emotionally driven and ruled by momentum. It is highly profitable for short-term traders and a deadly trap for new long-term buyers. Fundamentals are excellent at this stage, but warning signs are evident in numerous areas. The Federal Reserve and yield curve cycles are probably turning negative, valuations are stretched, and mutual fund retail flows are heavy to the buy side. Leading stocks show explosive short-term gains, the rally is typically narrowing to a handful of leaders, and churning commonly starts to appear under the market's surface. A new fad has probably grabbed hold of popular sentiment, and initial public offerings in the leading sectors will be foisted upon an eager public. As they say—feed the ducks while they're quacking. Financial prudence is frowned upon, cash is trash, bonds are for old widows, and irrational exuberance has run amok. This third and final phase is relatively short but can carry a solid distance to the upside. This is the peak of the bull market; now we turn to the dark side.

If the bull market completed all three phases, it is likely that the bear market will show symmetry and develop in three stages as well. The first stage in a bear market occurs because valuations compress rapidly as wildly bullish sentiment dissipates. This stage is short but violent to the downside, and many investors will still believe the bull market is intact and look to buy dips with enthusiasm. As a result, this phase can be painful, and the rapid and easy gains of the final stage of the prior bull market can cause many to be whirled away in these selling hurricanes.

In the second stage of the bear market, stocks move down on fundamental deterioration, and earnings and sales forecasts work gradually lower as the economic environment weakens. The negative interest rate cycle is biting, which feeds inventory destocking, increasing jobless claims, and weakening economic numbers.

The third and final stage is marked by panic, fear, and capitulation selling. Economic numbers are poor, layoffs prevalent, and the press is predicting the end of bull markets for the foreseeable future. Retail investors are being washed out with record mutual fund outflows, as "long term" investors can't take it anymore. The monstrous outflows during the 2002 and 2009 bear market bottoms, with a combined $100+ billion in withdrawals, highlight the dangers of an inadequate risk-control strategy and blind long-term holdings. In this phase, business failures, bankruptcies, and frauds are exposed; Enron, WorldCom, and Bernard Madoff come quickly to mind. In addition, the market not only will discount poor fundamentals but also will build in an almost unrealistically poor future assessment. Financing has dried up for even sound companies, financial prudence is in vogue, bonds and cash are king, and irrational pessimism has replaced the irrational exuberance that was seen at the bull market peak. As people sell in a pure panic, great values are created. As a result, many large stocks that traded at P/E ratios of 30x at the top of the cycle can be had for P/Es under 10x, and many small stocks can be traded for their net cash value on the balance sheet. Examples of all this include 1932, 1974, 2002–03, and 2009. The cycle is now complete.

As mentioned previously, not all bull/bear cycles will undergo all three phases detailed above, but human nature makes it likely that many will see this long-term cycle of greed, fear, hope, and revulsion play out on life's financial stage.

Macro Analysis

Remember to keep an eye on the big picture at all times—and remember also that the big picture extends well beyond the stock market and includes macro factors that are important in identifying both potential winners and potential risk on the horizon. The macro outlook and intermarket analysis tie the US stock market to the global markets represented by bonds, real estate, interest rates, currencies, and commodities. I've highlighted the importance of economic indicators, the yield curve, and Federal Reserve policy—and they are certainly part of macro analysis, as these tools act as a barometer of the larger economic cycle and are vital to top-down analysis of the stock market. In this section, I'll discuss some of the other important macro tools and indicators.

To begin, it's important to note that key economically sensitive commodities are particularly important to the macro outlook for the market. The price of such industrial inputs as copper, or Dr. Copper to experienced traders, and oil should be monitored daily. Why copper and oil? First, copper prices respond to industrial demand for the metal, and rebounds in copper prices from depressed levels can indicate a factory demand uptick. This was certainly the case in 2009, when the metal bottomed out well before the stock market, offering a clue that global demand was beginning to come back after a hiatus. Second, oil is important not only because it can indicate an uptick in demand but because it can also choke off an economic rebound. Oil is used in so many industries that rapid price hikes feed their way into depressed earnings and slumping retail sales. Historically, rapid oil price increases have served to depress the economy and send it into a funk, which was certainly the case in 1990 and 2008. Rising crude oil prices can also signal problems on the international front.

Another way to use macro analysis is to highlight potential winners in the trading environment. Thus, rising gold prices should point a savvy trader toward exploring gold mining stocks, natural gas shortages should lead her to profitable investments in exploration stocks, and so on. A good trader should make it a habit to scan the charts of the leading energy, agriculture, and metals commodities on a daily or at least weekly basis to identify emerging trends and risks in the investment landscape. Interest rates should also be watched carefully. They are just as important to the market as oil prices, as they represent the cost of servicing debt and future economic activity—particularly in our debt-driven economy. After all, it was extremely low interest rates that fueled the housing boom/bust sequence from 2003 to 2007 and drove the profligate lending practices that very nearly destroyed the modern capitalist system. All of this is to say that you should use macro analysis as a tool to identify both secular and cyclical investment themes, trends, and risks. Macro analysis should be part of any trader's toolkit, and you should study the key macro inputs weekly for potential shifts in the investment landscape.

Relative Strength Is King

In Chapter 3, I mentioned the importance of relative strength, and I wish to expand on the topic here. Relative strength can point you to the leaders in the current economy and market cycle, and it is an especially important indicator in a few select circumstances. After a secondary correction in a bull market, the first stocks to display leadership will often be different from those that ushered in the previous market advance and frequently will be among the new leaders in the next advance. Keep a close eye on strength coming out of a correction, particularly in industry groups, as it will highlight a potential leadership area and will also tell you important things about the economic cycle. For instance, if apparel stocks emerge from a correction quickly, you can infer that consumer spending will likely be stronger than consensus expectations. If large technology companies rally sharply, technology capital spending is likely to be strong as a whole. In essence, then, relative strength presents you with clues to both the economy and the market leaders. A similar thing happens when an advancing market enters a three- to four-week period of consolidation. You are likely to see both group rotation and a few key groups beginning their advance while the general market is still trading in its range, all of which is generally a healthy sign for the broad market. If, on the other hand, you see prior leaders showing relative weakness while the market churns, it may presage a selloff in the broad market.

Chapter 5 | Market Considerations

While I am an advocate of the importance of relative strength, as an indicator it can be taken too far, which is why I recommend staying with liquid, higher-quality mid- and large-cap stocks. There are a few reasons for this. First, low-price stocks as a rule do not function as well technically as more liquid mid- and large-cap stocks, and they are also subject to more extreme volatility. They can break very hard and gap 10-30% under your stop point, effectively taking your portfolio's risk control function out of your hands. In addition, even though you may be well aware that you should exit these types of volatility-driven situations as soon as possible, mentally it can be very difficult to do so. In the long run, grappling mentally with yourself over these decisions makes it much more difficult for you to size your risk/reward ratio. These issues rarely crop up with more seasoned growth stocks. Second, I avoid trading into earnings reports and other either/or situations in individual stocks, as this is akin to gambling, with highly uncertain outcomes. Again, such tactics skew the risk/reward ratio that is a key component of trading successfully over the long run. Remember: you must maximize your risk/reward equation, and trading higher-quality, liquid growth stocks is the way to do this.

Two main market conditions tend to get the investment crowd excited and in a mood to create the type of momentum that is necessary to drive relative strength. The first is a bright outlook, which can express itself as explosive earnings growth, revenue growth, or a robust product development cycle or pipeline. Organic growth is the best catalyst of a positive market outlook, although the conglomerate and REIT booms were fueled by merger and acquisitions activity. The second factor that drives robust stock price gains is incrementally positive change at the margin, by which I mean simply that reported results continue to exceed the expectations investors have built into their assumptions. To answer the question of whether 30% earnings growth is good for a certain company, you have to know what investors' expectations were. If investors were expecting 20% growth, then you can expect acceleration in the stock's price. If, however, they were expecting 35% growth, the stock is likely to plunge, even if the company's earnings release is glowing. As with most things in life, results are always measured relative to expectations. It's like a child who comes home with a B on her math exam. Are you relieved or disappointed? Well, that depends: did you expect a D or an A? It's the same with news items, earnings releases, and new product announcements. Relativity fuels the market's gravitational pull as well.

Short Selling

Short selling involves selling markets that one doesn't own in order to buy them back later—and hopefully lower, right? While that sounds easy, it is harder for most traders to short than it is to buy. For the short side, I have a few cardinal sins to mention and recommendations to make.

First: do not, under any circumstances, short strictly because of valuation! Shorting because a stock is trading at 40 times earnings is a flawed strategy. Why? Because you are assuming a stagnant earnings number—and that is just your first mistake. For stocks with high multiples, it is typical for the companies to understate their earnings power, and analysts tend to underestimate the upside potential when a business has real momentum. This deadly combination can cause your 40x multiple to turn out to be 20x in hindsight. The second problem with shorting based on valuation is that, when it comes to earnings multiples, stocks have no ceiling. During the mania stage of a bull market, stocks can trade at 200, 400, and even 1,000 times earnings! Rather than shorting stocks that are hitting new 52-week highs with high multiples, consider buying them as good long-side trading candidates.

If you insist on shorting, before doing so it is far better to wait for a stock group to exhaust itself and begin to show earnings deterioration, technical weakness that includes a three- to six-month top, and heavier volume coming on selloffs in the stock. As with longs, you should time the entry either on low-volume rallies into supply or as the stock breaks support on increased volume. Keep your stops in place just as you would with a long, so that your losses are limited. This, again, is the only infallible rule in trading. If you're in a market environment that is trending not too strongly or at all, you may be able to establish good long setups in some groups at the same time that you have good short setups in others. But if you are a newer trader, I would advise you to go slowly with shorting and stay with a long or cash position until you get more comfortable with operating in the markets. When you do short, go with the trend just as you would with your longs. Do not short strength—pick on the weaklings in the market.

Sizing Your Trades

There are many ways to size trades, but I will walk you through how I size trades for my discretionary trading in both stocks and futures. For stocks, the first step is to identify your risk tolerance, which will be unique to you and may change given your age, asset base, career situation, and time commitment. I would suggest two risk measures: first, risk no more than a certain percentage of your equity in each trade, and second, risk no more than a certain percentage loss of total equity in each trade. For example, for a $100,000 account and an aggressive trader, let's assume that you limit your position size to 20% of total equity and your loss to a stop of 3%.

Chapter 5 | Market Considerations

Capital = $100,000

Stock Price = $50

Position Size = $100,000 * 20% = $20,000 position / $50 price = 400 shares

Risk to Stop = 3% * $100,000 = $3,000 / 400 = $7.50 stop, or $42.50 stop price

Using this methodology, a trader with a $100,000 account would size a trade to the $20,000 level, which would mean 400 shares of a $50 stock. He would then set his stop at $42.50 or higher so that his maximum loss (excluding slippage and downside gaps) would be $3,000 per trade. Note that this 3% stop level is the maximum amount of risk that our hypothetical trader would take on. As I've shown by means of the numerous technical patterns discussed in this book, most stops would be much shorter and should be keyed off technical levels. But even at this more aggressive level, a trader risking 3% of capital per trade has to be wrong much more often than she is right to lose a significant amount of money. For those just starting out, I suggest that you take things slowly and set 1% stop levels in your trading. As with any endeavor, setting stops takes time and firsthand experience before you can become proficient. In perhaps a year, you will begin to feel more comfortable with setting stops, and the process will become second nature.

The sizing process for futures is similar to that for sizing stocks, although there are a few key differences. The first thing you should know is that each contract represents a specific unit of the underlying futures, and this unit varies for each market. For example, for oil, each futures contract represents 1,000 barrels of oil—a quantity we can refer to as our "big point value"—whereas for gold, each futures contract represents 100 ounces of gold. You can readily pull these big point values from the exchanges where the futures contracts are traded. Next, you will also want to be aware of the contract months that are traded for each futures contract. Financial futures typically trade on a quarterly cycle of March, June, September, and December. The third major difference is that when you are trading on a discretionary basis, you'll want to first determine your risk/reward in the trade.

Let's say that oil is in a triangle consolidation pattern, your target on the trade is $109, and your stop point based on the technical pattern is $97. With oil trading at $100, you have 9 points of upside versus 3 points of potential downside, giving you a solid 3:1 risk/reward ratio. You work out your trade size in terms of contracts by taking your maximum risk tolerance, in this case 3% of total equity, and multiplying that by your equity of $100,000, which gives you 3,000. You then divide this total by the current price minus the stop price and multiply this total by the big point value. In this case, 100 – 97 = 3, and 3 * 1,000 = 3,000. Next, 3,000 / 3,000 = 1, so you would buy one oil futures contract. The formula and calculations are shown below.

Capital	= $100,000
Oil Price	= $100
Oil Big Point Value (bpv)	= 1,000
Stop Price	= $97
Risk Per Position	= 3%, or 100,000 * 3% = $3,000
Sizing Formula	= (equity * risk%) / ((price – stop) * bpv))
	(100,000 * 3%) / ((100 – 97) * 1,000)
	3,000 / 3,000 = 1
Position Size	= 1 contract

You can use this simple formula to equalize dollar risk among contracts with different big point values. What you'll notice is that your stop is determined by the technical pattern at play, and your position sizing is determined by your potential risk. In systematic trading, risk stops are more sophisticated and must take into account the underlying volatility of the futures contract so that you can determine your volatility-adjusted position sizing. In addition, in systematic trading you limit your risk per sector and overall portfolio risk, or "heat." You should do this in your discretionary trading as well: limit risk per sector to a certain percentage or number of positions. In addition, you should limit your overall portfolio heat so that you aren't risking more than a certain percentage of your equity in open trades.

Before placing your first trade, work on these numbers and, by paper trading, determine the risk limits that fit your tolerance for losses and portfolio volatility until the numbers become second nature to you. A good broker should be willing and able to sit down with you face to face and walk you through this exercise. In addition, remember that if you trade a large enough account you may not want to trade on margin at all. Again, it's all up to you, so design your trading to fit your particular financial goals and individual circumstances.

Keep It Simple; Don't Press

Trading is a great pursuit that offers a lot to those willing to put in the work and play it intelligently. It is both easy and extremely hard at the same time. To extrapolate from that thought, almost anyone can learn the methods, chart patterns, techniques, and risk-control measures involved in trading. But the learnable aspects of trading are not the reason some traders ultimately fail. Maintaining your discipline when your mind tries to convince you otherwise, staying patient and in cash when opportunities don't present themselves, and remaining determined to buy only the highest-quality relative-strength names even though you are getting tips about any number of companies—all of this is hard. The sirens will sing to you and attempt to lure you onto one of the thousand sharp rocks on the craggy coast. And while keeping your focus may sound easy, you may find yourself drifting toward the sweet music during three times in particular: when you hit a lull and are looking for something to do, when you are trying to play "catch up" for an error you have made, and when you go on a serious roll and start to feel like you're playing with free money. A trader in the business of making money must guard against all of these temptations and K.I.S.S.—keep it simple, stupid.

Don't press; don't trade the market that you *wish* were there versus the market that actually *is* there. Reality trumps desire. Trade the market that is in front of you, not the one you imagine may be there a year from now—and certainly not the one a talking head is telling you is there. Trust the evidence of your senses to deploy your capital only when the time is right. Have the courage of your convictions, and commit to the trading-to-win philosophy. Take responsibility for every trade. All of your winners are yours; so are all of your losers. Own them all, as that is the only way to learn. If you take credit for your winners but blame others for your losses, you are effectively shielding yourself not only from the responsibility for the loss but also from the opportunity to learn from the lesson that it carries.

Over time, you will come across numerous new indicators, chart patterns, and technical, fundamental, and quantitative methodologies. My advice is: continue to learn but keep things very simple. Some traders have a tendency to hide behind 100 different indicators, putting off their trading decisions because there are conflicts among 10 out of their 100 indicators. Keep it simple, stick to what works best, attack when the opportunities are there, and maintain your risk control discipline at all times. Don't make things harder than they need to be. You are more likely to succeed by correctly executing a mediocre system than by creating a superior one that you constantly violate and execute poorly. You have what you need now; the question is trusting it and executing it well.

CHAPTER 6

Systematic Trend Following

Every truth passes through three stages before it is recognized. In the first it is ridiculed, in the second it is opposed, in the third it is regarded as self-evident.

—Arthur Schopenhauer

Tactical trend trading can be done on either a discretionary or a systematic basis, and the trader can apply these methods to stocks, bonds, commodities, and other traded liquid markets. As the title of this chapter makes clear, however, my focus is on systematic trend following, which entails gathering the best practices and rules of successful traders, incorporating them into a computer-coded trading system, and then following that system in a disciplined manner. Contrary to popular belief, systematic trading is not a mysterious black box to those who create and use its systems. Rather, it involves analyzing a wide variety of trading and risk control methods, applying the most reliable of these to various markets, and then combining these methods with your preferred approach to the markets in order to systematically identify and execute trading opportunities with little or no intervention on your part. In essence, systematic trading takes many of the best practices of successful macro trading and puts them into a rules-based system designed to ensure continued consistency and minimization of risk.

There are many ways to identify trends, and throughout this book we have highlighted numerous examples, including breakouts, moving averages, cycle work, momentum, and various other measures. Regardless of your preferred method of identifying trends, once your trading system identifies an uptrend or a downtrend, it should generate buy or sell signals to position your portfolio to capture the major part of a developing trend. The sizing of the trade is written into the system, so that, for a given equity level and a given degree of risk tolerance, a consistent method is used to determine your commitment level for each trade. In addition, as a trade is taken, an initial stop is set at a predetermined level to limit the risk per trade for losing trades. For winning trades, as a trend takes hold, trailing stops are used, and these are raised as the price increases. Finally, the trader selects markets to ensure proper diversification, liquidity, and exposure to attractive market vehicles. A systematic trading approach accomplishes each of the above functions methodically and unemotionally, employing the best trading practices at each stage of the investment process.

Complete System of Best Trading Practices

> "It is magnificent, but it is not war. It is madness." (Said of the charge of the Light Brigade of the British cavalry in the Crimean War)
>
> —Pierre Bosquet

Regardless of whether you trade on a discretionary or a systematic basis, you are most likely employing some type of rules-based system in your work. To a discretionary trader, many of the rules may be subconscious while others will be explicit, but every good trader works with a framework and a unique approach to the markets. Systematic trend following makes every rule explicit, with trading best practices coded into a computer that executes your trading system.

How does a trader go about creating a trading system? He or she should start by addressing the following seven questions:

1. What are the long-term goals of my trading?
2. What is my working philosophical framework?
3. Which markets or stocks should I buy and sell?
4. How do I size positions?
5. What are my entry rules?

6. Where do I place stop-loss levels?
7. Where do I take profits?

Systematic trend following and system design are not easy, nor are they a quick fix. You must be prepared to answer numerous questions and give considerable thought to each part of the process. The above seven questions are not meant to be inclusive but to provide a framework for designing a system. Although they are intended to help a trader develop a systematic trading plan, they would work for a discretionary system as well, forcing a trader to add a layer of trading discipline to his work.

Any trading plan should start with a trader's goals and flow naturally, brick by systematic brick, into the construction of a trading system. Designing a trading system in this manner adds a conscious layer of discipline to the trading process. It incorporates trading best practices, from risk control to entry rules to profit-taking rules, and it is an evolving process, so if you discover better rules and test them successfully, you can integrate them into the trading program. This focus on rigor, discipline, risk control, and best practices is the key reason I switched to systematic trading.

In addition to this framework, a systematic trader should have the right mental makeup to invest in this manner. Systematic trading requires a rigorous approach to developing trading rules, the even greater discipline required to follow those trading rules, and excellent money management and risk control skills. In addition, systematic trading demands patience, a long-term outlook, and the discipline to stay with the strategy through the inevitable sideways periods. This need for discipline and evolution in systematic trading is best summed up by Ed Seykota in his interview in *Market Wizards* by Jack D. Schwager (HarperCollins Publishers, 1988). In answer to a question regarding what trading rules he lives by, Seykota responds with the following list:

a. Cut losses.
b. Ride winners.
c. Keep bets small.
d. Follow the rules without question.
e. Know when to break the rules.

The first three rules are at the very core of conservatively run systematic trend-following systems and should be built into any system from the start. As trades are taken, initial stops are placed at levels that keep losses small, and a fixed amount is risked on each trade initially so that unsuccessful trades have limited impact on portfolio results. In this way, the systematic trading approach is similar to the risk taken by a casino operator. The house risks a certain amount on each slot machine, each roulette wheel, and each blackjack table. It knows that on balance, the risk of losses is small, and profits will come from the edge the casino has in its betting. Systematic traders approach markets in the same way, knowing that small losses will be outweighed by small winners and especially by the large winners that happen over time, when markets engage in larger trends.

Traders talk about cutting their losses and letting their winners run, but it's mentally tough to go against the grain of human nature, which is more inclined to take certain winners while holding onto losing trades in the hope that they will come back and become profitable. Nevertheless, the importance of riding your winners and cutting your losses cannot be overstated. Riding winners ensures that the trader can take advantage of the handful of larger market moves that occurs each year. These outsized moves happen with much greater frequency than modern financial models tell us they should, and the reason for this is that trending is a natural part of many systems, finance included, and the boom/bust nature of finance will ensure that we see many large trends develop over the years. Fortunately, trend-following systems are naturally designed to take advantage of these outsized moves because they encourage traders to hold onto their winners and give them a chance to work and grow.

The next rule in Seykota's list, "Follow the rules without question," means to act on all market signals and let your system make your trading decisions for you. This is an important rule, as the biggest dangers in trading a good system are decisions by a trader to override stops or to override new buy/sell signals. Falling prey to either temptation takes away your edge and compromises the foundation of your system approach. If you override your risk control process, you open yourself to significant losses and the destabilizing practice of second-guessing yourself. Overriding new buy and sell signals is equally dangerous. The large winners that come from adhering to a trend-following approach are at the core of the system's profitability. You simply cannot afford to miss the 5% of trades that will constitute the bulk of your profits over the long run. You also cannot forecast ex ante which markets and trades will work and which will not. A trade is just a trade. Some work, some don't. Much of your edge in trend following comes from your risk/reward ratio, so if you override your system and let your losers run or cut your profits short, this ratio will deteriorate, and your performance will suffer noticeably.

The last rule—knowing when to break the rules—points to system evolution. As you study markets and system building, you will come across system refinements and enhancements, which you can add after extensive testing shows that they can improve one or more aspects of your trading. You should make changes with care and forethought, not under the pressure of chasing the latest system style. Even the best system will go through periods of underperformance that are tied to the market cycle. If there is nothing wrong with the system, then you should leave the process in place—even if short-term performance is lagging. There are normal phases of the market cycle where trend following as a category or different types of trend-following systems will lag. Knowing this beforehand will help you stay with your approach through these times.

Not a Black Box

There are three classes of people: those who see, those who see when they are shown, those who do not see.

—Leonardo da Vinci

Systematic trend following is not a black box to the trader who creates and uses the system. Despite the common misconception that systematic trend following is mysterious, risky, and unproven to the average investor, nothing could be further from the truth. These misconceptions persevere, however, owing to the large quantity of advertising thrown at the investing public by mutual fund companies. In an effort to convince potential clients that they are both risk averse and disciplined in following investment rules, mutual funds hold themselves up as prudent stewards of capital. None of the aforementioned is true. Mutual funds employ no risk control, fully capturing the downside of every bear market, and they underperform consistently through each investment cycle. In addition, they don't employ systematic rules that offer any edge. If they did, they would outperform with less risk, but the opposite is clearly true. For the mutual fund investor, research has shown that it would be far better to invest with index funds via a conservative, low-cost company like Vanguard than it is to chase the marketing, asset-gathering machines of the mutual fund world.[1]

In truth, systematic trading has been generating solid risk/reward results for investors since the 1970s. It not only captures the upside of bull markets, but it produces good returns and provides alpha-generating performance in bear markets as well. In addition, systematic trading diversifies traditional investment portfolios by adding markets like commodities and currencies that are not typically offered in most investment vehicles. It also offers global diversification, as bonds, currencies, equities, and commodities from numerous global regions and countries can all be added to a systematic trading investment portfolio. Table 6-1 shows the historical performance of the BTOP50, which is an index

---

[1] Christopher B. Philips, "The Case for Indexing," Vanguard, February 2011, https://institutional.vanguard.com/iwe/pdf/ICRPI.pdf.

of the 50 largest managed futures commodity trading advisors (CTAs). The index performed impressively, providing positive returns through the worst bear market periods of 1987, 2002, and 2008 and highlighting the BTOP50's ability to generate profits in good times and bad.

Table 6-1. BTOP50 Historical Performance, 1987–2011

Year	Return	Year	Return
1987	57.6%	2000	6.6%
1988	12.1%	2001	3.8%
1989	2.6%	2002	13.7%
1990	15.3%	2003	15.5%
1991	14.7%	2004	0.9%
1992	2.5%	2005	2.4%
1993	13.4%	2006	5.6%
1994	-0.2%	2007	7.6%
1995	14.0%	2008	13.6%
1996	12.8%	2009	-4.8%
1997	12.0%	2010	6.4%
1998	12.4%	2011	-4.3%
1999	1.6%	Average Return	9.5%

Source: BarclayHedge

A systematic portfolio manager knows the investment inputs and processes behind his system, but in order to protect his research and trading method, he won't reveal its specific rules to another trader. Nonetheless, it is worthwhile to sit down and talk with a systematic portfolio manager. Why? Because he can give you an outline of his system's market selection, trading signals, diversification, and risk control measures, which will provide you with a generalized overview of what drives his investment process. Talking with a systematic portfolio manager is no different from interviewing a discretionary trader about her trading method. Like a systematic portfolio manager, a discretionary trader will not reveal all of her trading inputs and methods, but this doesn't mean her method is a black box to her. Yet her trading method is just as much a black box to someone unfamiliar with her investing style as any systematic trading method might seem to be. So don't be swayed by any notion that systematic trading is any more mysterious than discretionary trading.

A cursory understanding of a system's strengths and weaknesses is necessary for any trader so that he understands when and why a system will underperform or outperform at various points in the investment cycle. For example, if a trader is using a classic trend-following system, he can expect that system to outperform during bull and bear markets but underperform during large trend changes and sideways, trendless markets. Systematic trend following, like any other system, is only as good as the inputs that go into generating the trading system. That being said, a sound, longer-term system can stand the test of time and consistently work well, whether a trader is using it in the 1970s or the 2070s.

Be Consistent and Unemotional

It is a capital mistake to theorize before one has data. Insensibly one begins to twist fact to suit theories, instead of theories to suit facts.

—Sherlock Holmes in *A Scandal in Bohemia*, Arthur Conan Doyle

Systematic trend following is unemotional, providing the trader with consistent signals and risk control measures. A well-constructed trading system applies trading signals regardless of a trader's emotional state, the current news, tips he might have received, and any hunches or feelings she might have about a particular market. At the same time, it incorporates the system trader's best practices when it comes to market selection, position sizing, trading signals, profit-taking signals, risk control, and diversification. In this way, systematic trend following combines the finest of human thought and our capacity for creativity with the best attributes of a computer and its ability to operate in an unemotional, disciplined, consistent manner. As a result, if a trader is skilled enough to have designed a good system and is wise enough to follow it, he can avoid many of the psychological and philosophical pitfalls that trip up many traders at some point in their careers. I have traded on both a discretionary and a systematic basis, and it is amazing how much the systematic method reduces my stress levels. Disregarding the intraday mental scramble and the news cycle is truly liberating. It's not for everyone, but for me it has been a welcome addition to my trading toolkit.

In designing a trading system, you must keep in mind several important considerations. First, you must make sure that you design your system so that it fits with your risk/reward tolerance. There is nothing worse than designing a system that will experience 20% drawdowns once every three years and then giving up on the system when the first 20% drawdown happens. In this case, the problem is not with the system but with the system trader. You must be able to know and feel the sting of a drawdown so that, when real money is on the line, you can stick with your system as long as it is operating in a manner that is consistent with your testing and design.

Therefore, you must ensure that you design a system whose trading style fits your own, as we're all wired differently. I can trade my system with confidence, but I couldn't trade another, equally good system if it didn't mesh with my investing style. Using a system whose style does not align with your own will invariably cast doubt on that system and lead to overrides or abandonment of the system at the worst possible times. A system must also pass the common-sense test. I'm a firm believer in starting with market and technical analysis to first propose a trading theory that can later be tested, rather than randomly testing trades on a computer to see if they are successful. While engaged in the latter process you may stumble upon a true trading revelation, but you may also find yourself data mining and generating a system akin to the Super Bowl indicator. Arguing from false premises is an exercise in epistemological futility. A final factor to consider is that longer-term systems with fewer degrees of freedom (or trading parameters) tend to be more robust and hold up for longer than those that employ a shorter-term focus with greater levels of optimization. Shorter-term systems need constant engineering and optimization in order to stay current and profitable in successive market periods.

Diversification and Risk Control

Genius is nothing more than a greater aptitude for patience

—Benjamin Franklin

Macro trading exposes a trader to many global markets that are not traditionally included in stock/bond portfolios. A macro trader adds commodities and currencies to the traditional stock and bond mix, and macro systematic trend-following strategies include global portfolios with stock exposure to the major geographical blocks of the Americas, Europe, Asia, and emerging markets. In addition, a macro trader adds global bonds to domestic bonds and adds hard assets to financial assets. This amalgam of geographic diversification, asset class diversification, and long/short trend-following flexibility affords a tremendous amount of uncorrelated alpha to a traditional investment portfolio. In designing my systems, I incorporated a greater than normal exposure to commodity futures versus financial futures, with over 50% of the portfolio allocated to commodities. I also designed the system with the intent of allocating exposure equally among the Americas, Europe, and Asia, to the degree that was feasible. Underlying currencies, geographies, and instruments give additional layers of diversification to the systems I designed.

Built-in, consistent risk control is perhaps the biggest benefit of a well-designed systematic trading program. As each long or short is taken, the trader places an offsetting stop to limit the impact of losing trades. Doing so frees the systematic trader from the narrative fallacy whereby the same conviction that often allows a discretionary trader to outperform in one cycle may cause a lapse in her risk control measures in another cycle, which can lead to larger, destabilizing losses. If a systematic trader has the discipline to follow her system, its built-in risk control handles losing periods, limits individual losses, and allows the trader to continue to preserve capital during adverse periods. You can't win if you don't have chips to bet, and risk control allows you to set the chips aside when the markets aren't moving your way so that you can use them at a later date. Risk control at the position and sector level is likewise an important component of a well-designed systematic trading program. You will want to limit your portfolio heat, or overall risk level, and you can do so by putting your maximum risk exposure levels in place for a number of different inputs. For example, you'll want to pay attention to your market sizing on individual trades so that an adverse move in a single market has minimal portfolio impact. You should also limit your sector exposure, as many markets are highly correlated with their sectors.

A good trader works through these issues and potential risks well in advance of launching his trading program—and with good reason. After all, the foundation of a solid trading system is not generation of trading signals but multifaceted risk control measures based on best trading practices. This is a real advantage in systematic trading. When designing a system, a trader is forced to think more deeply about risk control issues, which means that once the system is running, these steps are operating without the trader's having to reinvent the wheel with every trading opportunity. Consistency and diversification go a long way toward ensuring that a systematic trading style gives a systematic trader a reliable and quantifiable edge over the vast majority of discretionary traders.

Portfolio Fit

Wisdom begins in wonder.

—Socrates

Taking a top-down view of financial portfolio construction, a trader's key goal should be to design a portfolio that is consistent with a client's needs and unique circumstances. He should thoughtfully analyze the risk/reward ratio of each investment class he is thinking about including in the portfolio, and he should consider these assets based on both their own merits and how well they will fit within the larger context of the overall portfolio. Risk/reward being equal, he should choose investment classes and disciplines on the bases of their sources of returns, risks, and correlations with the other components of the portfolio. As an example, owning a portfolio with ten different equity-only mutual funds is probably a poor idea because, while it is diversified across equity styles and fund companies, in a serious bear market this portfolio mix offers only a minimal level of diversification. Similarly, an all-bond portfolio can be expected to perform abysmally in times of rapid inflation or sovereign debt defaults and financial recession. Cash may be safe one day but devalued the next. In the last 15 years alone, the Russian ruble, Mexican peso, Argentine peso, and Hungarian forint have been devalued in different ways. Even the Swiss franc, a traditional safe haven, suffered a reversal in 2011, after it was pegged to the euro to protect trade. For those concentrated in that one currency, the move from 1.40 to the dollar to .95 was swift and brutal. All of this is to say: if your portfolio is extraordinarily heavy on any single asset class, you should probably reconsider your investment mix.

One of the least talked-about keys to portfolio diversification is investing in asset classes and instruments that behave differently at different points in the investment cycle. This process is as simple as finding assets that go up while other parts of your portfolio are going down. You should pay particular attention to periods when you need this diversification most, such as during investment panics and major bear markets. Building a portfolio from assets with different return streams, market components, and correlations is of paramount importance in maximizing the risk/reward ratio in your portfolio. As an example, Figure 6-1 shows the negative correlation between managed futures and stocks in the ten-year period ending December 31, 2007. With this -.23 correlation, the return streams are likewise negatively correlated, providing a portfolio with real risk/reward benefits. During crisis periods, this negative correlation becomes even more pronounced, offering a risk/reward advantage when you most need it.

CORRELATION OF SELECTED ASSET CLASSES*

	Managed futures	Bonds	U.S. stocks
Managed futures	1.00	0.30	−0.23
Bonds	0.30	1.00	−0.29
U.S. stocks	−0.23	−0.29	1.00

*Based on a 10-year period ending December 31, 2007
1) Managed futures: Barclay CTA Index;
2) Bonds: Lehman Brothers Long-Term U.S. Treasury Index;
3) U.S. stocks: S&P 500 Total Return Index;
Source: BarclayHedge, Ltd.

Figure 6-1. Managed futures are negatively correlated with stocks, offering risk/reward advantages.[2]

Systematic trend following is underrepresented in the vast majority of portfolios, as are managed futures in general. The traditional investment portfolio typically comprises a mix of stocks, bonds, and cash. Depending on her age and risk tolerance, an investor's portfolio split may be 50% stocks and 50% bonds. This is a good start and is better than buying single stocks on margin from the latest tipster, but this mix is still lacking in terms of diversification and risk control. While bonds have traditionally been a solid performer during bear markets, tending to rise in value while stocks sell off, this was not the case during the 1970s, when interest rates spiked, setting off a bear market in equities. During that period, stocks and bonds were highly correlated and provided little diversification. A similar situation obtains during the current period. At the time of this writing, bonds have been caught in a 20-year bull market, and much of the Western world is witnessing record low bond yields, with 1% yields for Japanese bonds, US Treasury bonds, UK gilts, and German bonds. There is simply little margin and scope left for bonds to fulfill their proper role during the next investment cycle. In fact, just as they do today in Greece, Portugal, and Italy, in the near future sovereign bonds are likely to begin pricing in sovereign risk for formerly safe-haven bond markets in developed markets. If bonds lose their function as a risk reducer in the future, where should an investor turn?[2]

Real estate, hard commodities, and managed futures provide an answer, in my opinion. Even though it has its ups and downs, real estate is a portfolio diversifier and the second-best asset class in terms of protecting your portfolio against inflation. Hard commodities provide protection from inflation and exposure to an entirely new asset class for most investors, and as a result represent a different return stream. Managed futures, especially systematic

---

[2] Figures 6-1 and 6-2 are used with permission from the Institutional Advisory Services Group, Inc.

Chapter 6 | Systematic Trend Following

trend following in a macro futures portfolio, provide the greatest protection against inflation for major asset classes, as they are positively correlated with inflation. Additionally, unlike real estate, managed futures also provide crisis alpha. In Table 6-2, you can see how each of the major asset classes correlates with inflation.

Table 6-2. How Major Asset Classes Correlate with Inflation (Source: Gorton/Rouwenhorst)

	Return	Inflation Correlation
Stocks	6.9%	(0.52)
Bonds	2.3%	(0.74)
Gold	2.4%	0.26
Housing	1.5%	(0.20)

One of the most unusual features of systematic trend following is that some of its strongest return periods are during secular bear markets, like the 1973–1974, 2001–2002, and 2008 bear markets. On their own, managed futures offer the potential for excellent returns, but they also come with volatile monthly numbers. As an addition to an overall portfolio, however, they increase the likelihood of positive returns while acting to *reduce* overall portfolio risk. The chart in Figure 6-2 highlights this portfolio benefit of managed futures.

You can see that adding managed futures to your portfolio, so that they constitute 20% of the mix, and taking stocks and bonds to 40% each increases your returns by almost 1% annually, while reducing your portfolio volatility by nearly 20%. Adding managed futures to the mix also puts your portfolio in a better risk/reward position. In addition, managed futures benefit performance when a trader most needs it—during bear markets—and correlate negatively during adverse economic periods. This is a real plus, as almost every other asset class is positively correlated with the economic cycle. Finally, bringing managed futures into your portfolio mix adds distinct asset classes that are not included in traditional portfolio choices. For all of these reasons, managed futures have earned a place in many portfolios and deserve consideration from sophisticated traders.

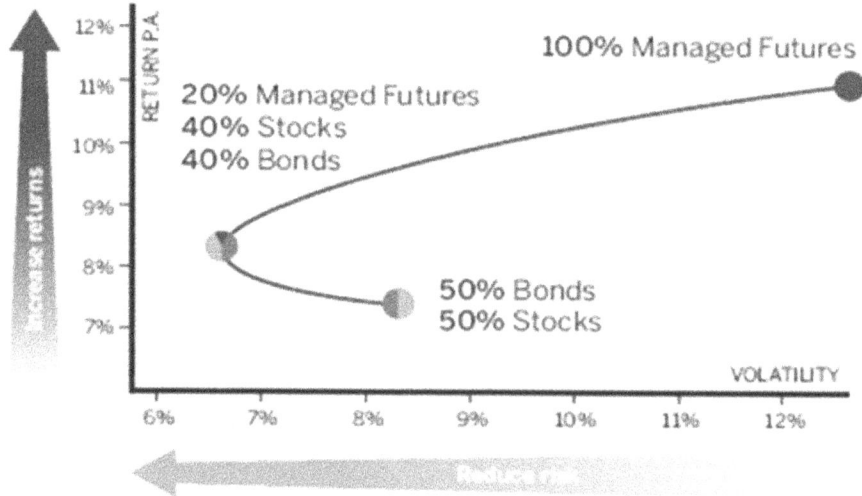

*1) Managed futures: CASAM CISDM CTA Equal Weighted;
2) Stocks: MSCI World;
3) Bonds: JP Morgan Government Bond Global;
Source: Bloomberg

Figure 6-2. Managed futures, when added to a portfolio, can increase returns while reducing risk.

Crisis Alpha and Black Swans

But we must learn to be equally good at what is short and sharp and what is long and tough.

—Winston Churchill

In addition to its ability to provide traders with global asset class diversification and uncorrelated investment returns, systematic trend following also gives traders exposure to two unique investment opportunities: crisis alpha and positive black swans.

You can observe crisis alpha in the positive returns and negative correlation that systematic trend following offered traders in lengthy bear markets and episodes such as 9/11, the flash crash of 2010, and the crash of 1987. This feature is what gives trend-following managed futures programs the potential to be a good fit for traditional investment portfolios, in spite of these trading systems' stand-alone monthly volatility. Remember that volatility and risk are two different things: volatility measures the variance of returns around the

Chapter 6 | Systematic Trend Following

mean return, while risk is typically associated with potential investment losses. Although managed futures certainly entail a risk of loss, as all investment classes do, this asset class is a true diversifier, impressively blending into the context of the larger portfolio. What's more, this uncorrelated investment class tends to deliver some of its best performance during the worst economic recessions and equity market declines. When this happens, managed futures provide true crisis alpha and demonstrate the main reason why they are such natural portfolio diversifiers.

In Figure 6-3, you can see the average annual returns on the top of each bar and the worst drawdowns at the bottom of the respective bars.

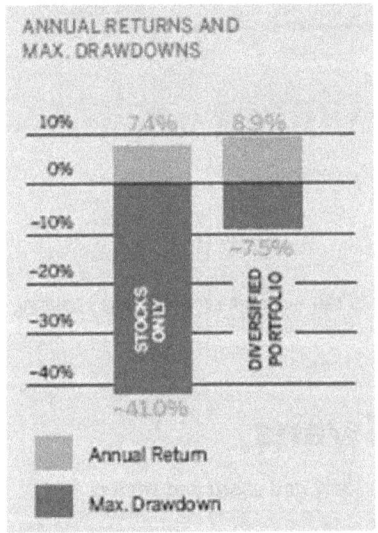

Figure 6-3. In the years 1987–2008, a diversified portfolio outperformed and reduced volatility. (Source: CME)

Notice that from 1987 to 2008, a stocks-only portfolio provided average annual returns of 7.4%, with a maximum drawdown of 41%. This is what mutual fund and equity-only investors had to endure during secular bear markets in 1987, 1990, 2001–2002, and 2008–2009. Compare this performance with a diversified portfolio holding of 20% futures, 40% stocks, and 40% bonds. The average return of this mix over the same period was 8.9% annually, while the worst drawdown was 7.5%! That's quite a contrast. As you can see, adding an uncorrelated asset category to your investment mix offers the investment free lunch (or nearly free lunch) of greater returns with less risk—which is why, despite the greater volatility of funds traded using systematic trend following, adding such funds to a portfolio may increase your returns while materially reducing your risk of loss. Think of how much better you would sleep knowing that a portion of your portfolio has the potential to offset most of your losses during periods of turmoil.

Systematic trend following also provides you with the opportunity to participate in black swan events, which could be anything from profiting from oil price spikes in the run-up to a war with Iran, to shorting bonds and catching the price gains that come from a sovereign default, to catching the heart of currency devaluation from a short position. By allowing you to participate in trends and then maintain your position until the trend changes, systematic trend following can capture the bulk of moves that few people, if any, saw coming or could reasonably have expected. For example, the great bull market in cotton in 2011, which saw cotton move from $0.20 to $1.70 in just eight months, was captured by trend-following programs.

It's also important to note that systematic trend following not only offers exposure to positive black swans but also provides extra returns during traumatic years like 2008, with the financial market crash, and 2010, with its extremely strong moves in the price of grain. This feature may be even more important in the future, as possible further stimulus programs and seemingly endless quantitative easing by central banks in the United States, the United Kingdom, China, Europe, and Japan, among others, are likely to lead to moves that we haven't seen before in oil, precious metals, currencies, and sovereign bonds. The instability of the financial system and its vulnerability to shocks, caused by exorbitant debt levels, increases the odds that many markets could witness moves on a scale not seen since the 1920s. For systematic trend followers, positive black swan exposure and crisis alpha have always been important in generating returns and negative correlations among asset classes, and they are likely to become even more important in the next five years.

In Sync with Change and Trends

Two roads diverged in a wood, and I – I took the one less traveled by, and that has made all the difference.

—Robert Frost

If you haven't noticed already, change has been a constant theme of this book—and with good reason. Change is the natural order of things. Nothing can be the same today as it was yesterday, so change is the underlying constant of the world we live in. You can look at change as either a disruptive threat or an opportunity, depending on your ability to position yourself to take advantage of it. If you want to be a successful systematic trend follower, you must embrace change, using it to capture trends as they develop and to profit from their larger moves—which happen with regularity.

Systematic trend following requires the flexibility to position yourself in the markets that are leading any advance and shorting those markets that are leading any decline. It requires the patience to wait for major trends to develop and then to follow along and hold your position until the trend has run its course. Having systematic rules in place to apply to this process simplifies the necessary decision-making and market selection. It keeps a trader in sync with the larger trends and at home in the investment landscape in which he finds himself.

CHAPTER 7

Discipline and Risk Control

What makes a great general? To know when to retreat; and to dare to do it.

—Duke of Wellington

So far in this book, I've addressed the markets and the attractive setups traders can use to play offense and create alpha for their trading accounts. But even if you master everything I have taught you thus far, you will have completed no more than a few steps in your journey to becoming a successful trend trader in the long run. Why? Because without risk control, you might as well kiss your profits goodbye. Risk control is *the* practice that ensures your long-term survival in the markets and keeps you profitably in the game, no matter how hard it gets. For this reason, I would recommend that you read this chapter on risk control several times so that you internalize the importance of this simple but powerful tool.

Risk control is what separates the trader who is hot for two to three years before he flames out and loses all of his winnings from the lifelong trader who will have fallow periods in the markets but never disastrous ones. Risk control is what keeps the magic of compounding alive so that you can realize truly significant long-term gains. It ensures that, no matter how wrong your positioning is or how many times the siren call of the crowd clouds your judgment, you will emerge from any market downturn with only minimal damage to your investment capital. If you learn nothing else from this book, you should learn never to underestimate the importance of risk control to your overall trading success.

The ONE Thing You Must Do—the Only Absolute Rule

> *Operate with a sense of peace and control. An investor who can accept what happens next, whether favorable or unfavorable, has a large emotional edge.*
>
> —John Hussman

I'm a firm believer in maintaining flexibility when trading the markets, which is why I am reluctant to offer up absolute trading rules. Using common sense, remaining flexible, and protecting your capital from the worst outcomes is more important to me. There is, however, one rule that I advocate adhering to: in every trade, exercise disciplined risk control by exhibiting a firm willingness to take losses at a predetermined price level. Risk control is your fail-safe point, the safety net for when your hands have slipped from the trapeze bars. It is the one thing that will protect your hard-earned capital, your ability to compound wealth, and your mental stability. Ignore it at your own risk!

Being disciplined about risk control has more to do with your mental approach to the markets than it does with cut-and-dried risk control rules, which is why it is important to adopt a big picture, odds-based viewpoint that allows you to see each trade you make in the context of your overall trading plan. You must adopt the mindset of the house at a casino, knowing that while you will have many losing trades, you will win in the intermediate and longer term by consistently applying your investment edge and maintaining flexibility and an ego-less approach to the markets. Take your losses in stride and look at them as a normal part of the trading process, not as an indication of failure.

After all, not every trade you make will work out. I've mentioned this statistic before, but it bears repeating: you can expect only 50-60% of your trades to be profitable. What's more, when you employ a systematic trend-following approach to the markets, you may be right only 30-40% of the time, so consider redefining investment success as taking small losses while letting your winners run. When you begin to see losses as a natural part of the trading process, their emotional sting will lessen, and you will be able to place each trade in its proper context. No one trade or position should be so important that you can't let it go (literally and emotionally) when it hits your stop.

Imagine that there are only five possible outcomes for each trade you make: a large gain, a small gain, breakeven, a small loss, or a large, potentially crippling loss. When you use a hard stop on every trade you make, you eliminate the fifth and worst outcome and protect yourself from the 20%, 50%, and 70%

losses that long-term investors routinely endure in their "core" holdings. On the other hand, if you let your losers run, the power of compounding will work against you.

As you can see in Table 7-1, to make up for a 20% loss, you would need to offset it with a 25% gain—and heaven help you if you lose 90% of your portfolio and find yourself having to hunt down a 900% gain! To make matters worse, each drawdown you suffer will erode your confidence level, forcing you to trade from a position of weakness. Remember that the only true hedge is a sale, because when you are safely cashed out of your positions, you will not sustain further losses, and you will be able to approach the markets again with a calm, detached attitude. After all, the markets will be there tomorrow, but it is up to you to make sure your capital is there to meet tomorrow's opportunities.

Table 7-1. How the Power of Compounding Can Work Against You

Drawdown %	Recovery % Needed
-10%	11%
-20%	25%
-30%	43%
-40%	67%
-50%	100%
-60%	150%
-70%	233%
-80%	400%
-90%	900%

Table 7-2 demonstrates the benefits of keeping your overall portfolio losses to a minimum. But how much room should you give each individual trade? I like to use a 1–3% portfolio impact as my stop-loss point. Now, the bulk of my trades are stopped out well before I ever reach this level, but my stop-loss point nevertheless functions as my risk control backstop. How so? Because I will automatically sell any given holding once the market hits my stop-loss level. This means that if a given trade makes up 10% of my portfolio, it can drop no more than 10% in price before it is automatically stopped out. You can adjust your stop-loss level to suit your risk profile and trading style, but once you have established your stop for a given trade, do not alter it to give the trade more room. Keep your edge and your discipline intact, and remember that each trade you make represents just a fraction of your overall trading activity. If you are forced to take a small loss, so be it. Examine the trade, see if it made sense, and then move on to the next idea and trade setup.

Table 7-2. Stop Levels and Examples

Portfolio Value	1% Equity Stop	5% Equity Stop
10,000	100	500
100,000	1,000	5,000
1,000,000	10,000	50,000
10,000,000	100,000	500,000

In addition to setting your risk tolerance for each trade that you make, I would also recommend that you establish an overall portfolio risk profile based on what would happen if, tomorrow, you were stopped out of every position you are currently holding. My personal overall portfolio risk profile uses 10% as a guideline, which means that I analyze my exposure and stop levels to limit my losses at any point in time to this percentage. (I also discuss diversification, risk control, and portfolio fit in Chapter 6.) This is another reason to trade more active markets, as it is easier to buy and sell them quickly. The last thing you want is for the market where you're long to resemble a roach motel—you can get in, but you can't get out. If you are having trouble determining how much of your portfolio is at risk at any given time, you can use sophisticated software analytic tools to help you measure your sector, country, and currency exposures and perform simulation drawdowns based on black swan events. The key point, however, is to have a plan in place that is simple and that you stick to at all times.

Although it may seem counterintuitive, the worst thing that can happen to you as a trader is to have a trade bounce back after you have violated your risk control strategy. Situations such as these will incorrectly teach you that it is sometimes acceptable to override your stops—even though it *never* is. Why? Because the moment that you do, you will have effectively thrown out your risk control discipline and put yourself back at the mercy of chance and the markets. Sure, in the short run the market often rewards bad behavior.

But over the long run, it severely punishes investors who lack discipline. Have a stop-loss sell discipline in place to ensure your long-term success.

Discipline Trumps Conviction

Do not fear mistakes. You will know failure. Continue to reach out.

—Benjamin Franklin

Just as a full house beats a pair of aces, discipline trumps conviction for the astute trader. The ego must submit to risk control in order to ensure long-term success. As a result, it is important to step back from your trading activities every so often and review your long-term trading game plan. When you are able to see each trade you make as just a small piece in a much larger puzzle, you will find it easier to take the necessary steps to stick to your trading strategy and maintain a healthy approach to the markets. Do you want to be right, or do you want to make money? The answer is obvious, so avoid making any trade personal or letting your conviction trump your discipline. Both traps are invitations to a beating.

There is another reason that your trading discipline should always come before your need to be right. The future is simply unknowable, no matter how smart you are or how much work you have done. Seemingly unrelated events have a way of ensnaring the stock market in a negative or positive feedback loop in such a way that even if your thesis is conceptually sound, external factors may override it. Take, for example, the Asian currency crisis of 1997. One day, investors were trading into a very strong bull market; six weeks later, the markets had undergone a major bear market correction due to slumping currencies in Thailand, Malaysia, and South Korea. What did Asian currencies have to do with technology stocks in the United States? Nothing, and yet everything, as tech stocks, caught up in the currency slump, underwent a severe short-term setback that no one could have anticipated before the onset of the currency crisis. But the unforeseeable connection between Asian currencies and tech stocks didn't matter to those who stuck to their trading discipline; they got stopped out with small losses and preserved their capital while other, less disciplined traders saw their trading accounts plummet.

While sticking to a trading strategy and maintaining hard stops are keys to achieving trading success, having the patience to wait for good trading opportunities is also a core component of a robust investment discipline. Why? Because avoiding marginal trades and waiting for solid risk/reward setups lower a trader's risk and exposure to his lowest-conviction ideas. There are times when no position is the best position, when uncertainty argues for taking a spot on the sidelines, and it is especially important that you maintain patience when confronted with these trying circumstances. Doing so serves three purposes: it preserves your capital, it allows you to view the investment landscape with a clear mind, and it keeps you focused on finding the next solid opportunity by ensuring that you are trading from strength. An expert trader has the ability to step back and wait for attractive patterns to develop. She doesn't jump the gun but rather holds back until a true move occurs and she can get an accurate picture of how the markets are developing. This keeps her capital and her mental state in an optimum condition for when prime opportunities do develop.

Constant Change Keeps You in Tune

> *By three methods we may learn wisdom: first, by reflection, which is noblest: second, by imitation, which is easiest: and third, by experience, which is the bitterest.*
>
> —Confucius

The typical investor in early 1929 learned that stocks always go up and that stocks that trade on the most margin make the best returns. An investor in 1932, on the other hand, learned that stocks are very dangerous. In 2002, gold was shunned completely after it had undergone a brutal 20-year bear market. Fast forward ten years into the future, however, and gold is one of the best-performing asset classes around. If history has taught us anything about investing, it's that investment classes, like fashion, have been and always will be subject to change. Meanwhile, the graveyard of bankrupt and battered companies is filled with the remains of formerly blue-chip stocks. WorldCom, Enron, Eastman Kodak, Delta Airlines, General Motors, Tandy, Circuit City, Blockbuster, Kmart, and Woolworths were all blue-chip stocks at one time or another. The stories of their declines are different, but they all fell victim to the same grim reaper: change.

Change is natural, yet long-term investors wish it away. It's as if it is simply too painful to acknowledge the temporary and fluid nature of the real world. But by committing to a long-term vision of the markets, buy-and-hold investors are effectively blinding themselves to the inevitable changes the markets will undergo, anchoring themselves to false assumptions, and leaving themselves vulnerable to enormous losses. The very strength of the conviction upon which their false assumptions rest makes them more likely to hold onto their mistakes for much longer than those who are flexible enough to regularly challenge their underlying assumptions about the markets and their investment theses. You cannot seek the truth and hide behind a lie at the same time.

Tastes, opinions, and technologies change rapidly, so you need to flow with change and implement a strategy that accounts for this very real feature of life on planet Earth. How can you accomplish this feat as a trend trader? By buying leading markets and selling poorly performing markets. This strategy not only ensures that you stay in tune with the times and own only those investment vehicles that are showing positive price movement, but it also forces you to flow with change as opposed to fighting reality. You will run faster with the wind at your back than with it blowing stiffly in your face. So it is in investing. A leading stock or market is telling you that its fundamentals are good and getting better. Conversely, you should avoid laggards that suffer repeated earnings misses and hit new yearly lows. At best, slumping stocks and markets will turn around after a significant amount of time has passed; at worst, they will be perpetual laggards that erode your capital month after month. Why endure the pain? Instead, accept and flow with change.

Remember: investing is cyclical, and industries and companies are in constant upheaval. Most of today's leading companies either will fall by the wayside or will become subpar investment vehicles in the future. An entire investment class could be subject to a 20-year bear market beginning tomorrow; today's top three economies may end up being the laggards of tomorrow. An entire continent—like Africa, which has been virtually stagnant and off the radar screen for investors for over 40 years—could be tomorrow's hot emerging market investment. Who talked about China in 2000? In 2002, who owned gold in any quantity? Change will come, and it is our job as traders to remain flexible and open to an infinite range of possibilities in the future.

Heed Warning Signs, and Remember, Market Action Trumps News

Tactics without strategy is the noise before defeat.

–The Art of War, Sun Tzu

Just as you would refuse a ride from a pilot who does not have access to the instrument panel, so too you should avoid navigating the turbulent investment skies without reading economic and sentiment indicators to warn you of approaching danger. I have developed proprietary short-term and intermediate-term readings comprising economic, technical, valuation, and sentiment indicators that guide my investment process and send loud signals at impending turning points in the stock market, but you don't need to develop your own if you have identified a few preexisting indicators that fit your trading outlook and style. The key point to remember is that the stock market is a discounting mechanism. It is forever trying to weigh the future prospects for the broad economy and ultimately for corporate earnings. The market does not care about the past and only occasionally does it worry about the present. Any indicator you use, therefore, should be chosen for its predictive value three to nine months into the future.

When selecting indicators to aid in your investment process, you should also remember that at a basic level, the markets are driven by the supply and demand of buyers and sellers. Have you ever noticed that the stock market tends to hit significant lows just after it has become the focal point of the local news? Doesn't it seem strange that the markets invariably suffer a bad break just when everyone is in a good mood about their investment portfolios and feeling like a guru? When market fundamentals are poor, but investors for the most part have sold out of their positions, leaving only longer-term holders in place, the markets may be primed to mount a surprisingly strong rally. The converse is also true; when the majority of investors are fully invested in the markets and the demand for stocks has been sated, the markets are ripe for sharp bouts of profit taking. How do we measure these extremes? What indicators have predictive value ahead of the curve? Some of the most important indicators to track regularly are put-call ratios, sentiment data, my proprietary overbought/oversold indicators, and volume and market breadth studies.

Figure 7-1 depicts activity in the stock market from 2006 to 2007. Notice the dashed line, which is the equity put-call ratio, and see how this ratio rises as traders purchase put options and declines as traders purchase call options. The equity put-call ratio is a sentiment measure and is meant to be used in a contrary fashion, meaning that as traders are fearful and rush to buy put protection, they may be signaling a stock market bottom, whereas when they are confident and are buying calls in droves, they may be signaling a stock market top. Readings over .70 should serve as bullish indicators, whereas readings under .60 should be seen as bearish reads on sentiment. While the equity put-call ratio is a secondary indicator to the trend, you can see that it identified several key turning points in the market, including a bottom in March 2007, as well as the bottoms in January 2006 and August 2007. It also did a good job of signaling several intermediate-term trading tops over a two-year span, particularly the July and October corrections in 2007.

I touched on the importance of indicators earlier in this book, especially in Chapters 2–5. But allow me to reiterate that it's essential not only to follow these indicators on a weekly basis through various technical services but also to look at them in a historical context. Only at extreme readings, however,

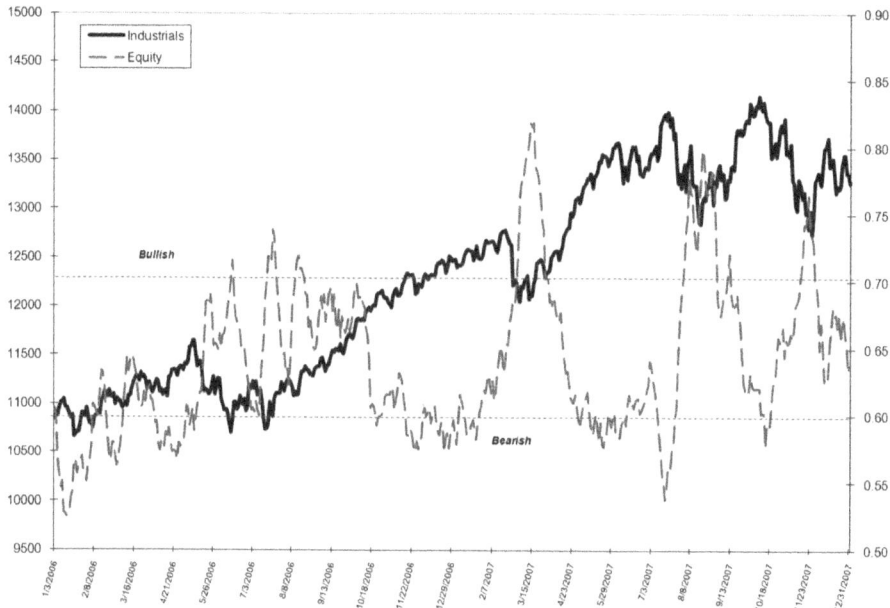

Figure 7-1. Activity in the DJIA in 2006-07 shows the usefulness of the equity put-call ratio as a measure of sentiment. (Source: everTrend Global, LLC; CBOE)

should you begin to act on their warning signs. When they are flashing a bright red warning that investors are too bullish, I strongly advocate raising your stop-loss levels and reducing your overall exposure so that you don't get trapped in short but sharp corrections. The end of a bull market can make for a great short-term trading environment, but you must shorten your time horizons, tighten your stop levels, and trade only the top opportunities available in liquid securities, so that you can move quickly to the sidelines as the markets become more volatile.

As a reminder, you should closely follow the Federal Reserve interest rate policy, the yield curve, high-yield bond spreads, and macro inputs. These indicators are more important than market news, as most news is typically filled with ex post facto excuses offered up by financial writers who are trying to explain away a given market event. More than once, I've seen two opposing headlines, one of which interpreted a market event positively while the other construed the same event negatively, based solely on the change in stock market levels. Action is more important than news.

Chapter 7 | Discipline and Risk Control

It's Your Capital—Stop Your Losses on Every Trade

> *It is the mark of an instructed mind to rest satisfied with the degree of precision which the nature of the subject admits and not to seek exactness when only an approximation of the truth is possible.*
>
> —Aristotle

Risk control wouldn't be necessary if you could always manage to be right with respect to trading, but who among us is *always* right about our trades? The fact of the matter is that no trader is right 100% of the time, but the good news is that if you can manage to be right just 50% of the time, you can make very good returns by following the simple maxim of letting your winners run and cutting your losers short. In fact, if you make a conscious effort to avoid the large losses that plague countless investors and traders, you will be more successful than 90% of your fellow market participants. Remember: your big-picture goal is to make attractive, long-term returns in the market, and the only way to do that is to avoid the large drawdowns that hurt traders on countless levels.

Earlier I discussed the math behind large losses. If you suffer a 20% loss, you need a 25% return to get back to even, while a 33% loss requires a 50% gain to get back to even. Isn't it incredible? Even if you suffer just one very bad year in the markets, several years may pass before you are able to recoup your monetary loss. What's more, recovering from your losses will exact a significant emotional toll, and there is a chance that you will become so discouraged that you will completely stop trading in the future—a decision that will cost you the very real potential to compound your wealth and attain financial freedom. Don't let this sorry situation happen to you. Stop your losses on *every* trade, take your losses quickly, and let your winners run. Cut losses, cut losses, cut losses, and you will earn the right to longevity in the trading arena.

Furthermore, do not fall in love with any market. Do not commit to gold or Apple or bonds. A market is just a vehicle that can help you reach your annual and longer-term goals. Paradoxically, if you research an individual stock or otherwise work too much on it, you can more easily fall prey to the deadly trap of convincing yourself that your position is right and the market is wrong. When a market violates your sell stop, do not call anyone to confirm your initial opinion, and do not do more "work" on the market. Instead, sell your position and move on. Once you are out of the position, the odds are good that you will realize the error of your ways. You will be wrong in this business, but that in itself is not reprehensible. The only serious mistake is staying with a losing position and compounding your initial error. In the long run, solid investment returns will accrue to those with a solid risk approach. Steady returns can be had only by those who avoid large losses and drawdowns. Treat your capital wisely, and it will be there for you in the future.

Eliminate Fat–Tail Losses

> *Everyone is a prisoner of his own experiences. No one can eliminate prejudices—just recognize them.*
>
> —Edward R. Murrow

A brief glance back at history confirms that change is incessant and can render the winners of today tomorrow's losers. As I pointed out earlier, the stock market's graveyard is littered with former blue-chip stocks. What went wrong? The tides of large-scale change swept in and knocked down even the best managed of these former greats, rendering their business models virtually obsolete in the blink of an eye.

Newspaper companies, for example, were considered safe blue-chip companies, with oligopolies or monopolies in their regional markets. They enjoyed tremendous long-term revenue growth and stability, they only occasionally suffered in the short run from recessions that caused them to pull back their advertising budgets, and they were well managed and enjoyed the capital support of both the equity and debt markets. Everything was going well, and the long-term outlook for the industry called for more of the same—until the Internet came out of nowhere. At first, the Internet was dismissed as a niche media market that didn't pose a serious threat to newspapers' advertising model, which hinged on readership and classified advertising. Within a few years, however, the world flocked to the Internet and pushed it into the mainstream. Since then, the Internet has managed practically to obliterate newspaper companies by leveraging real-time data and the interactive nature of the medium. It has captured each profit center that was once held by newspaper companies and has put a choke hold on their business models. Only ten years after it sprang into the mainstream, the Internet has forced newspaper companies to retrench and pushed them further and further into the Web to compete. In his seminal work, *The Black Swan* (Random House Trade Paperbacks, 2010), Nassim Taleb convincingly argues that change involves quantum leaps and is inherently impossible to predict. The newspaper companies would certainly agree with that assertion.

Why is this important? Because it makes long-term holdings in individual securities a much riskier proposition than is widely assumed. Each industry is subject to massive and rapid change that we cannot foresee today. Therefore, your investment method must be able to account for the risks and the opportunities associated with major change. As I discussed previously in this chapter, risk control and the use of stops-loss points will mitigate a fair share of your portfolio risk, but you should also focus on leading stocks, sectors, and markets if you want to eliminate fat-tail losses, by which I mean events that fall outside of three standard deviations—the odds of which are .03%, assuming a normal distribution. In the real world fat-tail losses are more prevalent, as mentioned numerous times throughout this book.

Another way to take fat-tail losses off the table is to move to a more nimble and less exposed position when technical and economic indicators are flashing ominous warning signs. It is important to remember that you are trying to eliminate the impact on your portfolio of the truly "unknowable unknowns," which means you are striving to eliminate the fat tails on the left side of the bell curve, as shown in Figure 7-2. Succeed in this, and you can remain in the game, enjoying the peace of mind that comes from a disciplined approach to trading the markets.

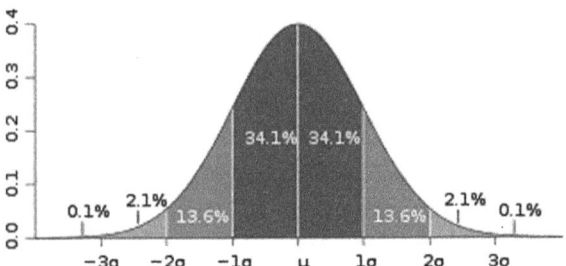

Figure 7-2. Strive to eliminate fat-tail losses, as seen on the left side of the bell curve.

Execute, Use Discipline—and Separate Your Ego from Your Trading Positions

> *Every man must patiently bide his time. He must wait—not in listless idleness, but in constant, steady, cheerful endeavors, always willing and fulfilling and accomplishing his task, that when the occasion comes he may be equal to the occasion.*
>
> —Henry Wadsworth Longfellow

Keep your eyes on the prize. It is easier to cross the finish line if you know where it is. If you keep your long-term and annual goals at the forefront of your mind at all times, you will be better able to view each trade you make within the context of the big picture, and it will be easier to take small losses and enjoy small and large gains. You will be able to refrain from giving in to the all-powerful ego and its constant need for stroking. You will avoid becoming emotionally and mentally invested in a situation in isolation from your bigger-picture goals. You will be able to operate in a disciplined fashion and flow with the markets.

On the other hand, if you marry your ego to your positions, you will be inflexible, closed to the message of the markets, and rigid in your investment opinions. You will not want to hear other opinions, as you will think you "know" the answer already. You will read only those research reports that confirm your position. You will feel the false strength that comes when a trader anchors herself to a false assumption. You will be lost and snow-blind. Now tell me: which of these two kinds of trader would you rather be?

If you are having trouble cultivating the correct "flow" mindset, I would suggest that you read up on the Eastern philosophies in Sun Tzu's *The Art of War*, *Living in the Now,* by Gina Lake, *Comfortable with Uncertainty*, by Pema Chedron, and *Zen Meditation in Plain English*, by John Buksbazen. The *Art of War* is especially beneficial to trend traders because it advocates the use of rules that are contingent on a particular environment. Given certain conditions, you should follow certain rules. There are no absolutes, no fixed rules that fit every situation. To apply the wisdom in *The Art of War* to trend trading, you must analyze the markets you are trading, know your current position, and then determine how best to position yourself for the market environment you see unfolding next.

If you are right in your analysis, your trades will be profitable. If not, you will take small losses and reassess your thesis. You must cut your losses at your predetermined levels, so that the damage from your incorrect moves costs you as little as possible. Remember: there is nothing wrong with making a mistake, only with staying with a mistake after you have been proven wrong. What if you really believe that you are right, but the markets move the other way? Discipline trumps conviction. You can always reassess the situation and reenter your position at a later date—but you should do so only after you have cleared your head. Do not tie up your ego in your trading decisions. *You are not your position.* Approach each day with an open mind and minimal assumptions, and you will spot opportunities, cut your losses, and realize profits you never thought possible. Accept and flow with reality.

Separate Winners from Washouts, and Stay in the Game

In financial markets, things always take longer to happen than you expect, but once they happen, events unfold much more quickly than you expect.

—Rudi Dornbusch, MIT professor

Chapter 7 | Discipline and Risk Control

An old rule of thumb states that it's easier to buy markets than to sell them, and that is patently true for the vast majority of traders. When you buy, you are moving from a neutral position of cash into a market. You have done your research, sized up your trade, and made a calculated decision to buy. Now you own it, and it's your baby.

If you have to let your position go at a loss, you are admitting that you have made an error. That is perfectly acceptable in the scheme of things; after all, none of us is perfect. But if you can't admit your error, if you allow your ego to enter into the trading equation, you will be unable to analyze the situation objectively, especially if you have not yet closed out of your losing position. And if you are holding onto a losing position that is quite substantial, your eventual loss might be so great that you'll be forced out of the game entirely. On the other hand, if you adhere to your risk control discipline, you will be able to stay in the game through thick and thin.

In your investment career, you will see hotshots rise like a phoenix and then crash like Icarus time and time again. These investors enter a certain investment cycle and capture the full returns on the upside, only to overstay their welcome and ride the cycle all the way back down again. In layperson's terms, they buy their own BS. Think back to the Internet bubble of 2000, when fortunes were made and then subsequently lost in hot stocks like Yahoo, CMGI, eBay, eToys, PMC Sierra, JDS Uniphase, and more. One-decision investors and traders bought the hottest stocks of the day and then assumed that the stocks were embarking on a new era, one in which they would be poised to rally indefinitely. They were wrong. Investors of this ilk will *always* be wrong over the long run, as each investment sector has its day in the sun, only to be replaced eventually by the next new thing.

Philosopher Karl Popper stated that if you can't see the flaw in your thesis, the odds are that you don't understand the problem. If you use risk control and stop-loss points, you don't need to be able to foresee each problem that will arise in the future because you will be stopped out of losing positions by the action of the marketplace itself. The market will tell you when you are wrong, saving you from significant losses so you can live to fight another day. In short, you will be a long-term survivor in the investment business.

CHAPTER 8

Pitfalls

> *Acknowledge your fears, manage your risk, accept your limitations, learn from your mistakes, and move confidently forward.*
> —Nassim Taleb

We all have different psychological profiles, which means that you bring a set of assets and liabilities to the trading arena that you do not share with any other trader. Despite your unique mental makeup, however, the odds are high that, during your trading career, you will encounter at least one of the mental trading pitfalls discussed in this chapter. Some of these pitfalls may be problems that have already presented themselves to you, while others may lie in wait stealthily for several years before you trip over them. Regardless of when you encounter the many traps that await you along your trading journey, I am confident that you can benefit from the lessons I've learned in my decades of blood, sweat, and tears in the markets—lessons that I'm sharing with you in this chapter.

Stock market lessons are expensive and painful, and no matter how successful you become, you will continue to have losing trades from time to time. Therefore, you should strive not for perfection but for improvement. To help you in your quest to become a better trader, I suggest that you read this chapter with an open mind and review it periodically, especially when things are going well and hubris begins to creep in. After all, it is in good times, when sloth and complacency lull the unsuspecting trader to sleep, that you are most likely to fall into one of these traps and be pulled into the trading bog.

We're Hardwired for Trading Failure

> *The financial markets generally are unpredictable, so that one has to have different scenarios. The idea that you can actually predict what's going to happen contradicts my way of looking at the market.*
> —George Soros

Chapter 8 | Pitfalls

Like golf, trading can be a difficult endeavor because it requires participants to act against their instincts. In golf, the natural tendency to stop a slice is to swing harder on an outside-in swing path. This results in—you guessed it—a bigger slice, as more right-to-left sidespin acts upon the golf ball. Similarly, the golfer who tends to top the ball will make the incorrect adjustment of trying to scoop the ball so that he gets under it and hits it higher. The result, of course, is that the golfer will top the ball even more or hit the ground well before his club reaches the golf ball. So it is in trading. More often than not, our natural inclinations serve to derail us from the track of trading success. In fact, we are predisposed to trading failure, which is why so few do it well. David Druz sums it up well—"Very few people succeed in this process. The learning curve is too steep and the correct psychology is too hard to implement. If you have any attachment to making money, and who doesn't, it is very tough to trade correctly." But fear not; all is not lost. To achieve trading success, half the battle is knowing what holds us back—and now you know that in many cases, it is *you* who are standing in the way of victory.

How, exactly, are we hardwired for trading failure? First and foremost, we want to win—and we don't want to win just once in a while, just sometimes, and just by small margins. No, we want to win big and all the time. Humans are naturally competitive, and those who gravitate toward trading tend to be among the most competitive of us all.

In trading, though, you will be wrong, and you will be wrong *a lot*. The very best traders are right only 50 to 60 percent of the time. The world's most successful hedge fund, which employs several hundred of the finest traders in the US, found that the top 10 percent of their traders were right just over 60 percent of the time. Remember: this fund is the crème de la crème of trading firms, and its success rate was *still* just a little better than a coin flip. There is little chance that you're as good a trader as those employed by that firm (or a better one), so recognize your limitations now and build them into your trading strategy. Always remember that trading is not about your ego, so check it at the door. Take your losses, and you'll win in the long run. Fail to take your losses, and you will be the loser.

In life, we are taught to try harder, to use our strength to fight through the tough times, and to persevere in the face of adversity, all of which are noble goals. In trading, however, acting in accordance with these maxims is the equivalent of flailing wildly about while stuck in quicksand: even though you feel as if you're improving the situation, all you're really doing is speeding up the sinking process. As Ben Franklin said, "Never confuse motion with action." We are programmed to work hard, to attack, and to get things done. The hard-charging caveman who woke from his slumber at 5 a.m., grabbed the biggest club he could find, and was first to hunt in the most favorable spots came home with the family meal. It worked for him. But it won't necessarily work for you.

Now, I'm not advocating that you take things easy, roll into the office at noon, and grab a cocktail by 4 p.m. You must work hard, but you must work smart first. In a bull market, there are probably four to six months when the conditions are favorable to trade with the odds firmly in your favor. In a bear market or a sideways market, you may have only two to three favorable months when the odds favor trading. Yet the cave dweller in all of us wants and craves action. In most work environments, doing more is admirable. In trading, however, doing more when the conditions clearly do not favor trading will only cost you money, increase your stress, and lead you to risk financial ruin. Is that what you want? Fight the urge to do more; in tough times, you will do more by doing less.

The society and institutions that surround us also hardwire us for trading failure. We are taught to be part of a team, to join the crowd, to cheer along with those from our group, our town, our country. Maintaining a team mentality is appropriate when you're backing your political party, when you are among sixty thousand strong packed into a football stadium, or when you're in a brigade of Army soldiers who are taught to follow strict orders. Sadly, it is not appropriate in trading.

In trading, you must stand alone and think independently. You determine your success or failure—you and not anyone else. There is no army of great traders you can join. There is no trading team. There is simply you, sitting in front of your trading screens with your skills and your talents, working to turn a profit. The good news is that *you* are all you'll ever need to succeed in trading. The bad news is that you must conquer the urge to frolic with the crowd. Stop your ears against the siren songs of others. When everyone else is being swept up by a trend in the markets, it's time to be extremely wary and move to the sidelines.

When Your Reason Is Invalid, So Is Your Position

When the facts change, I change my opinion. What do you do, sir?

—John Maynard Keynes

Before you enter any trade, you must have a valid ruling reason for doing so. Even if you end up making a losing trade, your reason for entering into that trade still could have been perfectly valid. What is *not* perfectly valid is holding onto a trade once your reason is no longer valid. If you bought a market because it was breaking out, but then it quickly fails, sell it! If you bought a technology stock expecting a large surge because of a robust earnings report from Apple Inc., but then techs begin to sell off, sell it! If you expect your airline stock to rally because you expect crude oil prices to decline, but they rally instead, sell it! If you are long corn because you expect an extremely favorable crop report, but then that report comes back negative, sell it! If you are short bonds because you are expecting strong employment numbers and they rally in response to strong employment numbers, cover!

Once your ruling reason for getting into a trade is no longer valid, neither is your trading position. John Maynard Keynes once stated, "When the facts change, I change my opinion. What do you do, sir?" So, what do you do when the reason for your trade is no longer valid? If you stay in your losing position, hoping your trade will turn around, then your position is lost. Remember that you must trade from a place of strength. Once you start flailing away blindly in the quicksand of busted trades, you will sink in your position of weakness. You will then be as lost as your positions are.

It's Not 9 to 5

It is a wise person who adapts himself to all contingencies; it's the fool who always struggles like a swimmer against the current.

—Unknown

We are creatures of habit, the whipping boys and girls of the industrial world. Thomas Edison's invention of the light bulb let us tame light and turn on the sunshine easily, effortlessly, and habitually. We rise to an alarm clock that we set, get into a car or subway at a predetermined time of our choosing, arrive at our destination, and power up our trading screens. Meanwhile, our computerized office calendars and smartphones alert us to our upcoming appointments. These pieces of our lives are neat, tidy, organized, and structured. However, the markets, opportunities, and important things in life are not. They ebb and flow to their own rhythms, blissfully unconcerned about waking or sleeping according to our artificial daylight and fitting into our even more artificial 9-to-5 rhythms. Days, weeks, and sometimes months will go by in the markets before even one ideal trading opportunity presents itself, yet the vast majority of traders continue to try to fit square peg trades into round holes as they struggle to fight reality itself.

We've managed to tame many aspects of our lives, but the markets aren't among them. They beat and pulse to their own rhythms and refuse to bend to our wills. The New York Stock Exchange may open every day at 9:30 a.m.

and close every day at 4:00 p.m. (except on those true "black swan" occasions, like September 11, 2001), but just because the markets are open doesn't mean that there are worthwhile trades to be made. Just because you can point, click, buy, and sell doesn't mean that you should. As Yogi Berra said, "We may be lost, but we're sure making good time." Take opportunities when they are there, not when you need them or want them to be there. Trade when your tools and your methodology indicate that conditions favor successful operation in the markets.

To the layperson, it may appear that you're sitting around idly as you wait for market opportunities to develop. So what? Forcing trades and demanding that the uncertain realm of the markets conforms to society's 9-to-5 system will lead to unforced errors, bad habits, and excess stress—not greater profits. Fill the valleys of inactivity with study. Read and hone your craft. Don't flail about. It has been said that true wisdom is fitting rules to circumstances. If the circumstances don't favor your operating in the market, don't trade.

Assuming and Anchoring—the Deadly A's

> *I followed a golden rule, namely, that whenever a published fact, a new observation or thought came across me, which was opposed to my general results, to make memorandum of it without fail.*
>
> —Charles Darwin

Just like the seven deadly sins, the deadly A's should be avoided at all costs, as each is the result of a mental hole in our thinking. The first deadly A, assuming, is a mental habit that pervades our day-to-day lives. But while we can assume that the sun will rise each day, we probably can't safely assume too much more than that. Why? Because change is too rapid and the world is too uncertain to maintain many other fixed assumptions. When it comes to the markets, one should never have *any* fixed assumptions. How many of the following assumptions have you found yourself falling victim to?

- A certain blue-chip stock won't trade under ten times earnings or yield more than 5%.
- Markets are inherently efficient and are driven by fundamentals.
- Low bond yields are good for stocks.
- High oil prices are bad.
- Stock buybacks are good for a particular stock.

Chapter 8 | Pitfalls

I'd wager that you would agree with most of the above statements, and yet these assumptions have been proven wrong numerous times in different stock market cycles. Why is it, then, that we continually fall prey to our assumptions? As Karl Popper stated: "Most people don't propose theories to be tested, they propose assumptions." No general framework or theory is permanent. Remember: you cannot prove anything, but you can disprove something with just one exception to a well-established rule. Just because you've seen a turkey live for a thousand days in a row doesn't mean that the bird will make it past this upcoming Thanksgiving. There is only change and your observations of reality. The second deadly A, anchoring, is related to assuming. Once you have taken hold of a golden, immutable, flawless (and incorrect) assumption, you can easily make the mistake of mentally anchoring to that assumption, regardless of whether it conflicts with unfolding reality. In fact, when reality threatens to undermine a given assumption, it becomes even easier to anchor that assumption, block reality, and mentally live within the reality you have created for yourself. Human beings crave certainty; we like things to be orderly and predictable. We are constantly in search of our own personal Rock of Gibraltar to cling to in dangerous seas. We need the beacon to shine from the lighthouse and show us the way when we are lost. We need to anchor our ship. But there is a problem that comes with the imagined safety of an anchor: anchors can keep you firmly committed to a bad position with a deceptive sense of misplaced confidence. As we've discussed previously, "wrong and strong" is a dangerous and vulnerable mental stance for any trader.

As an example, the consensus view in early 2008 was that high and rising oil prices would continue well beyond that year because the large emerging economies of the BRIC nations—Brazil, Russia, India, and China—would need an ever-increasing amount of energy to power their burgeoning economies. Extrapolating the BRIC countries' prior five-year expansion into the future, analysts projected an ever-rising daily thirst for oil in these nations. That growing thirst, combined with the preestablished energy needs of the rest of the developed world, would (it was argued) put pressure on the producing nations, which were at or very near peak oil production. Since producing nations couldn't possibly meet the increased energy needs of the world, prices would continue their stunning rally and possibly touch $200 or $300 per barrel. Ergo, the analysts held, one could safely buy and then hold energy stocks and crude oil futures through any market "dips."

When they made their oil price projections, however, the analysts made the same mistake they almost always make: they assumed that the BRIC countries would follow along a linear path to prosperity when, in fact, they didn't. Energy analysts weren't alone in this assumption. In fact, this line of thinking proved disastrous to many, including the best and brightest in finance.

As peak oil prices came and then went in July 2008, major holders of energy stocks disregarded the initial declines as being normal reactions to gyrating markets. Even as oil continued its "panic" declines to lower levels, these fundamentalists ignored reality, dug in more strongly than before, and clung ferociously to their Rocks of Gibraltar, their shining beacons, their anchors. While such tenacity had given them the strength to ride out previous market corrections in the group, this time it only served to ensure their failure, as it reaffirmed their faulty convictions and closed their eyes to the fact that the downturn was continuing in contradiction to every logical assumption they held. In the end, almost one third of long/short equity hedge funds went out of business because of the devastating losses they suffered in 2008. Most had been positioned in long-term holdings in energy and mineral stocks that proved to be their undoing.

As Ronald Reagan once remarked, "Do not be afraid to see what you see. Facts are stubborn things." Anchoring to a false assumption freezes the mind into a rigid state, keeping it closed to contradictory thoughts or realities. Anchoring keeps the truth at bay and closes our eyes to reality.

Fighting Trends and Outthinking Mr. Market

We have two classes of forecasters: those who don't know—and those who don't know they don't know.

—John Kenneth Galbraith

Our minds are truly amazing. We can process incredible amounts of data and draw varied and creative conclusions from this information stream, so we like to think we are smart, cunning, and sophisticated. Maybe we are. But it seems to me that we tend to be skeptical too often—and in the wrong ways. Even as we place excessive trust in our own assumptions and anchoring, we stubbornly fight dominant trends that are clearly evident in the markets, priding ourselves on our skepticism about what is right before our eyes.

In the example about oil prices in the previous section, market participants were fighting a downtrend and holding onto their positions even as the market was clearly telling them that their assumptions were wrong. The same phenomenon is just as apparent when a market is in the early stages of advancing to new highs. Instead of buying breakouts in an emerging uptrend, traders will tend to believe that the stocks are too expensive, too speculative, too early, or just plain wrong. They will be skeptical when they should be open to the messages that the market is plainly communicating to them. They will be dubious and distrustful rather than asking why a certain market event is unfolding and then buying into the advance (using risk control, of course). Rather than buying into a breakout, they will feel more comfortable buying supposed blue chips or taking further losses in a dozen other laggards that are "cheap." In short, traders are predisposed to do the wrong thing.

In any market cycle, only a handful of industry groups and leading markets are truly worthy of your investment dollars. The market will tell you where to put your capital, if you will only listen. To hear the message, you have to be willing to flow with the market and let it tell you where to go.

Guessing and the Big Score

I was gratified to be able to answer promptly. I said I don't know.

—Mark Twain

"I'm going to take a shot at XYZ reporting earnings tonight," says Sam. "Why?" you ask. "I just have a feeling that the numbers will be good," comes the lame reply. You've heard this before. In fact, you've probably even said this before. But the truth is that when you make trading plays based on hunches or intuition, you are guessing instead of making intelligent investment decisions. Worse, you're probably trading for no other reason than you have found a horse to bet on. As the saying goes, "You can't win if you don't bet." That's true. But you can't win in the long run if you don't have an edge, and guessing is not an edge.

We all get what we want from the markets. Some crave excitement and action. Some enjoy the feeling of playing on the big stage with millionaires and billionaires. Others are looking for the big score to attain wealth instantly. What do you want? If you can answer that question honestly, you can begin to implement a plan that will allow you to achieve your goals. Once you know what you want from the market, write down your plan for obtaining it, and make this plan as concrete and specific as possible. State your plan and review it at least quarterly so that you stay on track. Your big-picture goals should drive your daily trading activity. Don't trade just to trade or just to do something. Just because you've come to work, analyzed hundreds of charts, read through all the pertinent research you can find, and sourced investment ideas before the markets open, that does not mean you have to trade today—or even tomorrow. Flow with the markets and trade when your ideas fit the market environment. If you trade for the big score or for the thrill of the action, you will attain those things, but long-term profits will prove elusive.

Joining the Crowd, Buying the News

Men, it has been well said, think in herds; it will be seen that they go mad in herds, while they only recover their senses slowly, and one by one.

—Charles McKay

Buzz, noise, stories, rumors, tips, and news are all around us, nagging at the edges of our consciousness and tempting us every single day. Your broker calls to tell you that BioFuture is about to receive approval for a major drug or that InPlay is about to be taken over. On television, you hear about a major earnings release that will be made public tonight and potentially spark a big rally in technology stocks. Your friend calls to tell you that you should be fully invested to take advantage of a sharp rally that his indicators are telling him is just about to unfold. A news report mentions that copper is going to rally big on Chinese buying. A newsletter writer sends you an email reminding you that her subscribers were up 50 percent last year based on her sharp investment insights. When you get home, your neighbor tells you that his friend John just heard that RumorMonger's business is booming and the company is hiring all the bright people they can. Noise, noise, noise! And none of it matters. They are all selling, talking, and buzzing, but the smart trader isn't buying. Why?

As Friedrich Nietzsche once wrote, "Insanity in the individual is something rare ... but in groups, parties, nations, and epochs, it is the rule." People are social animals, and the pull of the crowd is strong. It is so strong, in fact, that people are known to be more easily swayed and manipulated when they are in a group setting; their intelligence levels drop and their basest cravings prevail over their rationality. Carl Jung expressed the view that crowd-herding behavior was natural in *The Undiscovered Self*, when he wrote,

> *All mass movements, as one might expect, slip with the greatest ease down an inclined plane represented by large numbers. Where the many are, there is security; what the many believe must of course be true; what the many want must be worth striving for, and necessary, and therefore good. In the clamor of the many there lies the power to snatch wish-fulfillments by force; sweetest of all, however, is that gentle and painless slipping back in to the kingdom of childhood, into the paradise of parental care, into happy-go-luckiness and irresponsibility. All the thinking and looking after are done from the top; to all questions there is an answer; and for all needs the necessary provision is made. The infantile dream state of the mass man is so unrealistic that he never thinks to ask who is paying for this paradise. The balancing of accounts is left to a higher political or social authority, which welcomes the task, for its power is thereby increased; and the more power it has, the weaker and more helpless the individual becomes.*

Chapter 8 | Pitfalls

I've seen the herd mentality firsthand in that great invention of the investment world: the investment conference. In my opinion, there is no better place to witness the madness of the crowd than at an investment conference, where a normally staid group of investment professionals comes together and rapidly mutates into an investment mob. During quiet market times, there is little news, either positive or negative, for an investment conference to feed on or feed into, but at turning points, the mob is unleashed.

During my investment career, two particular conferences left an indelible mark on me, as they vividly illustrated the contrasting investment psychology at the top and bottom of the markets.. In March 2000, I attended an impressive investment conference in San Francisco that was held just weeks before the ultimate peak of the technology boom and the 18-year bull market in stocks. The conference was held at the Ritz Carlton in Nob Hill, and the trappings were out of a Scott Fitzgerald novel. As investors arrived at the conference, the driveway was jammed with Porsches, Ferraris, and Lamborghinis as they made their way to the valet stand. Once inside, the tech CEOs and CFOs who were the stars of the conference seized upon the opportunity to display themselves in all of their stock option glory.

The conference itself was overflowing with attendees, and the presentations drew standing-room-only crowds. You literally couldn't move without bumping into an analyst or portfolio manager from one of the hottest mutual funds or hedge funds in the world. All the top names were salivating to buy the latest bullish presentation, hoping to make contacts and glean the next bullish sliver of news. Even waiters were looking for stock tips as they served attendees an impressive array of snacks, drinks, lunches, and lavish dinners. The nightly entertainment for the weeklong conference included the top names in entertainment, who were flown in and paid six-digit fees for the night. The crowd's bullishness about investing in technology and stocks in general was at a crescendo, and analysts were forecasting ever more gains, ever more innovation, ever more of everything. Greed and euphoria were palpable.

In February 2009, just weeks before the bear market bottomed out, I attended a very different investment conference, in Geneva. The day before, as I took a taxi in from the airport, the driver asked me if people in America were all poor and slept in boxes. That set the tone. At the conference, there was no nightly entertainment. There was no bumping into people. Food came in little boxes, and you could drink coffee, water, or soda. During a conversation with a Greek pension fund manager, I asked if his fund planned to reallocate some of its investments to stocks given the significant overweight position bonds now represented in his portfolios. He looked at me like I was crazy. No one was bullish. Stocks were universally despised, and the worry wasn't about making money; it was about whether the system itself could be saved. Fear was palpable.

You will see this cycle, from greed to fear and back, again and again. Ignore it. The only news that matters is the action of the stock market itself. So remember: your observations and insights—based on your study of trends as I've outlined in this book—should have a greater impact on your trading decisions than any other outside information. Of course, the tendency among amateur traders to grasp at expert opinion is understandable. After all, in most fields, knowledge is more absolute. In math, 1+1 always equals 2. In the stock market, however, there are only odds to success. As a result, knowing how to manage losing trades is infinitely more important than any piece of information you pick up from a friend, colleague, or television personality.

More experienced traders also have a tendency to buy the news and the opinions and thoughts of others, but this behavior is not the result of a belief in absolutes but rather comes from feelings of insecurity that the trader harbors about his own methods. It is especially easy to fall prey to the noise of the crowd after suffering through a losing period in the markets, but it is important to remember that even the best trading method will go through cycles where it is less successful.

Thanks to the pervasive reach of the Internet, more news and information are available to investors than ever before. Use the information that is available to you, but filter any ideas or data you unearth through your trading process. Your opinions, observations, and method should be the only things you use to make buy and sell decisions. Take responsibility for both your good and your bad ideas. Be honest with yourself. Don't buy the hype; you've got everything you need between your own two ears.

It's Not Different This Time, Because People Don't Change

Those who cannot remember the past are condemned to repeat it.

—George Santayana

As discussed previously, the investment world is in a constant state of flux, with different industries, markets, and countries coming into and out of favor very quickly. The change that continually roils the investment landscape is not new. At various times in the last hundred years, different groups of stocks and market sectors have captured the imagination of the investing public. Rails, the "Nifty Fifty," radio stocks, casinos, the technology bubble of 2000, the

Asian "miracle," tulip mania, the South Sea bubble, silver, gold, bonds, the Swiss franc, Japanese stocks, big-box retailers, oil stocks, and emerging market stocks have all seized the attention of the investment public at one time or another. Change, upheaval, and the ongoing quest for progress will continue unabated, and Adam Smith's process of creative destruction will lead to the inevitable rise and fall of countless industries in the future.

The face of the markets may change, but the game will remain the same. Traders may have computers and online accounts instead of ticker tapes and a phone, but market participants will always cycle through the primal emotions of fear and greed. Bernard Baruch summed it up nicely when he commented, "Two and two still make four and no one has ever invented a way of getting something for nothing. When the outlook is steeped in pessimism I remind myself two and two still make four and you can't keep mankind down for long."

During the latter stages of a bull market, traders tend to position themselves aggressively. With their confidence running high, they will chase high-beta markets at every turn. At the depths of a brutal bear market, on the other hand, the opposite is true. So-called long-term investors will swear off stocks and sell at any price to avoid the pain of losing. Then they will tell you that the economy and the stock market are mired in a long-term slump and have little chance of recovering in the future. You will see this psychological ride repeat itself time and time again through each and every investment cycle the market undergoes. Perceptions in the markets change more rapidly and to a much greater degree than market fundamentals change. In many ways, this business is even more cyclical than the economy it loosely forecasts.

Reality vs. "Should Be"

When one door closes, another opens: but we often look so long and so regretfully upon the closed door that we do not see the one which has opened for us.

—Alexander Graham Bell

Hope is not an investment strategy, yet many substitute it for analysis and proactive risk control. When you hope for an event to unfold in the markets, you are effectively declaring that you are at the mercy of the whims of other traders and investors. You cede your thought process to chance, which is tantamount to fighting a losing battle while praying for victory. And let me tell you, you won't win. Larry Hite, a trend-following legend states it well when he says, "We have no bias. We don't believe anything 'has to' happen; we look at what has happened, and what is happening to our money." At all times, you bear responsibility for your successes and failures in the market. Whenever you catch yourself blaming someone or something else for a loss you have suffered, step back, take responsibility for your decisions, and learn from the situation. Do not dwell on the loss for any longer than it takes to learn from it, then move on and don't look back. You can only live and trade in this moment. You cannot trade the past, but you must learn from it.

You may not like the market you are dealing with, but it is the only one there at any given time. Therefore, you must trade within the context of reality and not according to what you wish or think reality should be. Then, when market opportunities do arise, seize and profit from them. You can only trade today within the market environment surrounding you. Accept this fact, analyze the best moves you can make given the reality of the markets you face, and take responsibility for all of your actions.

It's Not All Fundamentals, Schoolboy

> *Not everything that can be counted counts and not everything that counts can be counted.*
>
> —Albert Einstein

Do you remember my earlier discussion about anchoring to assumptions and how this bad habit can affect your perceptions of reality? A related error is assuming that every move in stocks or the markets as a whole is related to changes in fundamentals. Nothing could be further from the truth. For example, think about how futures selling takes over and drives stocks down sharply during a normal correction. In these waves of selling, supply simply overwhelms demand. As a result, virtually all stocks that are tied to a given index, like the S&P 500, will be driven down in price. In this case—and in many other cases as well—it is not fundamentals but rather supply and demand that bears responsibility for short-term movements in prices. In the long run, fundamentals do matter, but as John Maynard Keynes stated, "In the long run we are all dead."

Figures 8-1 and 8-2 illustrate market scenarios where purist fundamentalism failed market participants who adhered to it. Anyone who follows sell-side research knows how often fundamentalists advocate buying high and selling low, but what good does buying high do if those same stocks subsequently undergo startling declines of 70–90% before the recommendation to sell is made? If that's their contribution to investing, I say pass!

Chapter 8 | Pitfalls

Figure 8-1. U.S. Steel – Fundamental Buy and Sell Recommendations

Figure 8-2. Fundamental Natural Gas Outlook

The markets are driven by myriad factors, and the savvy trader uses all the tools she has at her disposal without digging in her heels and closing her mind to other successful methods of trading. I've found that my trading is most effective when I use a combination of technical, economic, sentiment, fundamental, and liquidity measures in concert with one other. The bottom line, however, is that you must approach this business with an open mind and continually seek to learn the latest tricks of the trade from successful operators.

Taxes—Pay the Man

Be thankful we're not getting all the government we're paying for.

—Will Rogers

Ask a room filled with a hundred investors to shout loudly if they like to pay taxes, and you will be greeted by the sound of silence. No one likes to pay taxes, but they are part of the tab that is part and parcel of being successful, and the bill will always come due. You can minimize your tax bite through tax-deferred vehicles and retirement accounts and by maintaining some longer-dated investments outside of the markets. Beyond deploying those strategies, however, you should not concern yourself with taxes—and they should not drive your investment decisions, as allowing them to do so will almost certainly lead to calamity.

My old boss, Ralph Bloch, used to joke that if you hold your positions long enough, your tax problems will go away, but many investors and traders seem to treat the sentiment behind this joke as dogma. During strong bull markets their focus shifts from making profits to avoiding taxes, leading them to refuse to let go of their winners. Their stocks have treated them well so far, and even though they can see warning signs on the horizon, they ask themselves, "Why shouldn't the stock keep going up forever?" In a catastrophic decision, they allow their false sense of security to intermingle with their misplaced fear, and eventually they wind up surrendering all of their gains. Sure, they've solved their tax problem, but they've sacrificed their returns and profits in the process. When you are successful, you pay the man and move on. Remember to focus on your analysis, not on tax avoidance.

Chapter 8 | Pitfalls

I'm Never Wrong, or the Fallacy of Intelligence

> As far as the laws of mathematics refer to reality, they are not certain; and as far as they are certain, they do not refer to reality.
>
> —Albert Einstein

The investment field draws intelligent people with the lure of profits and open-ended success. Entrants to the career bring strong personalities and skills coupled with degrees from the most prestigious universities on the planet. Once they're on the job, the top investment professionals in the field work for blue-chip firms that employ the latest technological advances. The money these firms spend on research, consultants, and strategists could fund a small army. All of their apparent advantages, however, tend to give investment professionals a false sense of their own intelligence, which often leads to their downfall during times of dramatic change.

During inflection points in the market, high-ranking professionals within the world's best investment firms often know less than the cabbie who whisks them to their next power lunch. Why? Because their unprecedented access to the best information money can buy carries two potential pitfalls. First, because these firms tend to be isolated from the real world and the real economy in a small bubble that includes New York, London, and Tokyo, the information they rely upon necessarily comes from second-hand sources. As a result, they are especially vulnerable during larger shifts in tastes and emerging trends.

The second and much larger danger is the false sense of infallibility their so-called information "edge" gives them. I've said it once and I'll say it again: "long and strong" is the most dangerous investment stance you can take. When you have access to the best analysts, the most powerful technology, and real-time information from well-connected thought leaders, it is easy—and incredibly dangerous—to assume that you are right and that the market is wrong and will come around to your viewpoint. Even the most intelligent and well-connected investment professionals—and the firms they work for—can fall prey to this form of hubris.

Just look at Long Term Capital Management (LTCM). The principals of LTCM literally wrote the book on modern finance theory and option pricing, and the firm employed no fewer than three Nobel Prize winners. LTCM was widely regarded as one of the few free lunches on Wall Street and promised investment returns of 20% or more with little risk and volatility—until the firm blew up in spectacular fashion in the fall of 1998. In addition to failed risk models that convinced the firm to use ever-increasing amounts of leverage, hubris and a belief in its own infallibility burned a cool multi-billion-dollar fund to the ground. LTCM is just one of many firms that have collapsed spectacularly in the past ten years, and the common denominators among them all include a sense of infallibility, blindness to their own assumptions, excessive leverage, and a market event that exposes these shortcomings to the harsh light of reality.

So, how do you avoid the fate of the LTCMs of the world? The key is to recognize your weaknesses and realize that no one holds a monopoly on the truth or the markets. We will all be wrong from time to time. But if you're wrong and flexible, you can minimize the damage from your mistakes. And remember: when you're wrong, risk control is your backstop.

It's not only financiers that have a tendency to exhibit a sense of infallibility. The medical field is similarly rife with intellectual arrogance and inflexibility. In the late 1940s, before the development of a polio vaccine, public health "experts" noted that upticks in documented polio diagnoses corresponded with increases in the consumption of ice cream and soft drinks. As a result, doctors recommended eliminating these threats as part of an anti-polio diet. Public health officials later learned, however, that correlation is not the same thing as causation when they put two and two together and realized that the consumption of ice cream and soft drinks was related to polio outbreaks only insofar as both markedly increase during the hot months of summer. Only then did they resume looking for the real causes, having wasted time on the wrong ones. A similar circumstance unfolded in the 1960s, when doctors thought that infant formula was healthier for children than breast milk and told an entire generation of women to abandon breast feeding. Only recently has the medical field reversed course and changed its tune, as research has shown that not only do breast-fed children develop healthier immune systems, but mothers who breast-feed enjoy reduced cancer rates as well. The lesson here is clear: question authority, suspend judgment, and use your own mind after you have done your research and taken everything you've learned into consideration.

Have a Backstop

Focus on losing, focus on dollars at risk. Don't hope or think about how much you can make. You must be competitive. It has to hurt when you lose, and you should have quiet confidence when you win. Buy new highs; buy when action is better than news would indicate. Continue to monitor and analyze the herd. Monitor crowd sentiment and know expectations versus your viewpoint.

—Paul Tudor Jones

Chapter 8 | Pitfalls

The tactical trend trading methodology I advocate need not be applied only to the markets. In fact, it is intended to encompass a systematic framework for success, which is why, in my epistemological structure, I have repeatedly stressed the importance of harmony, realism, and a positive psychological approach to overcoming obstacles. The flexibility to adapt, grow, and survive errors in your day-to-day life is just as important as the successes that come when you execute well within a favorable market environment.

But if you want to enjoy long-term success, you must continually balance risk and reward—especially within your personal financial affairs. Make allowances for owning a variety of assets, and do not be afraid to approach your personal finances from a much broader viewpoint than that espoused by the financial mainstream. The world is an uncertain place, but if you remain open-minded and flexible, you will be prepared to tackle any uncertainty that comes your way. Countries as well as companies rise and fall, and using a 20- or even 50-year time horizon is taking a naive view of reality. Read the history of the twentieth century. Talk to someone who has fled a country that underwent rapid, unforeseen regime change. Inform yourself about global politics and economics. Remember that the post World War II world has only been around for sixty years. Remember that change is continual; it is the natural order of things.

Because change and uncertainty are natural and unending, I advocate splitting your financial assets into two general classes: currencies and assets. In the category of currencies, you can include any item that has purchasing power, as long as it displays ready convertibility and portability. Among these are cash, gold, silver, collectibles, watches, jewelry, and diamonds. In the category of assets, you can include stocks, bonds, art, real estate, commodities, hedge funds, managed futures, and business ownership. If your outlook for the future justifies adding further categories, don't be afraid to include them in your own financial framework. Just make sure that you maintain at all times a broad view of your financial picture so that you can be flexible and adaptive when change comes your way.

To enjoy true long-term success, incorporate a margin of safety and true diversity in both your investment account and your personal finances. Take a big step back and look at your financial situation from the widest perspective possible. How comfortable are you about your finances when you do this? Are you focused on a relatively minor battle while losing sight of the war? Are you building an impressive fortress on ground that is sliding into the ocean? Take the broad view, and you can build a more robust personal and professional financial system.

CHAPTER 9

Philosophy

Chaos is a name for any order that produces confusion in our minds.

—George Santayana

Your philosophical outlook on life is the foundation upon which you build the system and plan the actions necessary to reach your goals. If you use sound thinking to formulate your personal philosophy, you will lay the bedrock upon which success can build. If, on the other hand, you approach life with a flawed epistemological framework, you are no better off than you would be if you launched a magnificent boat with a cracked hull or built a castle on quicksand. I'm a pragmatically rational person, and when something isn't working, I realize there is a gap between what is "supposed" to happen and the reality of my experience. When I see this gap start to form, I step back and attempt to address the flaw in my mental model. I also recognize that outliers are part of reality, and I don't fight reality. Instead, I avoid becoming emotionally entangled in any given situation and learn to incorporate outliers and other eventualities into an improved mode of thought. I am able to do this only because I approach the world with an open mind, the ability to change, and a willingness to accept reality as it unfolds. I urge you to do the same.

Accept Reality

A man should look for what is, and not for what he thinks should be.

—Albert Einstein

The market is an emotional amplifier that turns success into euphoria and setbacks into despondency. Market gyrations pale in comparison with the mental fluctuations traders and investors experience throughout the course

Chapter 9 | Philosophy

of a full boom/bust cycle. One day you're riding high and the market is doing what it's supposed to do; the next day, things change, and serendipity's evil cousin Murphy is at your door—and he doesn't have a grin on his face. When your trades start going south, it's easy to blame the market for your troubles, but the problem isn't the market. The market is not supposed to do anything; it owes you nothing. The problem, rather, is the reality/expectations gap that you create in your mind. It is your creation, so you must tame it, and in order to do so, you must make an effort to align your expectations with the ongoing reality. Reality will not meet you halfway, so you have to accept reality by seeing things as they really are and, as much as possible, by leaving your personal biases and desires outside the door.

The greatest source of frustration for most people, regardless of the endeavor they are undertaking, is the desire for reality to be something other than it is. But reality is always what it is, and your wish that it be something else is your problem. After all, you created the expectation that reality would somehow be different or that something external would rescue you from it. The places in your mind that hold onto the false hope that reality will bend to your will are the source of the expectations/reality gap. Peace comes only from accepting and flowing with reality.

There is no magical place in the past or future that will save you. The only time that matters is now. Your actions now are all that you can control. You cannot do anything in the future today or change the past today. Right now, all you can do is control your thoughts and your actions. As Jean-Paul Sartre said, "I am nothing other than my actions." It is only when you know reality without illusions and desires, complete with all its pain and danger, that you can achieve real freedom and security. Clinging to false hopes and desires will only lead to further anxiety and insecurity. I have found the Eastern teachings particularly helpful in my efforts to adopt the mental attitude necessary to accept reality for all that it is. Below I offer some essential guidelines for accepting and ultimately flowing with the realities of both life and the markets.

- Don't expect anything. See what happens and don't obsess about your expectations or the results.
- Don't strain or force anything.
- Don't rush.
- Don't cling to anything; don't reject anything. Let it all come to you naturally.
- Let go. Learn to flow with all the changes that are bound to occur. Relax.

- Accept everything that arises. Accept your feelings, reality, and experiences.
- Be gentle with yourself. Accept who you are.
- Investigate yourself and question everything; take nothing for granted. Only your experience counts; be awake to the truth.
- View all problems as challenges. Don't run from negative events; look upon them as opportunities to learn and grow.
- Don't ponder. You don't need to figure everything out.
- Don't dwell on comparisons between yourself and anyone else. Giving in to egotism and a focus on contrasts lead to pride, envy, greed, jealousy, and hatred.

The reason I highlight this approach to accepting reality is that the practice of meditation can help you open your mind to seeing and accepting the reality of the real world that is in front of you. You may be skeptical of meditation, but my experience shows that it can allow you to grow not just as a person but as a trader as well. How so? Meditation can help you be more open and receptive to the opportunities that arise before you each year. Change is a positive force if you have the ability to accept and flow with it. New ideas, industries, products, and economic cycles are unfolding before you every day. If you accept them, you can then take the next step and position yourself to take advantage of them. If, however, you choose the other path and continue to believe that reality must conform to your desires, then you will be closed to new and profitable trading opportunities, and your portfolio will probably be cut down by the lawnmower of change that wiser investors are pushing. An inflexible mind is like a snow-blind soul careening down a black diamond slope. Good luck with that mentality—you will need it.

If you accept reality with all that it entails, in today's markets you will be in a better position than ever before to trade effectively. A trader with an unskilled mind trades the markets of tomorrow or yesterday. He trades yesterday by looking at historical P/E multiples and expecting a return to glory days. He looks at historical earnings power and sees an inevitable mean reversion. He sees craziness and longs for a return to normalcy. In short, he sees nothing and hopes for everything.

The only thing that would help investors who trade the markets of yesterday is a time machine. Industries grow, die, prosper, and suffer, and new industries scarcely imaginable will rise up in the future to replace today's leaders. Darwinism rages in the economic world, evolution in the financial markets is real, and permanence is as illusory as the Easter bunny. Just think about the fact that the media industry—and especially newspapers—will likely never be the same after the advent of the Internet. No one in 1980 could have imagined that this vaunted, blue-chip industry would be largely displaced by the online world. Who could have guessed that we would get our news, hunt for jobs, and search classified ads on a computer? The past is useful only for study, and even then, it can lead to the narrative fallacy that the past is more similar to the present than it is.

No less ineffectual than those who trade yesterday's markets are those who trade two to three years into the future. You will hear perfectly smart and logical people fight reality by concocting macro problems that don't exist and may never happen. While it is good to plan for contingencies, it is not good to get too far ahead of yourself or today's reality. Neither you nor anyone else knows what tomorrow will bring. Just as, five years ago, you couldn't have foreseen what today would look like, you can't hope, today, to see the unfolding landscape of the future. Don't rush reality. Trade the market that is before you today. Straying into the past or future will only serve to blind you. Many people trade yesterday's or tomorrow's markets subconsciously to avoid making decisions. They are afraid to commit and to see what they see. Remain in the flow with reality and accept it for what it is in all its forms. Stay in the now; it is the only time in which you can control your thoughts and actions.

Flow, Don't Force

Tension is who you think you should be. Relaxation is who you are.

—Chinese Proverb

Flow, that state of easy, natural brilliance, is a rare but beautiful sight to behold. In the public domain, it is Michael Jordan and Tiger Woods on their best days. It is the Cirque de Soleil "O" show. It is U2 performing live on stage. In our personal world, flow occurs when your unique talent is percolating at its peak in harmony with your surrounding environment. It is an amazing feeling of ease and symbiosis where nothing is forced. It is like water flowing effortlessly down a ravine, moving along the path of least resistance. Contrast this picture with that of a boulder crashing clumsily down a hillside, meeting resistance with one bump after another, forcing its way down in a noisy series of shocks.

The same concept applies to the trader who is facing his monitor on any given trading day. Each day the trader faces myriad stocks and markets in which he can deploy his capital. If his method is sound and his mind is trained, his work environment will be positive, enjoyable, and connected. If his method is sound but his mind is untrained, tension, stress, and fear will rule him, and he will be stuck in an emotional state that renders him unfit to operate successfully or at least optimally. The trader who cannot first accept and then flow with the markets and the changes that occur therein is wearing concrete shoes and expecting to move with speed and success, an error that causes a hopelessly large gap between expectations and reality.

How does a trader achieve flow and regain control over the stresses and uncertainty that plague the financial markets? Paradoxically, you gain control by letting go, and dispel fear by acknowledging its existence. Accepting and flowing with reality are tough mental states to achieve, but there is hope. First, realize that positive changes in your mental framework will not happen overnight, and that it takes patience and self-awareness to achieve this frame of mind. Further, it is likely to take three to six months of daily effort before flowing with reality feels more natural, and probably a year or more before doing so becomes second nature. Be gentle with yourself and the process and realize that you will suffer setbacks along the way. Perfection is not the goal, nor is it a livable reality.

The process of proactive, positive change is a journey with no destination. It is about continual improvement, not about arriving at some future point and declaring victory. Victory is yours now, and setbacks are part of the landscape. When you suffer a setback, acknowledge it, learn from it, and resume your journey forward with confidence. Remember that breakthroughs frequently result from breakdowns, so it is critical to view every failure you suffer as a learning opportunity. Even if you have a star-studded year with 100% returns, you will experience scores of missed opportunities, a couple of negative months, and many weeks that you'd like to forget. Keep it all in perspective and do not feed the emotional monster. Anger gives energy and life to negative experiences. If you can step back and see your failures as a necessary part of the trading process, you will find it easier to maintain your stride and sustain your pace. The unexpected will happen, and you should adapt and adjust accordingly.

Fear in all its forms chains us to mediocrity and blocks our pathway to success. They say that there are only two emotions on Wall Street—fear and greed—but greed is really just the mirror image of fear. Greed stems from a fear of inadequacy. It stems from the fear of trusting in your ability to do well over time. It springs from a fear of never having enough to satisfy your cravings. The fear we experience during a panic selloff is also very real. It is the fear of the abyss, of emptiness and the possibility of losing our possessions. Your work, your livelihood, and your assets are all under attack during panic selloffs, and as a result, you will be strongly pulled toward emotional outbursts of fear and panic. Your friends will be selling their holdings and you won't want to be left behind, so you'll be tempted to throw your assets at the market in the hope that you will be able to cling to something. If you follow that course, you will fail. In tense market situations, it is far better for you to let go, relax, and be proactive. Acknowledge fear and it will lose all power over you; pretend it isn't there, and it will lie in wait for the next opportunity to ravage your psyche. Below I list some steps you can take to gain a measure of control over the fears we all face.

- Acknowledge your fears. Bring them into the light of day by writing them down.
- Relax and realize that most fears are both irrational and unimportant in the bigger picture.
- Accept yourself and your shortcomings. Work to improve, but accept what and who you are.
- Operate from an egoless stance. Do not feed your fear by bringing your emotions, wants, and desires into everything you do. Operate from an objective, easy position.
- Let go. By accepting that you can't control everything, you gain mastery over those things that you can control. Don't invite nonexistent problems.
- Remain patient and flexible. If you can accept and flow with any contingency, you have real power to trade today's reality.

There is one final point I would like to mention: accepting and flowing with reality is not a pessimistic stance of resignation. It does not mean closing your eyes and helplessly resigning yourself to your fate while hoping for the best. It is not surrendering to apathy and inaction. It is the opposite of all these things. It entails keeping an open mind and seeing things for what they are. It is sight, not blindness; it is the eternal path of knowledge, the quest for truth.

Embrace Change—It Is the Only Constant

This is one of life's packages: there is no freedom without noise – and no stability without volatility.

—Nassim Taleb

Inherently we are torn between a desire for stability and equilibrium on the one hand and a desire for change and vitality on the other. This psychic push-pull is behind many of the anxieties and fears that present themselves when we confront the changes that we realize are coming but that we wish we could tame and save for some far-off future. Both psychologically and emotionally, we desire an anchor that will hold us in a secure, familiar position. Fear of the unknown and the unfamiliar drive countless people toward lives of sameness and routine. Yet we must all accept the reality of change and develop a positive mindset to cope with and benefit from its resultant upheaval. As I've noted many times before in this book, change is the only constant in our world. Nothing can be the same tomorrow as it was yesterday—not even our memory of yesterday. Yet people are reluctant to see and accept change, and this forces a series of tragic emotional purges as human beings lurch from one accepted worldview to the next.

Human beings cherish their beliefs, and many people are more concerned with establishing stability and fixed viewpoints than they are with seeking the truth. Max Planck stated that science advances one funeral at a time. History is rife with examples of the reluctance of the establishment to accept change. When Galileo, in the seventeenth century, challenged the belief propounded by the Catholic Church that the Earth was the center of the universe, the Inquisition tried him for heresy. The view of the Earth as center of the universe was so deeply held, in fact, that the authorities in Rome eventually accepted it only with great reluctance and unease. It is easy to see why, as the truth that Galileo presented challenged established authority, centuries of teachings, and humanity's cherished role at the center of the universe. Now, that represented real change!

While changes in economies and markets are less profound, the beliefs that practitioners hold concerning their pet markets or stocks are no less rigid. The ego is a powerful thing, and once a trader becomes personally invested in a certain market outlook, she will lose all her objectivity and flexibility. At that point, she loses the ability to think and act and becomes a victim of change rather than its beneficiary. If you long for stability and equilibrium, I urge you not to seek it in the financial markets. Markets change much more rapidly and dynamically than the economic world that they only loosely represent. Boom/bust sequences play out in a micro fashion on a quarterly basis. Markets regularly experience drops of 10–20%—even in bull market years. Therefore, to operate in this environment, a trader must have both an epistemological framework and a trading process that are adaptive to change and its embedded risks and rewards.

Try this as an exercise: be honest with yourself and write down the ten changes that you did not see coming in the last year in your personal or professional life. I suspect that you will have no problem coming up with such a list. How many of these ten changes could you have foreseen? Precious few, if you are being honest with yourself. Do you think the future will be any different, that the process of change will suddenly stop, or that it will be more predictable? Would you even want it to? Change is constant, and you must account for it if you wish to succeed from the standpoint of both risk and reward.

The attitude one has toward change is also crucial. Let's face it; we all play a game of mental masturbation in our daily lives. We each have our own fertile fantasies that we entertain. I have not known anyone, including myself, who was perfectly rational and objective in all phases of his life, and we bring our biases and individual quirks to the investment world as well. A skilled trader learns to get comfortable with his biases and manage his tactics accordingly. He can see change as both an eventuality and an opportunity and searches for it in all of its forms, regardless of whether it is large-scale change or subtle change at the margin. He incorporates a positive outlook and an open mind, which allow him to see changes to which those around him are blind. Most of us operate with blinders on, seeing only that which our mind has placed before us and excluding the larger landscape all around us. But it is far better for you to assume that you know very little and open your mind so that you gain the eyes of a child, which are ever open to new things. As Socrates said, "Wisdom begins in wonder." As applied to the markets, you may operate with a particular worldview and a thematic stance, but you should occasionally take another look at the action around you and listen to what the markets are telling you. The markets are an invaluable guide if we will only keep our minds open to their messages and stay in synch with the opportunities they offer.

Change Leaps—There Is No Equilibrium, No Fair Value

> *"Financial capitalism is inherently and endogenously given to bubbles and busts."*

> *"Stability is ultimately destabilizing, because of the asset price and credit excesses that stability begets. Stability can never be a destination, only a journey to instability."*

> —Hyman Minsky

Humans are built to see the world in a linear fashion and have trouble with abstract concepts that do not fit this straightforward mold. Consider the difficulty traders experience when they try to grasp the concept of exponential growth. The power of compounding is the eighth wonder of the world, but why is it so powerful, and why can't most traders wrap their minds around the enormous returns that can generated by exponential growth?

To answer that question, consider a few simple examples. The story goes that in ancient India, a mathematician who had performed certain services to the ruler of a province asked for a reward that the king thought was a pittance. The mathematician wanted one grain of wheat for the first square on a chessboard, two grains for the second square, four grains for the third square, and so on, doubling the number of grains with each subsequent square. There are only 64 squares on a chessboard, so you can imagine that the king thought he was getting a terrific deal. With a laugh, he granted the mathematician's wish. Now, how much wheat do you think the king owed the mathematician? Stop for a second and try to come up with an intelligent guess (hint: it is a large number), and then compare your response with the actual results. The exponential growth of one grain growing at 100% per square times 64 squares = 18,446,744,073,709,551,615 grains of wheat—the equivalent of 80 times what would be produced in one harvest at modern yields if all of Earth's arable land could be devoted to wheat production. The eighth wonder of the world indeed! Even if you're good with numbers, you can see why it might be difficult to grasp the remarkable scaling power of exponential growth.

Consider, as a second example, the exponential growth of capital that I illustrated Chapter 1. Remember that $100,000 growing at 20% for 17 years multiplies the initial investment 22-fold to $2,218,611. Exponential growth is truly astounding. To see how quickly an investment can double in size, divide 70 by the percentage growth you are expecting, and you will get the approximate doubling factor. Therefore, an investment that grows by 10% per year will double in 70/10 = 7 years. It takes only 35% growth to double your investments every two years! As another example, inflation running at only 2% for 10 years would decrease the purchasing power of your currency by 25%. No wonder we have difficulty grasping the power and speed of exponential growth.

Regardless, the ability of the value of our portfolios to leap with small, constant percentage increases, combined with our inability to recognize the power of compounding, leads to planning and investment disasters of all stripes. Instead of leveraging exponential growth to their advantage and steadily growing their portfolios by 10% or more each year, people take excessive risks so that they can "get rich quickly." But as you already know, high-risk long shots taken with the bulk of your portfolio are both dangerous and tactically flawed. You simply don't need to go "all in" to realize large gains, as long as you keep the intermediate and longer term firmly in your mind. Exponential growth will take care of your profits if you manage your risks correctly.

There are other ways in which change leaps much faster and farther than we can predict. The pro-cyclical nature of change ensures that as one factor changes and reaches an inflection point, its growth will sharply and visibly accelerate. Networks like the Internet, for example, as a rule scale rapidly and grow exponentially. Meanwhile, linear growth remains a myth concocted in an accounting spreadsheet. While long-term growth will appear linear on a logarithmic graph, it will tend to exhibit stagnation for a period of years before galloping higher in a more creative, more energetic period for another stretch of years. I like to call this exponentially explosive growth "the linear leap."

In the financial markets, you will often see linear leaps on display. In fact, I've witnessed several linear leaps in just the last 15 years. Technology, for example, experienced a robust period in the 1990s as the world embraced the sector's productivity-enhancing aspects. Brand-new industries within technology emerged, including database management, fiber optic networks, business intelligence software, computer services, wireless communications, and the big one—the Internet. In this way, technology experienced something like a quantum leap that allowed consumers and businesses to operate in a manner that was completely unimaginable before these emerging trends evolved.

Keep in mind, too, that technology isn't the only area where linear leaps have recently occurred. We've seen similar booms and subsequent busts since 1990 in oil, housing, and stocks. The linear leap is powerful fuel for rapid, short-term growth and outperformance. While it is next to impossible to predict a linear leap before it develops (my crystal ball is no clearer than yours), if you stay aware of your surroundings and open to the inevitable changes the future holds, you can take your positions early and enjoy the rewards that unforeseen change affords investors who accept and do not fight reality.

Like linear leaps, procyclicality also causes change to surge, not crawl. To see procyclicality at work, consider the following example from the financial sector, which highlights the extent to which this phenomenon is inherent in lending. Banks lend to consumers and businesses with the expectation that they will be compensated and receive a profit for taking the risk in extending credit and debt financing to the marketplace. They are profit-seeking enterprises that look to maximize their individual profits while ensuring that they are compensated for their risk of default. To measure this latter factor, they analyze consumers' credit scores, assets, income to debt service ratios, earning power, and more.

To understand how the housing bubble evolved in such an explosive fashion, the procyclicality of bank lending in the period from 2002 to 2007 needs to be examined and explained, because in hindsight it seems blatantly obvious that this was a credit bubble for the ages. Let's look at lending during the housing bubble from the viewpoint of the banks. Thanks to record low interest rates in the aftermath of the 2000–2002 recession, housing affordability rose quickly as monthly mortgage payments plummeted. Suddenly, due to a lowered ratio of income to debt service ratio gave individual consumers access to more credit, the same $300,000 mortgage loan became much more affordable. With lower costs to finance the same house, consumers reacted by buying ever-larger homes and, in many cases, second homes, which led to a procyclical rise in home prices. Now, not only did income to debt service ratios look better than ever before, but asset values did too, which allowed for greater borrowing capacity from the bank's viewpoint. Banks and other lending institutions readily extended home equity lines of credit, making credit and debt financing much more easily available, and consumers willingly took equity out of their homes, saved less, and increased their spending levels in response to their newfound wealth.

The next step in this lending cycle was that the increased profits enjoyed by the banks brought in a flood of hypercompetitive consumer lending companies that were aggressively seeking short-term profits and market share. In search of these gains, they eased credit terms and lowered or eliminated the down payment requirements traditionally mandated by banks. This brought in the next wave of buyers who were less creditworthy, and it also encouraged real estate speculation and house price "flipping" by those eager to capitalize on supposedly ever-rising home prices. All the while, the enormous demand for homes continued to inflate the underlying asset prices, which only further validated and propagated this procyclical process. Notice that the further the housing bubble evolved, the more powerful the forces that perpetuated and accelerated the mania became. Tight credit conditions, high deposit requirements, high relative payments, stable home prices, and apathy toward home prices were replaced by ever-greater levels of easy credit, lower monthly payments, accelerating home prices, and belief in a never-ending up cycle. Nowhere along the line did external forces attempt to staunch the upside and act as a countervailing influence to the boom cycle in home pricing and lending.

For these reasons, the housing bubble is a perfect example of the upside of a procyclical boom/bust sequence. The bust happens because each of a variety of forces is ultimately sated and reverses course. In the case of a credit cycle, the downside can be devastating, threatening the entire financial system. In the case of the technology cycle, the effects were less devastating but no less severe in localized economies across the globe. A boom/bust sequence is a normal part of human nature and change, but that doesn't mean it isn't destructive. Great upheaval can result from the boom/bust nature of procyclical moves in politics, sports, religions, belief systems, and many other human institutions, and in each of these cases, change leaps and accelerates as it gathers exponential force.

Part and parcel of procyclical changes are feedback loops, which encourage and propagate the actions of market participants. In the example of the housing bubble, profit motives and capitalist incentives encouraged a tremendous surge in activity that ultimately led to rampant speculation and a near freeze in global credit and the capital markets. The housing bubble is an example of the downside of capitalism. But just as, in Winston Churchill's words, democracy is the worst form of government except for all the others, capitalism is the worst economic system except for all the others. In a market-based economy, capital is allocated where it is treated best, with little distinction or foresight as to *how* it will be treated best. Short-term gains are emphasized and rewarded over long–term benefits, with the result typically being a boom/bust sequence when the good thing is enjoyed too long and exploited too thoroughly.

Profits and prestige are the primary feedback loops that encourage market participants' aggressive actions to exploit profit opportunities in modern capitalist systems. While these feedback loops do a great job of providing the seed and expansionary capital necessary to meet the needs of billions of worldwide consumers and businesses, they also tend toward extremes and overzealousness at the tail end of a rising secular tide. Human nature drives these speculative urges, and the animal spirits identified by John Maynard Keynes will bubble up as long as the human race continues. It's amazing how quickly one boom follows another and how little people actually learn from the last bubble. If you recall, the housing bubble began to percolate only two years after the greatest bubble the stock market had seen in 70 years began to subside. Similarly, the oil bubble formed only two years after the housing bubble peaked. As George Santayana said, "Those who do not remember the past are condemned to repeat it." The evidence suggests that we do not learn from history.

In most scientific endeavors, the scientist stands apart from his experiment. A physicist peering through her telescope at the heavens does not interfere with the rotations of the planets, nor does she have an impact on other solar systems light years away. In the markets, however, investors are both participants and observers, and as such, they operate with the inherent biases and stresses that such a dual role demands. George Soros, the brilliant captain of the Quantum Fund, has a term—"reflexivity"—for the push/pull relationship that participants-practitioners are subject to.

Let us first examine what reflexivity entails and then distill its implications for the financial markets and the concomitant strategy it dictates for market participants to be successful. Reflexivity occurs because of the dual roles that investors play as both participants and observers of the financial markets, and it is inherent to the feedback loop wherein the flow of capital both reflects and at the same time has an impact on the underlying fundamentals that investors observe.

Brief examples of positive and negative reflexive processes will illustrate both the point I'm making and the strategies necessary to take advantage of reflexivity's implications. A positive reflexive process occurs when increased capital flows positively affect the underlying fundamentals. An example can be found in the conglomerate boom of the 1960s, where rising stock prices allowed companies to acquire more competitors with inflated stock values. These acquisitions led to increased earnings, which in turn led to greater investor confidence and expansion of price-to-earnings multiples for the underlying stocks. Accelerations in their stock prices made it easier for companies to fund more stock takeovers, which are earnings accretive, perpetuating the cycle in a positive reflexive feedback loop. You can readily see that in the case of the conglomerate boom, positive fundamentals and the capital inflows from investors worked in a positive feedback loop and not in isolation from each other.

A similar thing happens in a negative reflexive pattern. Debt-ridden companies often find themselves subject to such a pattern. Let's take the example of a company with a heavy debt load that has misread the economic landscape or is suddenly hit with an unexpected change in the fundamentals that support its debt service burden. In this case, the company is subject to negative fundamental factors at the same time that it is in a vulnerable financial position. To raise needed capital, it approaches the capital markets. Investors looking at the situation respond by pulling capital lines and providing further credit, but only on onerous terms. The company's credit rating is subsequently cut, and its stock price begins to plummet. This negative reflexive process then creates a negative fundamental and investor feedback loop. Since the company's equity price is collapsing, it becomes prohibitive to raise capital through an equity offering, and with its credit rating under pressure, the increased cost of capital adds to debt service costs, even if the company is able to raise debt financing. The confidence of customers and employees is also tested, often resulting in a loss of orders to financially stronger competitors. Further, the company's top talent may begin to flee, as employees pursue greater economic opportunities. All of these negative occurrences then feed back into another negative reflexive cycle, putting still greater pressure on the company and making bankruptcy a distinct possibility, particularly if it needs to roll over large amounts of existing debt. We are social animals, and reflexivity accounts for this fact. Fundamentals and investor capital flows interact in a reflexive process that quickens the process of change.

While reflexivity certainly has implications for the financial markets, it has an impact on investors as well. For an investor, the clearest implication of reflexivity from a risk/reward standpoint is never to underestimate the speed with which a formerly sound company or industry can unravel. Change happens, and reflexivity ensures that its ramifications are felt and exaggerated in a negative fundamental/capital feedback loop. As in nature, the sick and wounded are starved of capital and left to fend for themselves while the strong and growing garner ever-greater access to cheaper capital and growth opportunities. Strength begets strength and weakness begets weakness as the process moves further from equilibrium. For those steeped in the wisdom of letting winners run and cutting losers short, the pain of this process will be minimal. For those who allocate capital in step with financial and societal momentum, reflexivity will reward your efforts. On the other hand, for those who employ mean-reversion strategies and fight important trends, reflexivity results in a jarring ride that will occasionally be marked by disaster.

This second derivative nature of change involves such rapidity and far-reaching social feedback mechanisms that it can render once sound industries impotent in short order. For those who scoff at this last point, I urge you to look again at the Dow Jones Industrial Average and remember that not one company has been an uninterrupted member since the DJIA's inception just over 100 years ago. Tremendous upheaval is the norm, and experience bears this out.

To summarize, here are the large forces that ensure that important changes leap and grow more quickly than our linear brains assume they will.

- Exponential growth
- Linear leaps
- Procyclicality
- Feedback loops
- Reflexive participation

Thanks to the five forces listed above, change not only will happen but will evolve and expand at a rate that exceeds academic assumptions. Change will also tend to last longer and very often reach a point of oversaturation that perpetuates its subsequent fall from grace. The boom/bust sequence is a part of our human DNA. We are social animals who flock from one thing to the next. Social proof is a powerful motivator in influencing our collective actions, much as a herd of cattle follows in the wake of the lead bull. As we have already pointed out, the human mind is looking for shortcuts, or heuristics, to aid our thinking, and following the actions of the collective "other" is one way to make quick, but not necessarily thoughtful, decisions.

The flip side is that the crowd is correct in the middle stage of this process, and a trader should seek to participate in this dynamic power with the foreknowledge that all trends change and the bust part of the boom/bust sequence is inevitable at some point. The 100-year flood will happen once every five to ten years. Count on it, and build a system in your personal and professional life that reflects this reality. Gradualism, linearity, and predictability are the hobgoblins of the small mind. There is no safety in numbers. Change is constant, and it leaps constantly. Protective stops, risk control, diversification, and a keen curiosity that seeks to find the flaw in consensus thought are necessary to avoid overstaying one's welcome in future cycles of change.

History Repeats

There are decades when nothing happens; and, there are weeks when decades happen.

—Vladimir Lenin

When was growing up, I spent many years in Heidelberg, Germany, a beautiful city that is home to Germany's oldest university, which dates back to its founding in 1386. The city exudes charm. With its cobblestoned pedestrian downtown that winds several miles until it leads to the main square, and its castle that sits above the square and overlooks the city along the Neckar River valley, the city is a joy to behold. As you climb the narrow side streets and ascend gradually to the castle above, the view only improves. Mark Twain, who was enamored of Heidelberg and the view from the castle, observed, "I have never enjoyed a view which had such a serene and satisfying charm about it as this one gives." Nothing has changed since Twain enjoyed it. From the castle ramparts, you can look down at a truly spectacular view of the city along the banks of the river. The vantage point affords an excellent perspective of Heidelberg and its picturesque surroundings. The romantic cobblestoned street cuts a lengthy, delicate trail between the Baroque buildings as it edges against the river and trails off and blends into the rest of the cityscape.

Looking at the world from the perspective of history provides a similar broad view, where you see the parts of the whole as a piece of the larger picture. With this viewpoint, possibilities and perspectives open up that are not available to the person at street level, who can only take in a limited view. All of this is to say that when you step back and view today in the context of history, your viewpoints and understanding open up. People haven't changed much in terms of psychology and actions throughout the course of history. Only the trappings of their surroundings and their technologies have changed. With this understanding and backdrop, you can use the lessons of history to

Chapter 9 | Philosophy

forge a useful framework for understanding today's problems and their possible outcomes.

One of the key lessons that history holds for us is that for vast stretches of time, the status quo has reigned, and only superficial changes have been evident. Then, seemingly without warning, several hundred years of tradition are swept aside in days. Such is the lesson of historical events such as the French Revolution, the Arab Spring, the US War of Independence, World War I, and the fall of the Berlin Wall. These events, some of them barely predicted, swept aside the preceding order and ushered in rapid, profound change in the historical blink of an eye. Why are we so blind and so slow to react to these impending changes, and what can history teach us about the current problems facing the financial system? I will attempt to answer each of these important questions in turn, knowing full well that the future is uncertain and unpredictable but believing that perhaps history can provide us with some alternative scenarios.

Each of the above historical cases was characterized by a simmering groundswell that, *ex post facto*, argued for the potential for such large changes. Yet, *ex ante*, they were not predicted or widely anticipated. After the fact, experts offered readily digestible analyses explaining the inevitability of the changes and implying that anyone could have readily predicted them. Before the fact, however, such experts were silent, dead silent. Before the fact, they offered no sure predictions.

Take the Arab Spring uprisings of 2011. The North African region that encompassed the countries of Tunisia, Libya, and Egypt was politically stable, ruled by dictators who had held power for over 20 years without interruption. There were no warnings of impending regime change. Then, in December 2010, Mohamed Bouazizi set himself ablaze in Tunisia to protest police corruption and the confiscation of his wares. Already struggling, Bouazizi could not morally accept the injustice of further theft at the hands of a corrupt dictatorship. He resisted the treatment with the only power he had left and took his own life in the most visible and demonstrative statement of defiance humanly possible. He lit himself ablaze and in doing so became a flaming symbol of defiance and a burning sacrifice to change.

Bouazizi's public suicide swiftly and unexpectedly set off a chain reaction. The act resonated with his fellow citizens and awakened deep resentment and anger directed at the status quo. The anger thus unleashed grew quickly, leading to the swift ouster of the dictatorship weeks later. As dominoes fell, unrest spread from Tunisia to Egypt, Libya, Bahrain, Syria, and Iran, among others. Dictatorial powers were toppled in Tunisia, Egypt, and then Libya, where iron-fisted absolute power was swept away by the waves of anger and passion released by the mass of the people. The change unleashed by the Arab Spring uprisings is still simmering.

A similar uprising happened in 1989. At the end of the World War II, Germany was split in two, with West Germany falling under the influence of Europe and the United States, and East Germany under the direct power of the Soviet Union. West Germany ultimately rebuilt itself into an economic world leader, while East Germany stagnated under Communism. As the Berlin Wall was built, splitting East and West Germany into two halves, the lives of those in the East were literally and symbolically cleaved from the Western world. As the decades passed, the economic and social differences between East and West Germany grew markedly. Eventually the Soviet Union broke up, and its absolute power over its Eastern European empire loosened. At the same time, the desire for freedom and opportunity began to take hold and grow in East Germany. On the night of November 9, 1989, these forces combined with a serendipitous event to emancipate that spirit of freedom. A radio broadcast inadvertently stated that the wall had opened, allowing East Germans to visit West Germany. The word spread, and thousands of people from both sides hurried to the Berlin Wall. Guards, taken by surprise and unwilling to offer resistance, stood aside as East met West and the wall fell, first psychologically and then physically as the people dismantled it over the ensuing months.

The examples of the Arab Spring and the toppling of the Berlin Wall help explain why some of the largest changes in history are so unpredictable. The underlying conditions may support unrest and discontent, but until a trigger event occurs to set change in motion, people tolerate existing conditions, and no change occurs. Then, suddenly, a small event occurs, resonates, and unleashes profound change that spreads like a firestorm, and although *ex post facto* analysis often suggests that these types of wholesale changes could have been predicted, the reality is that it would have been tremendously difficult to do so. Even those who participated in bringing about the enormous changes that occurred during the Arab Spring and the fall of the Berlin Wall admit that they had no inkling of the profound changes that were just around the corner.

A similar phenomenon can be observed in the price of bonds in the period leading up to World War I. When Franz Ferdinand, the Archduke of Austria, was assassinated on a street in Sarajevo, no one could have predicted that his death would lead to full-scale war between more than 18 countries, leave over 10 million dead, and cast a shadow over Europe that wouldn't fade until the end of World War II. While the fallout from Franz Ferdinand's assassination may seem obvious in hindsight, newspaper accounts of the day suggest that the Archduke's contemporaries were not expecting a significant impact. There was no panic in stock and bond prices in the time leading up to the impending cataclysm. Contrast this reality with the conventional view that the war was all but preordained because of a decade of escalating rivalries. Had investors known then what was supposedly so obvious, bond prices surely would have dropped materially in price instead of holding value.

Why are we are so slow to react to material changes? The following is a nonexhaustive list of reasons why humans fail to accept change rapidly and respond to it effectively:

- Problem of induction: even though there are ample historical precedents, people react to what they see and know.
- Status quo bias and tradition: we are naturally creatures of habit, assuming that what we see and know will continue ad infinitum.
- Narrative fallacy: we create stories to explain change away and make things easier to understand *ex post facto* versus *ex ante*.
- Appeal to authority: when faced with uncertainty, we turn, sheeplike, to strong leaders to guide our actions or to reassure us.
- Cognitive dissonance: we ignore or try to discredit news and information that are too tough to accept.

Since we are creatures of habit, most of us crave comfort and the status quo over better solutions. The comfort of a bad system is that we at least know our place in it and how it works. The prospect of an unknown system, on the other hand, frightens most people—even if the new system is potentially better. Many people around the world hold dearly and strongly to their traditions. We are brought up with certain belief systems, which are reinforced through multiple institutions and authorities in our formative years and beyond. At home, at school, and in public, a child who grows into adulthood learns the customs and traditions of her birthplace and country over a lengthy period. It takes a traumatic series of events and a strong push to overcome this natural inclination to prefer traditional ways and thought patterns. The problem of induction intensifies our tendency to cling to tradition, as we put more faith in our firsthand experiences than we do in things we cannot experience for ourselves. We create narrative fallacies that act like logical red herrings to explain events in terms and motivations in keeping with our traditions and consistent with our thought patterns. But this bad habit leads us astray and perpetuates misunderstanding, as we can't see things from a different perspective. Cognitive dissonance also plays an important role as a self-defense mechanism. Rapid change is too traumatic for us to handle and process, so our minds keep the disturbing new information at bay, disdaining logic and rejecting change. Authority figures play to these weaknesses, reassuring us in terms that appeal to our interests and reliance on tradition, so that they can maintain their positions of political and monetary power for as long as possible. You will see regimes everywhere create straw men and external enemies to explain away economic recessions and hardships of every imaginable kind.

So what can history teach us about the current problems facing the financial system? Let's start boldly with the largest systemic problem facing our financial system today: excessive sovereign debt levels. Investors seem confused about what to do about the exorbitant and unsustainable levels of global debt. Battle lines have generally been drawn between austerity and growth, but neither seems likely to work as a solution by itself.

So what will solve the world's debt crisis? In *This Time Is Different: Eight Centuries of Financial Folly* (Princeton University Press, 2009), Carmen M. Reinhart and Kenneth Rogoff wrote a wonderful historical study recounting the episodes of external debt default throughout modern history compared with the levels typically associated with some form of debt devaluation and default. There were notable spikes in debt defaults in two distinct periods—during the Napoleonic Wars and around World War II. In both cases, almost half of countries worldwide experienced debt restructurings or external default. The timeline of 1800 to 2008 shown in Figure 9-1 reveals that steady levels of debt restructurings and defaults are the norm, with most years seeing at least ten percent of countries in sovereign debt trouble.

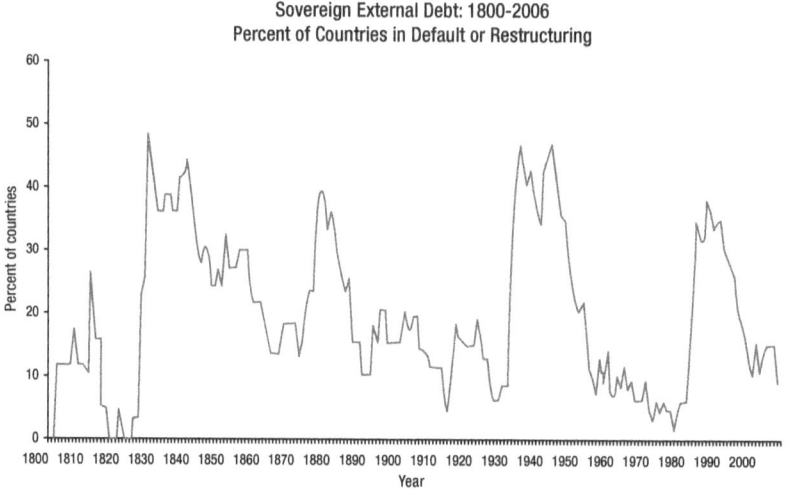

Figure 9-1. Steady levels of debt restructurings and defaults are the norm. Source: *This Time Is Different*, Carmen M. Reinhart and Kenneth Rogoff.

Chapter 9 | Philosophy

More recent history includes debt defaults by Argentina in 2002, Russia in 1998, and Greece in 2012. In each case the debt destruction was astounding, with loss levels of 70%, 82%, and 70%, respectively. In addition to suffering losses in bonds, Argentine and Russian investors witnessed currency devaluations of 75% and 85%, respectively, which led to inflation rates that approached 100%, large increases in unemployment, and social instability. In these cases, savings were destroyed, and much of the middle class was forced into poverty. According to Reinhart and Rogoff, history tells us that when sovereign debt levels rise above 90%, they lower potential GDP by more than 1%. History also shows that public debt tends to soar after a financial crisis, rising by an average of 86% in real terms. At what levels are debt ratio problems likely to arise? History tells us this too, as seen in Table 9-1.

Table 9-1. Levels at Which Debt Ratio Problems Are Likely to Arise

Ratio of External Debt to GNP at End of 1st Year of Default	% of Total Defaults
< 40%	19%
41-60%	32%
61-80%	16%
81-100%	16%
> 100%	16%

Source: *This Time Is Different*, Carmen M. Reinhart and Kenneth Rogoff.

Next, take a look at Table 9-2, which details the current debt levels of the largest countries and the biggest sovereign debt offenders globally.

Table 9-2. Current Debt Levels of the Largest Countries

Country	External Debt Level (USD in billions)	Debt/GDP
Japan	2,441	233%
Greece	532	189%
Spain	2,166	179%
Italy	2,223	121%

Country	External Debt Level (USD in billions)	Debt/GDP
USA	14,825	101%
UK	8,981	75%

Taking both history and the information in Table 9-2 into account, we can arrive at one conclusion: a massive wave of sovereign debt defaults and restructurings is *likely*. While investors operating today have never seen the United States, Japan, the United Kingdom, Italy, or Spain fall into default, this does not mean that they won't. The problem of induction, our status quo biases and traditions, our narrative fallacies, authority figures in all these countries, and cognitive dissonance all conspire to tell us quite convincingly that *we will not default*. Logic and history, on the other hand, tell us that it's likely that the majority of the above-mentioned countries will default and/or restructure their debts in a material way. Logic and history argue that pension plans, savers, banks, insurance companies, and currencies will be obliterated in the process and that financial chaos will reign until the system resets and adjusts with more sustainable debt levels.

What solution does history offer to the problem of too much debt? It is neither austerity nor growth, but rather some form of significant default and financial pain to the holders of this debt. It also argues for currency devaluation to pay back the debt in cheapened units of money. You can see in Table 9-3 that as early as 2006, before the financial crisis, Standard & Poor's incorporated significant debt rating downgrades into its baseline assumptions. Of all the major economic powerhouses, Japan is forecast to be the first nation to become noninvestment grade by 2020. To make matters worse, the bleak picture painted by Table 9-3 has only deteriorated for each country, thanks to quantitative easing and GDP contraction brought on by the crisis.

Table 9-3. S&P 2006 Long-Term Baseline Scenario: Sovereign Debt Ratings

	2005	2020	2030	2040
Australia	AAA	AA	BBB	Non-IG
Canada	AAA	AAA	AAA	AAA
France	AAA	A	Non-IG	Non-IG
Germany	AAA	AAA	A	Non-IG

	2005	2020	2030	2040
Italy	AA	A	Non-IG	Non-IG
Japan	AA	Non-IG	Non-IG	Non-IG
S. Korea	A	A	Non-IG	Non-IG
Spain	AAA	AAA	BBB	Non-IG
Sweden	AAA	AAA	A	Non-IG
UK	AAA	AAA	A	Non-IG
USA	AAA	BBB	Non-IG	Non-IG

The picture is not pretty. People don't like it, so they ignore it and focus on the next set of quantitative easing-induced "hopium." So it goes.

History also sheds light on another problem: currencies. In a system of fiat currency regimes, it is in the best interests of an exporting nation to maintain a competitively low exchange rate for its currency to keep its exports strong. When a nation's currency appreciates too much, its exports become less competitive, which hurts economic growth. The solution that history offers to a nation confronting this problem is to devalue its currency and thereby regain cost competitiveness with other nations—and some countries are taking note. Take Switzerland, for example. The Swiss franc appreciated substantially in 2010 and 2011, from 1.170 per US dollar to 0.707, as investors sought a currency refuge from the weakening and troubled euro. In a stunning move, in 2011 the Swiss National Bank pegged the franc to the euro at a rate of 1.20 Swiss francs per euro and in doing so devalued its currency by 26% from free market values. More recently, in early 2012 the Bank of Japan intervened in its currency, announcing its intention to target a 1% inflation rate, in a move that stunned the markets and sent the yen materially lower, dropping 8% in under a month. And that probably won't be the last of yen depreciation. Once seen as a currency safe haven, Japan faces an existential choice. Although it cannot afford to run trade deficits, Japan's export-dominated economy ran its first trade deficit in 30 years, throwing the country into possibly the world's worst fiscal situation. To make matters worse, the nation has lost competitiveness relative to the rest of the developed world—and especially relative to its Asian neighbors. What this means is that full-scale currency intervention and continued aggressive currency devaluations are likely in this former leading economic power. After all, history shows that its debt and currency values are at unsustainably high levels and are likely to fall significantly lower in the future.

If you're skeptical that Japan's currency can fall any further, take a look at Figure 9-2, which illustrates the currency debasement that occurred in Europe from 1400 to 1850, culminating in a large debasement during the time of the Napoleonic Wars. You can see that over this 450-year stretch, the silver content in the average European coin dropped from 8.5 grams to 1.0 gram. This represents a stunning 88.2% loss in purchasing power over time.

The Romans did the same centuries before as their empire crumbled. The denarius, Rome's coinage, was pure silver at the beginning of the first century

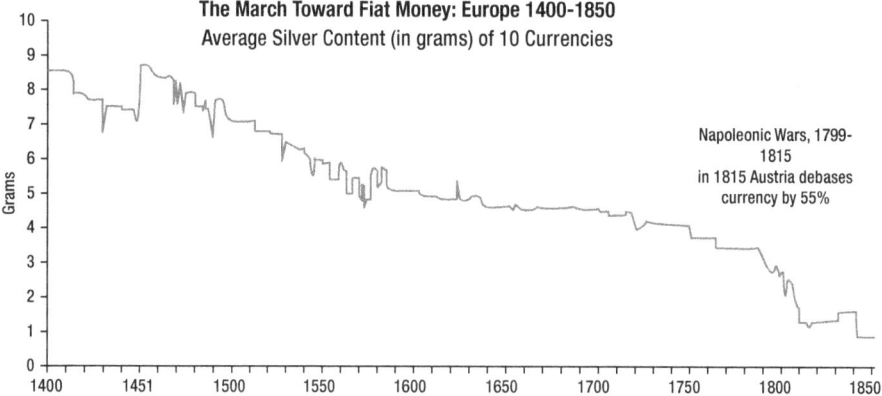

Figure 9-2. Europe showed a stunning 88.2% loss in purchasing power over time. Source: *This Time Is Different*, Carmen M. Reinhart and Kenneth Rogoff.

A.D. By about A.D.100, the silver content was down to 85%. By A.D. 218, the denarius was down to 43% silver, and by A.D. 250, the silver content dropped to 0.05%. Talk about devaluation! As an investor looking to preserve and grow your assets, you must tune out the opinion of vested interests who might be arguing that a similar outcome is impossible in the present day. History does indeed rhyme.

The Logic of Failure

You may be right and I may be wrong, and with a little effort we may get nearer to the truth.

—Karl Popper

The modern world is far more evolved and complex than our human minds can fathom. We just can't keep up with the speed and complexity of the world, and we are lost if we try to do so. To compensate for this inadequacy, our minds perform numerous tricks to simplify, codify, and distill this complex world into piecemeal bits that are more palatable to mental digestion, and we use these inputs to make efficient and mostly correct choices. Think about walking in midtown Manhattan during a busy Monday morning. Your mind is able to quickly identify potential dangers among the thousands of people you encounter by making quick assumptions based on facial features, dress, and mannerisms. You can cross a busy intersection and your eye will catch any movements from a car or bicycle that jumps out at you. You can process all of this external information quickly and efficiently without letting it overwhelming you. These mental shortcuts are wonderful at moving us through everyday life, but this same ability to selectively focus and dismiss certain inputs can also lead us into trouble in complex situations.

A solution to this gap in our ability to fully assess and plan for contingencies in complex situations is offered by Dietrich Dörner in *The Logic of Failure: Recognizing and Avoiding Failure in Complex Situations* (Henry Holt & Co., 1996). Dörner's solid decision-making model, which can be used in situations that are too complex to handle with our mental shortcuts, or heuristics, is as follows:

Complex Decision-Making Model

1. Formulation of goals
2. Formulate models and information gathering
3. Predict and extrapolate
4. Plan actions; decision making; execute actions
5. Review effects of actions, revision of strategy

Dörner's model is solid in that it takes a step back from the day-to-day battles we fight in order to assess two notable additions to normal thought. The first is big-picture goal formulation. What is it that you wish to accomplish in your trading? Write it down, make sure it is a concrete goal, and keep this roadmap in front of you as a guide. The second critical aspect of the model is that it can help you assess the success, or lack thereof, of a decision and revise future courses of action and planning. If your method isn't working, challenge yourself to explore why, and if your strategy needs changing or notable flaws have surfaced, by all means correct your methodology. Do not be afraid of mistakes. You should seek them out and look for the flaws in your plans. Trust me; they are there. Everyone makes mistakes, but the key is to review these mistakes and revise your methodology and epistemological framework accordingly.

Take a look at Dörner's model again, and notice that executing actions is part of step 4. Our mind, left to its generalizations, would probably respond quickly in an act-react sequence. While this leads to faster decision making, it has a few notable and potentially devastating drawbacks.

1. It doesn't take account of the big picture.
2. It doesn't factor in system effects or context.
3. It can lead to tactical victories but strategic blunders.
4. Implicit goals are omitted.
5. It doesn't reassess our decision making.

In other words, left to our own devices, our minds can lead us to execute a given investment strategy without determining where this strategy fits in achieving our overall financial goals. Each decision we make in the markets must be made in the context of the system, and the act-react model that we are equipped with doesn't make adequate use of big-picture thinking.

John Locke defined a madman as someone who argues logically from false premises. There are several variations on this theme in the stock market. One is our tendency to apprehend false knowledge in our trading. For instance, in a bull market, stocks tend to rally strongly, while selloffs tend to be short and shallow. The market itself often quickly bails out traders when they make mistakes, which can teach careless traders to ignore their stop-loss rules after a long winning stretch in a strong market.

Let's say that the last three stocks that you sold when they hit your stop-loss point managed to quickly reverse and then traded higher. That experience will lead you to believe that the next time your stock hits its stop-loss price, you can simply ignore your stop and wait a while to see if it comes back. After a few months of the bull market rewarding you for taking off your safety controls, you may decide that it's generally better to let your stocks rebound before selling them. Your decision to be lax about your trading discipline and avoid hard stop-loss points appears to be vindicated by the positive experience of enhanced profitability and less emotional pain, as you find you have fewer losers to sell. As you continue down this slippery slope, the bad behavior you have learned continues to be rewarded as the bull market roars on.

The consequences of induction, where experience leads us astray, are exposed eventually, but until that time comes, those who perform with less discipline will often be rewarded, sometimes more than those who are disciplined. These bad actors can even put pressure on those who stick to their discipline, as their performance may exceed that of disciplined operators over a short period of time. Just look at the experience of many mutual funds at the end of 1999 and in early 2000. Mutual fund managers learned that to outperform the stock market and keep up with the heady performance of their investment peers, they had to buy large-capitalization technology stocks to the exclusion of all other sectors. Those who failed to heed the siren call of the crowd underperformed and witnessed asset outflows as the public chased performance and rewarded the "winners." The problem of induction can lead us into some strange places.

Another area where logic and arguing from false premises can lead us astray is when we become "assumption blind." To simplify a complex environment, we are quick to accept common assumptions and use these as a basis on which to model our behavior. While these heuristics can be useful in everyday situations, they can make us blind in more complex situations or during times of dramatic change. The ancient skeptics maintained the dual goal of suspending judgment on all things and achieving a sense of quietude from doing so. Practice this habit in your market operations. Listen to the arguments of your friends and fellow operators, but withhold judgment until you have time to reach your own conclusions. Challenge both the conclusions and the underlying assumptions of consensus thought.

The nation's top business schools embed several assumptions in their models and their teachings, one of the more egregious of which is the fallacy that you can assume that the markets are efficient and investors are rational. Only an academic, buried in models and detached from reality, can argue either point with any seriousness. Rational investors wouldn't have poured record amounts of mutual fund money into stocks at record high valuations during the four-month stretch from November 1999 to March 2000. Nor would rational investors have sold a record amount of mutual fund holdings in the summer and fall of 2002 at the low point of a grueling bear market. Yet numerous investors did both. "Homo rationale" is indeed a fallacy of the ivory tower. He doesn't exist. Not convinced? Look at the housing bubble, the oil bubble, and the more recent flight to "safety" in the Treasury bonds bubble.

Irrationality is commonplace, and as a result, efficient market theory lacks validity. Academics and fundamental analysts assume that markets are self-correcting and that any excesses on either the downside or the upside will be corrected in short order. A strict efficient-market theorist won't even go that far; she will assume that markets are always efficient—never mind the reality. If she models it, it must be so. But instead of being self-correcting, markets tend to follow boom/bust and self-perpetuating models much more closely. Trend following, heuristics, memes, and performance anxiety are only some of the reasons that higher prices beget higher prices and positive feedback loops take hold. You have only to look at oil prices, which moved from $50 per barrel in early 2007 to a high of $145 per barrel in the summer of 2008, to appreciate the extreme inefficiency of the financial markets. This kind of inefficiency can be seen repeatedly on the macro level, and it is even more pervasive on the micro level as individual stocks and sectors swing from emotional highs to despondent lows.

Critical Thinking

> Whenever a theory appears to you as the only possible one, take this as a sign that you have neither understood the theory nor the problem which it was intended to solve.
>
> —Karl Popper

The greatest foundation of successful modern societies is the ability of human beings to think critically and rationally and take responsibility for their own actions so that they may evolve, solve their problems, and march to progressive improvement. We owe a debt of gratitude to the ancient Greeks for establishing the tradition of critical thought and discussion. Socrates paid with his life for leading the argument that man could use his own mind to seek the truth. He questioned authority and challenged other thinkers' assumptions to find the flaws in their arguments. He did this with the truth in mind and taught that while we may never arrive at perfect truth, we can evolve and come closer to it by questioning and challenging our assumptions and theories. History has not been kind to those who have sought the truth and advocated for change. Those with a vested interest in maintaining the status quo have erected barriers and doled out brutal punishments to thought leaders in an effort to deprive human beings of the moral freedom and educational opportunities that they require in their quest for knowledge and improvement. Thankfully, the importance society places on authoritarianism, mysticism, and violence has decreased to such an extent that true and lasting progress is now possible.

In just the last 100 years, the world has witnessed an unsurpassed degree of freedom and progress. The West has led the charge, contributing the mental ballast needed by other societies to embark on a similar path, and personal and economic freedoms are now opening up for an unprecedented number of people on a global scale. And what do we have to thank for this explosion of innovation and personal freedom? The answer is our willingness to think, grow, and expand our horizons and our ability to try new things, make necessary mistakes, and reach out anew with better solutions. This attempt to know our world in an imperfect way was best summed up by Xenophanes of Colophon, a philosopher who was born over 2,500 years ago.

Chapter 9 | Philosophy

Through seeking we may learn, and know things better.
But as for certain truth, no man has known it,
Nor will he know it.
The perfect truth, he would himself not know it;
For all is but a woven web of guesses.

I should point out that this skeptically rational approach to thinking is not a pessimistic thought process that leads to the general belief that humanity cannot progress and evolve. On the contrary, it speeds up progress and evolution by quickly alerting us when we begin to veer down the wrong path.

There are many worthy modes of thinking and approaches to logic, but for the purposes of this book, I would like to highlight the wise, adaptive methodology advanced by Karl Popper, who postulated that life itself is problem solving. Popper came of age during the 1900s, the greatest period of scientific advancement the world has ever seen, and melded philosophy with scientific inquiry in his approach. Central to his methodology was an optimistic belief that humanity can progress and that knowledge can expand by a series of conjectures and refutations. To that end, Popper would advance and then subsequently test bold theories to ensure their validity and robustness. If a theory underwent the critical process of attempted refutations and survived, it could then be accepted tentatively as accepted knowledge.

The *tentative* acceptance of knowledge was key to Popper's philosophy, for it approached knowledge, all knowledge, with a sense of limits and humility and accepted the fact that our knowledge is imperfect and likely to be improved upon in the future. Popper's belief in both the potential expansion of knowledge and the limits of our knowledge stands in sharp contrast to the mindset of most thinkers, who cling to their beliefs and set themselves up for disappointment and disaster at the hands of inevitable change. Remember, the ideas of even the most brilliant and innovative thinkers are often superseded in time. Galileo was superseded by Newton who was superseded by Einstein who will be superseded by someone else with a better, more precise understanding of our universe.

In markets, the same phenomenon applies. Trading methods and beliefs that hold the promise of profits today are likely to lose validity over time or at least undergo periods of underperformance. Traders can fall off the trading cliff unless they accept the limits of their own knowledge and constantly strive to critically examine their methodologies and the theories upon which their methods are built.

It is an easier mental exercise to look back at historical mental follies and see their flaws than it is to conduct theoretical tests of cherished and accepted beliefs in real time. We can laugh now at those who thought that the world was flat. We can snicker at the fact that Columbus was trying to find a shorter route to the trading centers of India when he accidentally bumped into the New World. We can shake our heads smugly at the unwillingness of the religious establishment to accept that the sun, not the Earth, was the center of the universe. Yet, can we challenge our own beliefs and trading and investment systems and see their flaws before our inflexibility leads us to disaster? Do you have the mental strength and flexibility to adjust as the environment around you changes?

One good way to test divergences between your beliefs and reality in the financial markets is to flag your performance numbers. Yet most people will blame the markets for their underwhelming performance. The market is reality, they claim. Rather than question their cherished methods, they would prefer to continue down the same less painful (though less profitable) well-worn path each day, even if it doesn't get them to their destination. People crave certainty and anchor themselves to assumptions in spite of reality, but we must fight this tendency if we truly desire to improve our personal and financial performance and enhance our growth. Change may be painful in the short run, but denying change is far more harmful in the long run. Knowledge is ever in flux, and if you are having trouble remembering that, turn to Karl Popper's ten theses of epistemology[1].

1. There are no ultimate sources of knowledge. Every source is welcome; and every source is open to critical examination.

2. The proper epistemological question is not one about sources; rather, we ask whether the assertion made is true—that is, whether it agrees with the facts.

3. All kinds of arguments may be relevant. Typical procedure is to examine whether our theories are consistent with our observations.

4. By far the most important source of our knowledge is tradition. We learn most by example, by being told, by reading books, by learning how to criticize, how to respect truth.

5. Every bit of our traditional knowledge is open to critical examination and may be overthrown. Yet without tradition, knowledge would be impossible.

6. Knowledge cannot start from nothing—nor yet from observation. The advance consists in modification of earlier knowledge.

---

[1] Karl Popper, *Conjectures and Refutations* (1963; reprint, London: Routeledge, 2002).

7. When recognized, our own errors provide the dim red lights which help us in groping our way out of the darkness of our cave.

8. Neither observation nor reason is an authority. Their main functions are to help us in the critical examination of those bold conjectures which are the means by which we probe into the unknown.

9. Although clarity is valuable in itself, exactness or precision is not: there can be no point in trying to be more precise than our problem demands.

10. Every solution to a problem raises new unsolved problems.

Submit your methods to constant tests, challenge your underlying assumptions, and above all remember that you are not trying to prove your theories. Rather, you are seeking the truth as a way to a more profitable path.

How can you find your way to a more profitable path? Instead of trying to prove that your theories are correct, you should attempt to *disprove* them with conflicting information. Of course, this latter strategy runs counter to most people's way of thinking. Generally, people postulate a theory and then seek corroborative evidence to support their original belief. Just look at the political realm, where those on the right seek the encouraging sounds of Fox News and those on the left seek the comfort of MSNBC. Neither camp is seeking the truth, nor are they looking to challenge their assumptions; instead, they are searching for confirmation and the unchallenging and comfortably reinforcing view of their cheerleader hosts.

When it comes to the financial markets, you must constantly challenge your tendency to seek confirmation. Once you take a position, you should spend as little time as possible confirming your original ruling investment position and as much time as you can trying to challenge it, searching at every turn for the flaws or alterations that will render your investment hypothesis invalid. Failure to do so will eventually lead to unpleasant surprises in your portfolio and investment results, and even, occasionally, to complete disaster.

Since there are no ultimate sources of knowledge and no one has a monopoly on the truth, you must do your own thinking and challenge your own work. It is good practice to find out what the smart money is doing and actively seek out as many ideas from those investors as possible, but it is not good practice to blindly follow even the most successful operators. You must live and die on your own hook, as they say. Every investor and investing style goes through both fat and lean times, so take the ideas of others but submit them to your own thought process so that you can validate those ideas and continuously challenge them. When you perceive market action that runs counter to your assumptions, it is time to question the investment and enact your exit strategy.

No one in this business will spoon-feed you the buy and sell information on every new investment idea. As a result, it is incumbent upon you to develop your own profit-generating and risk-control methodologies and manage your funds accordingly. Own your ideas and take credit for both your successes and your failures. Taking responsibility for your own actions and becoming an active, thinking market participant will reward you with long-term success that is independent of other investors.

Follow George Soros's lead, and actively seek out the flaws and vulnerabilities in your market positions so that you can exit them when the time comes. Let's use an example to illustrate this point. Assume that you have done your work and think that copper prices can rise 30% over the next six months because of increased Asian demand. To take advantage of this robust pricing outlook, you buy copper futures and metals stocks in expectation of strong performance. But if you hold fast to your assumptions and do not subject them to revision and further review, you could be setting yourself up for dramatic failure—even if your original thesis was based on sound fundamentals. Why? Because there are myriad ways your thesis could be upset, including a war suddenly breaking out that causes a sudden 20% drop in equity prices along with a sudden decline in prices for economically sensitive metals like copper; the demand you were looking for could be postponed; or you could see a slower rise in the copper price, yet watch your metal stock holdings drop in price. In short, many events can unfold to either disrupt or invalidate your thesis and expectations.

If, on the other hand, you hold your investment position with a flexible outlook, you can still enter your trades with the same amount of gusto but leave yourself "outs" if market action or events don't confirm your original thesis. In this way, you can remain more flexible in the face of potential changes and adapt your actions to align with the unfolding reality. When you use conjectures and refutations, you are privy to an adaptive epistemological system that can change when the facts do—and in the investment world that is absolutely vital. Adaptation is a true edge.

You should critically challenge your ideas and market positions with one overriding goal in mind: to ensure mental flexibility so that you can stay in tune with the markets. Rigidity and epistemological arrogance are occupational hazards. Stay alert, open, and critically rational so that changes can be incorporated and seized upon in your work. Treat existing positions as tentative truths that may be supplanted by different truths when you find them to be more valid. Write down your operating investment thesis so you can more readily challenge it and ensure that it's still valid. If it is not, then

Chapter 9 | Philosophy

adjust your holdings to reflect the new market reality. Most market participants let the media lead their investment decisions, operate without working investment theories, and aren't willing to critically challenge their positions in a proactive fashion. If you don't fall into the same traps that most investors do, you will be miles ahead from the standpoint of both risk and reward.

Network Effects: Think "System"

Out of clutter find simplicity; from discord make harmony.

—Albert Einstein

The world is not a random place, even if it is unpredictable. Under the chaos of systems and networks (and the markets are just one of them) there is a structure that binds the parts together. Einstein was right when he said, "God does not play dice with the universe." Although we trade individual markets, at the end of the day we do so only after we have analyzed the system within which these markets trade. This is why I start my investment process from a macro viewpoint, move on to the broad futures markets, then study sectors, and finally look at individual stocks. If you trade the other way around, you are likely to watch your tech stock get hit by a breakdown in the Thai baht that you never saw coming. You think it can't happen? Think again. In 1997, a large failure in a minor currency served as the tipping point that set off a deep recession in Asia. In the process, the currency breakdown took roughly a third of world demand out of the global economy and led to downward GDP revisions, lower earnings growth, and plummeting oil prices. This wouldn't make any sense to the fundamental analyst who wears blinders or the investor who looks at the markets from a bottom-up perspective instead of as a network. The reality is that global economies and markets are an intricately linked network, and to be successful as a trader, you need to see them as such.

In *Linked: The New Science of Networks* (Perseus Publishing, 2003), Albert-László Barabási states that clustering is five times more likely to occur in the real world than would be the case with random networks. You can observe this reality in cities that become exponentially larger once they reach a certain critical mass, in our highway and aviation networks, and certainly in markets. The Italian mathematician Vilfredo Pareto discovered that the network effect applies to the distribution of wealth in a given society. He formulated the concept of the 80/20 rule, whereby roughly 20% of the population holds 80% of the wealth. Book sales work the same way, with a few winners garnering the lion's share of total book sales each year. Networks are not random but display an order that conforms to the power law discussed in the next section.

Suffice it to say that size begets size and connectedness begets further connectedness as systems grow.

Network effects are relevant to our epistemological framework in several ways. On the positive side, networks are governed by two fundamental laws: growth and preferential attachment. Networks prefer to attach to nodes that house more links, and this offers the first mover an advantage. Knowing this, it makes sense that companies like eBay and Facebook have succeeded in the online space. Each was first to market its respective product, and as such, each enjoys a tremendous advantage over its competitors in continued growth and relative success. In fact, eBay has garnered so much traffic that its network serves as the de facto standard and dominates the online marketplace.

Efficiencies in selling and buying quickly become so large that all other players are crowded out unless they offer an extremely compelling advantage. Microsoft enjoys such an advantage, with nearly ninety percent of the marketplace using its operating system as the standard platform. Even though users complained about Microsoft's Vista operating system, because of its enormous network advantage, the company didn't lose its edge. Google holds an advantage over its competitors in Internet search, while Visa and MasterCard have an edge in credit payment systems. Apple enjoys a similar advantage, thanks to a combination of iTunes, the App Store, and simply brilliant industrial design. Given these efficiency advantages enjoyed by certain companies, an investor who is targeting companies that are in the early stages of growth in a given category will want to place her capital with the early adapters and winners while avoiding the challengers. The "me-too" player will tend to be marginalized rather quickly and fade further as the contest intensifies, but network winners will be great investments for those who get aboard early.

Network effects also help investors by bringing home the concept that the world and global markets are connected and interdependent on each other. Wars, crop failures, technological developments, currency failures, bond market selloffs, and political battles are all within the relevant scope of the trader. Everything is connected, and small changes at the margin can have an outsized impact on the larger landscape. As a result, the ability to see the interconnectedness of the markets will put you one step ahead of average investors, who tunnel into their fundamental worlds.

Think back, for example, to 2008 and 2009, when the collapse of the housing and debt bubbles triggered selloffs in global stock markets and led to routs in crude oil and copper. Since the world is so interrelated, the collapses also led to budget problems at both the state and federal level; 30-year highs in unemployment; failures in levered companies; a government bailout of numerous financial firms; and challenges to the capitalist system. As history has shown, within networks a failure, or even a small event, can trigger a cascade of failures in a vulnerable system. If you had been aware of the ways in which the housing and debt markets were connected to the rest of the financial system, you would have been able to avoid the subsequent fallout. So, the next time you see problems building on the horizon or come across an interesting news item, see if you can put the problem or information into the context of the network of the global system. It could be the canary in the coal mine warning you that oxygen is being sucked out of the room.

In nature, systems are dynamic, and the species that survive for centuries are those that can adapt and display a certain level of flexibility. This adaptability explains the longevity of the mouse and the cockroach, but it also reveals why the Tyrannosaurus rex and the saber-toothed tiger are now extinct. The first two can survive in variegated climates and feed on myriad food supplies, while the latter two, for all their awe-inspiring killing abilities, were optimized for specific climates and large prey.

In the human world, our tendency to optimize systems leaves them with flaws and weaknesses that make them more susceptible to failure during times of stress. This is why you should always be on the lookout for systemic risk. It is also why I advocate a higher margin for error, less optimization, and greater flexibility in both your trading system and your personal affairs. During tough times, correlations among asset classes increase almost uncontrollably, leaving you with greater risk and less diversification when you can least afford it. Hold some cash and hard assets in reserve, and by all means do not use margin in your overall positioning. It will come back to bite you and leave you at the mercy of a systemic event. The realities of change and the interconnectedness of our frail human networks demand that we make our portfolios more diverse and flexible so that we can meet change from a position of strength.

The Fractal World We Live In

There are three kinds of prevarication: lies, damn lies, and statistics.

—Mark Twain

I have made the case quite strongly that change, not equilibrium, is the rule. Equilibrium is a conceptual tooth fairy concocted in ivory towers. If equilibrium is the rule, why is it never reached? Why is the world in such a constant state of evolutionary flux? Why is change so rapid and disruptive?

The bell curve does a great job of depicting the reality of the physical world. Take a look at the bell curve in Figure 9-3 with its familiar bell-shaped distribution of events. When the Bell curve is used to demonstrate factors like the height of people, it depicts a "normal" distribution, where the bulk of people would range in height from 5' tall to 6'6" tall. It will also show some outliers on the low end, with 3' or 4' tall people, and some on the high end, with people who are 7' to 8' tall, but you can see that the number of outliers tails off rapidly as you get under or above these rarer heights. The extreme outliers are nonexistent, according to the bell curve, as you would never expect to pass a 25' tall person or a 1" tall person on the street. So far, so good, but what impact does the bell curve have on stocks and your investment account? The truth is that the bell curve and the notion of equilibrium and efficient markets are absolutely flawed and dangerous epistemological approaches to the financial markets.

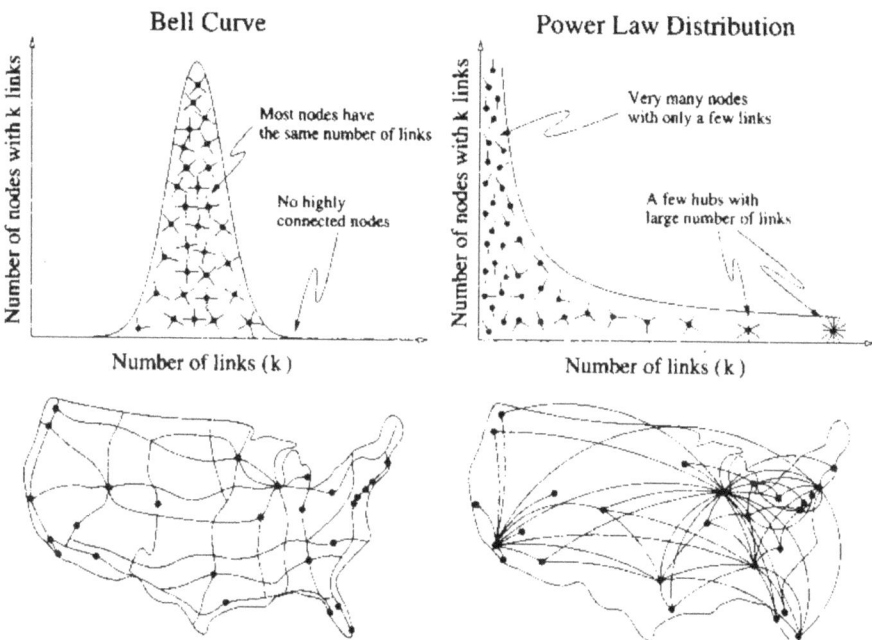

Figure 9-3. Power law distribution is more accurate than the bell curve in depicting the US highway system.[2]

Take another look at the distribution curves shown in Figure 9-3. The left-hand panel shows the familiar bell-shaped distribution curve, while the right-hand panel depicts the probably unfamiliar image of a power law distribution. Underneath each of the two distributions shown in the figure is a corresponding map of the US highway system. The map on the left demonstrates how the highway system would look if it developed under a bell curve distribution, and

---

[2] Figure courtesy of Albert-László Barabási from *Linked: The New Science of Networks* (Cambridge, MA: Perseus, 2002), p.71.

as you can see, most cities on this map have roughly the same number of links, with the exception of a few larger and a few smaller highway hubs. Now look at the map on the right, which shows how the highway system would look if it developed under a power law distribution. You can immediately see that this map is a more accurate reflection of the real highway system, as a few large cities dominate the structure, with Chicago and Los Angeles noticeable for their sheer highway density.

Notice two major differences between the two systems of distribution. First, under a power law distribution, most of the plotted data points represent small values. Second, under a power law distribution, these data points are extremely large in scope and dominate the topography. The fact that the bell curve does not account for an increased number of large events and the greater size of those large events means that this system of distribution exponentially underrepresents risk in the traditional financial model. The implications of the bell curve's shortcomings are not superficial; as a distribution system, it is completely incompatible with the reality of the financial markets.

What about the power law distribution system? Does it more accurately reflect the financial markets? Take a look at the lists below, which highlight the characteristics and assumptions of both the bell curve and power law distributions, and decide for yourself.

Bell Curve	Power Law
Mild randomness	Wild randomness
Typical occurrence is average	Atypical, winner-take-all effects
Change is slow	Change leaps
Predictable	Hard to predict
Equilibrium, mean reverting	Scalable

First, let the math show that the bell curve fails as a representative model of the reality of financial market history. Remember that a model is only a theoretical framework that attempts to explain observable reality. If the observed facts do not support the model, then a critically rational person must discard the flawed model and work to improve it in the hope of reaching a theoretical framework that better explains the real world. Note that the model must fit reality; reality stands as the final arbiter of truth. An incorrect model, no matter how elegantly it is constructed, no matter how many reputable people believe it, is still false. Reality is the truth, and the reality of observable financial market history simply shatters the illusion that the bell curve and modern financial theory can explain market movements.

In his book *The (Mis)behavior of Markets: A Fractal View of Financial Turbulence* (Basic Books, 2004), Benoit Mandelbrot highlights several important examples that demonstrate the inadequacy of the bell curve in explaining the financial markets. According to Mandelbrot, under the bell curve model, the odds of seeing the August 31, 1998, decline in the stock market were 1 in 20 million. In other words, such a decline theoretically should have been seen only once every 100,000 years. Similarly, the odds of seeing the three large declines that occurred in the month of August 1998 were 1 in 500 billion. A year earlier, in 1997, the Dow Jones Industrial Average fell 7.7% in one day, and the odds of that occurrence, according to the bell curve, were again 1 in 500 billion. If those examples aren't extreme enough, let's segue to the 1987 crash. The odds of such a staggering drop were 1 in 10 to the 50th power, a number that is outside the scale of nature. If you still believe that the financial models offer any semblance of quantitative control or explanatory power over observable financial reality, then you will be doomed to reap the whirlwind of change that is coming your way.

Figure 9-4 indicates the impact of rare events on the long-term rate of return of an entire asset class, in this case US stocks. You can see that one line in the graph in Figure 4 shows outperformance that is double that of the other line over a 20-year period. Yet as we know from history, that outperformance is illusory—it didn't happen. What is the cause of the difference in performance? The line showing outperformance eliminates the ten biggest *one-day* moves from a period covering over 7,200 days. Nothing could be a clearer illustration of why rare but high-impact events matter significantly. In the risk/reward conversation, these events cannot be called outliers and avoided, and their concentrated impact should be the starting point for financial analysis.

Chapter 9 | Philosophy

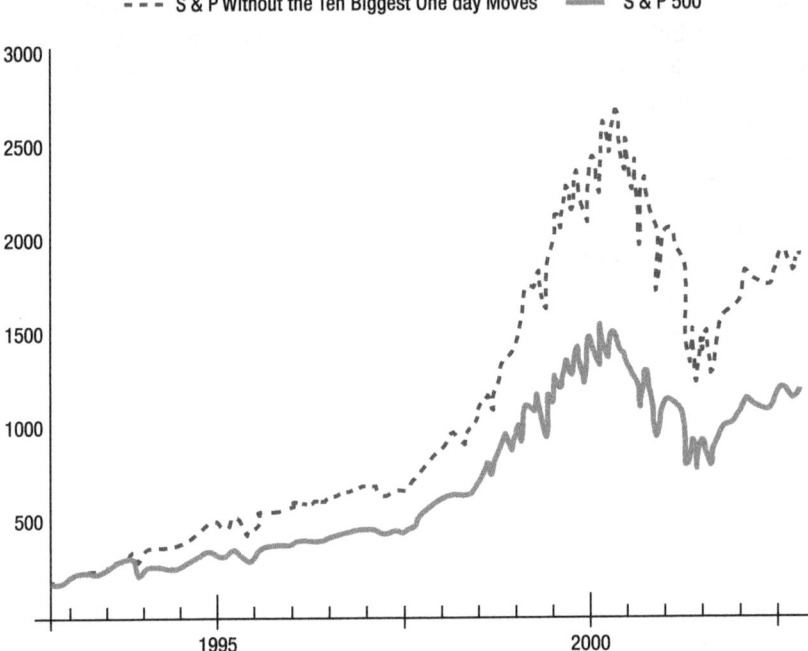

Figure 9-4. Eliminating the ten biggest one-day moves shows outperformance by the S&P 500—but it's illusory. Source: Fortune.

You can perform the same exercise shown in Figure 9-4 by plotting a financial chart that eliminates the largest positive-return days in a given period and seeing the dramatic impact on later periods. In the ten-year period from April 1, 1996, to March 30, 2006, for example, eliminating the ten largest positive-return days from the S&P 500 cuts the market's rate of return from an annualized +7.1% to -3.2%. This astounding impact—an almost 10% reduction in annualized returns—comes from simply eliminating the ten largest positive-return days from a period that encompasses roughly 2,650 days. It is another reminder that the outliers, the improbable events, drive reality.

In the real world, the impact of important, catalytic events is no less stark. What would the former East Germany look like if the Berlin Wall had not fallen on November 9, 1989? Can you eliminate D-Day from World War II? Is 9/11 not an important day in the war on terrorism? Is Albert Einstein important to the development of nuclear weapons? Was Dr. Martin Luther King, Jr., an important figure in the civil rights movement? Important days and people shape history as much as they do the financial markets, yet we continue to believe that the "average" and the "normal" are suitable explanations for reality. We think of change as happening slowly and incrementally, when it actually leaps and lurches from holes that we never saw in the tapestry of the future.

As I write this in 2012, it is clear that the financial industry has not learned its lesson. Instead of treating the market events of 2008 and early 2009 as additional painful examples of the inadequacy of current financial theory and risk modeling, investors are looking at them as outlier occurrences. The myths surrounding efficient market theory and the human tendency to anchor to flawed financial models are too strong to shake. The majority of market participants walk around spellbound, like tribesmen worshipping idols that can't speak and offer no help in explaining their world. They are unwilling to move to a more effective method of thinking. The flawed methods are all they know, and to imagine a different way is too difficult a prospect. It is far better, they think, to continue fumbling in the dark with a broken flashlight.

For those of you who are willing to step out of the dark, however, what exactly can you do moving forward? How do you prepare for events and changes that are unpredictable and that have the potential to alter the future in a dramatic fashion? How can you prosper in a world of constant change, a fractal landscape that is beyond your comprehension? When designing and thinking about your personal financial and trading goals, it is important to build a portfolio that is both strong and flexible. Imitate the natural world and create a trading system that is capable of absorbing shocks. The traditional asset allocation mix of 60% stocks and 40% bonds is not robust enough, nor is a leveraged stock-only account or a mix of ten stocks that you hold for the long term. Trade according to your own financial situation, but in broad terms your portfolio should be diversified, should maintain short-term liquidity in various stores of value, and should comprise a noncorrelated asset mix. Furthermore, your short-term liquidity should include cash in one or more currencies as well as a combination of hard assets, such as precious metals or coins, diamonds, or art, depending on your means. Maintaining this liquidity mix makes for a more robust portfolio than simply holding cash, and it will leave you in a stronger situation in the event that your home currency comes under devaluation pressures.

Within your cash holdings, you should diversify among different financial institutions. On the asset side of the ledger, mixing stocks, various bonds, managed futures, hedge funds, and real estate is a healthier approach than just owning stocks. On the bond side, diversify among types and maturities, seek only the top-tier credits, and don't passively assume that sovereign debt is risk free. Within your stock holdings, it may help to spread your risk among different brokerage houses and asset classes, but remember that during shocks to the system, correlations have a way of moving rapidly toward 1 and destroying portfolios. Flexibility is paramount. Hold more liquid stores of value than the common wisdom suggests, and work with portfolio managers who have shown an ability to navigate change. If you sense that your portfolio manager is arrogant or believes he's infallible, find a new steward for your capital. Rigidity and intellectual arrogance have a way of meeting the grim reaper and his sickle. Perhaps the best piece of advice I can give you is that you must remain intellectually open to the changing landscape and maintain a sense of balance in your positioning. Fads come and go, but a strong position characterized by flexibility and diversification should stand the test of time and change.

The Art of War

> *If you know the enemy and know yourself, you need not fear the result of a hundred battles. If you know yourself, but not the enemy, for every victory gained you will also suffer a defeat. If you know neither the enemy nor yourself, you will succumb in every battle.*
>
> —Sun Tzu, *The Art of War*

With its advocacy of skilled, flexible thinking and its requirement that leaders understand both themselves and the environment in which they find themselves, Sun Tzu's *The Art of War* has tremendous applications to the financial markets. Read the quote that precedes this section a second time. Notice that in explaining how to succeed in battle, Sun Tzu advocates knowing both yourself and your enemy. This implies that good warriors maintain the mental flexibility to carry out different battlefield tactics to suit different enemies and when working with different resources. In much the same way, skilled traders adapt their trading strategies to give themselves the greatest odds for success in the financial environment in which they finds themselves. Many financial practitioners, having fallen victim to the academic charade of "all else being equal," seem to work on the mistaken assumption that one trading strategy will work in any economy and when applied to any market. But in what realm of your life is it safe to assume that all else is equal? In a global economy, where different stocks and industries and even regimes rise and fall with regularity, you should assume that "all else is changing" and work accordingly. History and economic cycles may rhyme, but the verses are scarcely similar.

> *There are armies that must not be attacked, positions that must not be contested, commands of the sovereign that must not be obeyed. The art of war teaches us not to rely on the likelihood of the enemy's not coming, but on our own readiness to receive him; not on the chance of his not attacking, but rather on the fact that we have made our position unassailable.*
>
> —Sun Tzu, *The Art of War*

There are two primary ways to make sure that you are prepared for the market of tomorrow. The first is to flow with the changes and trends that prevail, which requires many of the traits that I outlined earlier in this epistemological section. Flowing with change allows you to thrive when others are merely trying to survive. It allows you to capture the opportunities that present themselves every week, every month, and every year. When you flow with the changes and trends, your world becomes easier to navigate, and your profitability will increase dramatically. The second way to prepare yourself for the market of tomorrow is to ensure that your financial position is robust enough to handle those times when you find yourself out of synch with current conditions, which, in spite of your best efforts, will happen with some frequency. Maintaining the health of your position and its ability to absorb shocks will ensure that you will experience minimal risk and capital loss when your conjectures are proven incorrect by the realities of the marketplace.

What are the key elements that characterize a robust approach to the markets? Another term for robustness could be "survivability quotient." First and foremost, maintain your stop-loss discipline and ignore your ego. Remember, your ego wants to be right. Your ego doesn't like to take losses. Your ego wants to sell your winners quickly and wait for your losers to break even before selling them. But the road to profitability and effective risk control begins when your ego ends its interference in the pragmatic realities of the risk/reward equation. Second, remain diversified in uncorrelated assets in both your personal and professional trading portfolios. Now, when I say that you should diversify your portfolios, I don't mean that you should simply hold small-cap US stocks alongside large-cap European and Asian stocks. This type of diversification may work well when the markets are up, but it will utterly fail you during market stresses, when fear will throw global equities into tighter correlations than your models could ever foresee. No, true diversification works during good times *and* bad times. It can be achieved by balancing cash with hard currencies, stocks with bonds, and real estate with managed futures. Diversify not by optimizing your risk frontier but rather by optimizing your survivability quotient. Finally, strive for portfolio balance. The best ways to do that include corralling your sector exposure, avoiding leverage, using stops when your trades become more directional, and staying on the sidelines during binary events.

> *Military tactics are like unto water; for water runs away from high places and hastens downward. So in war, the way is to avoid what is strong and to strike at what is weak. Water shapes its course according to the nature of the ground over which it flows; the soldier works out his victory in relation to the foe that he is facing. He who can modify his tactics in relation to his opponent, and thereby succeed in winning, may be called a heaven-born captain.*
>
> —Sun Tzu, *The Art of War*

Chapter 9 | Philosophy

If you learn nothing else from this chapter, remember this: approach the financial markets with an open mind. Assume nothing. Take in the landscape of the financial markets from as many vantage points as you can. Seek contradictory opinions, evaluate the best thought leaders, and use their input. Look for the black holes in the consensus view and challenge them. What factors are they "assumption blind" to? Only after sizing up the landscape that lies in front of you should you formulate a trading plan that will give you the greatest returns for the least amount of effort and risk. As the Sun Tzu quote above suggests, flow like the water and seek out the easiest path by buying the leading instruments within the leading asset classes. Move along the lines of least resistance, buy what is in demand, and short, or avoid, what is in abundant supply. This game is hard enough without trying to take profits in out-of-favor groups that are in clear downtrends. The trader who can operate most flexibly and seek out the best opportunities puts herself in a position to seize opportunities through myriad market cycles in an ever-evolving financial environment.

CHAPTER 10

Summing It All Up

Execute Your Plan—and Keep It Simple

A good plan violently executed now is better than a perfect plan next week.

—George Patton

Now that you are armed with the tactical trend trading system I have outlined in the pages of this book, the time has come for you to finalize your plan of attack against the financial markets. Your battle plan should incorporate your methodology for generating returns and your risk control measures, and simplicity of execution is paramount. After all, events unfold quickly in the financial markets, and simplicity allows you to adapt to these changes as they present themselves. While I analyze myriad indicators, statistics, and various market inputs in my trading, the core of my work simply involves buying leading markets, shorting the weakest markets, and using a stop if my positions move against me. The simplicity of my trading approach keeps me in synch with changes whether or not I can anticipate them. It enables me to react to changes rapidly, protect my positions and my portfolio, and stay in tune with the ever-evolving nature of the markets. It promotes the dynamism and longevity of my portfolio in a way that would not be possible with an overly optimized and complex system.

Trade to Win

Your time is limited, so don't waste it living someone else's life. Don't be trapped by dogma, which is living with the results of other people's thinking. Don't let

> the noise of others' opinions drown out your own inner voice. And most important, have the courage to follow your heart and intuition. They somehow already know what you truly want to become. Everything else is secondary.
>
> —Steve Jobs

In this book, I have spent a lot of time discussing risk control, various trading pitfalls, and the epistemological framework a trader needs in order to profit from leaps of change. And with good reason: maintaining risk control and employing stop losses are the two basic keys to achieving long term-trading success. Still, if you can't generate alpha, what's the point of playing the game?

The trading-to-win philosophy has been a major influence on my own trading style, and I would recommend that you trade according to this mentality as well. How do you trade to win? You must commit to finding the trading instruments and emerging ideas that put profits on the board. You must put yourself in a frame of mind that frees you to commit more capital to trades that are moving in your direction and cut back quickly when the market turns against you. You must trade markets that can move rather than holding back to play it safe. You must find the markets that are going to treat your capital best. You must believe that you can accomplish the goals that you set forth and commit to excellence in your trading and your life. Trading to win is not about safety and timidity; it is about putting yourself out there and seeing what happens. You must have the confidence to buy into leading markets, sectors, and stocks. If you do all of the above and maintain a sound belief in your trading system, you will be doing everything you can to achieve success. Ironically, trading to win not only allows you to trade more proactively, but it also allows you to do so with less fear and uncertainty. It will put you in a position that is in tune with the financial world around you, giving you the confidence you need to cut your losers more quickly, and decreasing your overall trading stress. Trade to win!

Accept and Flow with a Changing Reality

> Many of the assumptions of modern society are based on shared illusions.
>
> —Leonard Mlodinow

If you accept change as the natural order of things, you will find it easier to flow with change as it happens. The more easily you can accept changes and flow with them in a positive manner, the stronger your mental state will be.

Psychiatrist Elisabeth Kübler-Ross developed a five-stage model for dealing with life-altering situations. Those stages are as follows:

1. **Denial**
2. **Anger**
3. **Bargaining**
4. **Depression**
5. **Acceptance**

The last step in coping with dramatic change is acceptance, but the four steps leading up to acceptance are mentally painful and financially hazardous for many traders. However, if you maintain balanced risk control measures and use stop-loss orders on every trade, you can speedily and relatively painlessly short-circuit the road to acceptance. In doing so, you will be able to preserve your capital, reduce your exposure when conditions change, and remain in synch with the financial markets. Your mind will probably not be ready, willing, or able to accept every emerging change that it confronts, but if you have proper risk control measures in place, you'll find the path to acceptance is much easier to travel.

Mentally, there are other ways to move quickly to acceptance of change. First, realize that change is the natural way of the world. Stagnancy and stability are unnatural, and the status quo doesn't last long. Second, when you see potential change looming on the horizon, do not immediately brush it off as unimportant. Instead, picture the change occurring, take note of the possibility that the future will be different than you imagined, and spend some time watching to see if significant change develops. Third, view change as a positive. Too often, I hear people referring to the "good old days." You know what? Today is the only day that matters, and *these* are the good old days. You can't live in reverse, so you must see change as something that will help you in your trading. Change is negative only for those who fail to learn, grow, and adapt. The future is infinite in its possibilities, and change is the agent of infinity.

If you accept change quickly and readily, you will be able to flow with it instead of battling its inevitable tide. To be in a state of flow feels natural, easy, and fun and keeps you in tune with the rhythms of the world. Fighting against reality, on the other hand, leads to extreme anxiety and fear as the reality/expectations gap widens, draining your energy, increasing your stress levels, and leaving you disconnected from the world around you. The next time you encounter a potentially threatening change, see if you can adjust your response to reframe the change and accept it in a more positive light. If you make a habit of this, you will find change easier to deal with and the investment journey more profitable and less painful.

Risk Control

Learn to fail with pride — and do so fast and cleanly. Maximize trial and error — by mastering the error part.

—Nassim Taleb

You will frequently be wrong about your trades and investments, but if you have proper risk control measures in place, you will be able to ensure your longevity in the markets. Risk control is your protection against the fallibility of your best efforts to identify profitable investment opportunities; it will allow you to realize the truly remarkable power of compounding investment gains. But the benefits of a sound risk control strategy extend well beyond your profit and loss statement, as they also will enable you to maintain a healthy mental state and undergo personal growth. Traders who experience dramatic drawdowns tend to become worn down mentally over time, with every new significant loss causing their expectations/reality gap to cast a real shadow over their psyches.

Since downside risk can be so great, a trader who is looking for a solid risk/reward strategy that works over myriad market cycles should avoid market approaches that rely on excessive leverage, mean reversion, or bottom-fishing. Instead, he should employ solid risk control on his individual positions. Doing so will enable him to avoid potholes along the path to investment success and improve his performance in good years to levels he never thought possible. Above all, risk control is vital to ensuring a trader's survival and longevity for those times when he is wrong; it mitigates large drawdowns and keeps a portfolio performing decently even when the markets are falling apart. A trading or investing methodology that does not incorporate risk control is not a strategy but a flawed method whose shortcomings surely will come to light in the next bear market.

Change and the Margin

It's not the strongest of the species that survive, nor the most intelligent, but the one most responsive to change.

—Charles Darwin

Change, like many things in life, is a process, not an event. The world we inhabit and the markets we trade are in constant motion and a constant state of flux. They cycle from one movement to the next. They shift from one consensus to the next, one linear leap at a time. The status quo itself is change. What determines the next price of anything traded? How do we arrive at today's price, the one that incorporates all the hopes, thoughts, and prognostications of market participants? It is through incremental change, or change at the margin. Change at the margin is what slowly checks an advancing uptrend as it segues to a top, and then sets prices on the next downtrend. Change at the margin is the driver of the *next* move—and the next move is all that matters to the markets. Change is constant, and change at the margin is the tip of the spear of the forces of change.

Change at the margin is why major stock market bottoms occur while the economic outlook is still negative. If you look closely, bottoms coincide with the release of the worst financial news forecasts, and rallies take off from those lows even though the general market sentiment is still gloomy. By the time the economy and corporate profits are on the upswing, the markets have already rallied in anticipation of this news, and the most powerful move of the upswing has passed. Change at the margin is also why stock markets peak and begin to sell off when trading conditions are still excellent and the economy is the picture of perfection. Traders who remain in their positions when the market swings from great to good are particularly vulnerable to losses, but those who are keenly aware of both the consensus expectations and the changes occurring at the margins can capitalize on this downtrend.

Remember: markets are discounting mechanisms. They are flawed and emotional, yes, but they continually look to the future, which advances slowly and incrementally because of the events unfolding at the margin. As such, a trader who stays in synch with marginal change can flow with the markets as they trend in one direction, reverse, and then trend in the next direction.

Seizing the profit-taking opportunities that change engenders in the markets is the very essence of trading. As a result, it is essential that you continue to develop two key personality traits that will enable you to stay in tune with change. First, you must maintain a flexible, open mind that is willing to see change as it develops in the markets. Entering situations with few assumptions and few (or no) fixed, inflexible biases aids the trader who wishes to stay in synch with the latest market developments. Second, you must see change within the proper epistemological framework. Recognizing that change leaps, is inherently procyclical, and is subject to the network effect allows a trader to benefit from both the speed and scope of change. Remember that changes are more far-reaching and reflexive in nature than is accounted for by the linear models that most traders use in their work. Change is the positive force that allows you to profit in markets.

Chapter 10 | Summing It All Up

Traits of the Winning Trader

> It takes a very intelligent and non-parochial fish to realize that his environment is wet.
>
> —Daryl Bem

Over the course of my investment career, I have studied many successful traders and their methods. While each has his own distinctive trading style, these traders share a set of six common traits:

- They love the markets and maintain a positive outlook.
- They have a macro view and see the big-picture implications.
- They stick to their method and keep things simple.
- They are patient as they wait for opportunities to develop, then are aggressive in seizing them.
- They respect risk and the chaos of the markets.
- They maintain the mental flexibility to adapt to a variety of market environments.

I have seen the above six traits often enough in winning traders to know that adopting and developing them can give you an enormous advantage, while failing to cultivate one or more of them can hold you back from your full potential. Trading, after all, is a mental game. It doesn't matter if you are trading from a fundamental or a technical perspective, nor does it matter if you approach the markets systematically or on a discretionary basis. In the end, maintaining the correct mental outlook is the key to trading success. Remember: a mediocre trading method combined with a great mental approach to the markets and a solid risk-management framework will dramatically outperform a great trading method combined with a poor mental approach to the markets and a mediocre risk-management framework. The traits listed above encapsulate many of the points I have highlighted throughout the book. Risk control, flexibility, psychology, philosophy, a trading-to-win mentality, systematic thinking, and the ability to flow with trends are in synch with the six traits of winning traders.

Let's go through each of the six traits of winning traders and determine how they contribute to trading success and how they can be incorporated into your trading repertoire. The first trait is love of the markets and the ability to maintain a positive outlook. If you love what you do and commit your heart and your head to your trading endeavors, you will awaken each day with more energy and reduce the likelihood that you will give up because of short-term setbacks. Being positive about your abilities and believing you will ultimately be successful will keep you going through the inevitable drawdowns and obstacles that the markets will throw your way. I have had to trade throughout the greatest secular bear market in equities in the last hundred years, the 9/11 attacks, two bear markets when stocks were down 40%, the bankruptcy of one of my primary brokers, the bursting of the technology bubble, the crash of the housing market, the near collapse of the credit market, and numerous accounting scandals and stock frauds. Working through these events has not been easy, but I have been able to muddle through the bad times on my way to the good times, when everything is easy, flowing, and in synch, because I have maintained a positive outlook and have committed myself to the game of trading as long as I enjoy it. If you find that you deeply enjoy and connect with the markets, trading will become an exciting part of your life and work and you will be driven to succeed.

The second trait of winning traders is that they look at the markets from a macro, big-picture viewpoint. Macro traders, of course, see the markets in terms of the big picture as part of their daily routine, but in my experience, successful traders of all stripes do the same. Even fundamental investors, when they are successful, tend to have a global viewpoint they can express in three minutes, and they are able to assemble a portfolio that reflects this view. Maintaining a big-picture view of the markets is not as difficult as it sounds. In fact, it can be as simple as realizing that globalization has opened up foreign opportunities for multinationals and then seizing those opportunities by investing in Coke and McDonald's. Successful futures and equity traders develop themes, stay in synch with the markets, and position themselves to benefit from their macro viewpoints.

The third trait of winning traders is that they stick to their trading methods and keep their investment process simple. Success does not equal complexity—and vice versa. The investment wheel does not need to be reinvented every year. If you find yourself drifting from style to style and method to method, odds are high that you are overdoing it with your trading and reacting to events instead of anticipating them. Every trading style will go through periods when it underperforms the market and periods when it outperforms the market. Therefore, instead of giving up on your trading strategy the minute it begins to falter, maintain the discipline and the patience to stick to your method so that you can enjoy the next up cycle. Develop a theme, analyze markets, invest, maintain risk control—lather, rinse, repeat. Don't become discouraged or completely change your style the minute your method is out of favor. Do not add unnecessary complexity to your process. There is power in simplicity.

Chapter 10 | Summing It All Up

The fourth trait of winning traders involves remaining patient, waiting for opportunities to present themselves, and aggressively seizing them. Many amateur investors are too impatient to wait for opportunities to develop. Then, when circumstances are such that they can take profits, they reach out for them timidly, substantially diminishing their profit potential in the process. They overtrade and churn their accounts to such an extent that by the time a great trading opportunity presents itself, they cannot fully take advantage of it, as they are trading with reduced capital and decreased confidence. They chase, they grasp, and they flail about. They are like a lion running wildly at every movement on the plains, exhausting herself before a prime target presents itself. Great traders, on the other hand, wait, wait, and wait some more, and then pounce on attractive opportunities. If they are proven wrong, they back out and wait again until the next opportunity comes along, all the while reading and researching to uncover their next investment gem. Patience is a difficult trait to master and requires tremendous self-confidence. The markets are always rising or falling, which can make impatient traders feel as though they're missing out on scores of profitable trades. It takes real conviction to wait until you're thrown a fat pitch to swing at, but the rewards of remaining patient are significant.

The fifth trait of winning traders involves respecting risk and the chaotic nature of the markets. Anything can and will happen if you trade the markets for any length of time, which is why it is important to remember that you can't win if you don't bet, and you can't bet if you don't have any chips. Risk control, stop losses, diversification, and patience will all ensure that you have the chips you need to stay in the trading game on a long-term basis. We cannot divine the future. Wars, fraud, bankruptcies, bond defaults, currency devaluations, crop failures, oil supply shortages, and countless other shocks will shock the markets with frightening regularity, and it is only with the benefit of hindsight that it will seem that anyone could have predicted these events. But in the end, retrospective predictability is useless. Risk control and respect for the unknown are necessary to long-term success and survival in the financial markets, however chaotic they become.

The sixth and final trait of winning traders is that they maintain the mental flexibility to adapt to different investment climates. The financial markets cycle on an ongoing basis, and the only thing you can count on is that the leading sectors and stocks from one cycle will be replaced by entirely new leaders in the next. Oil led commodity markets in 2008, but in 2011, silver emerged as the leader. Technology led the stock market in 1999, but in 2005, housing stocks led the charge. New leaders will come to the fore with every new cycle in the markets, and you will be able to position yourself to take advantage of these new opportunities only if you use the same successful mental approach, risk control measures, and trading methods that you used in the last cycle. Doing so will ensure that you stay on the path of successful operation in the markets

Stay with It, Don't Force It, and Enjoy the Journey

> Defeat is a state of mind. No one is ever defeated until defeat has been accepted as reality. To me, defeat in anything is merely temporary, and its punishment is but an urge for me to greater effort to achieve my goal. Defeat simply tells me that something is wrong in my doing; it is a path leading to success and truth.
>
> —Bruce Lee

I have battled through countless hard times in the financial markets, including the most difficult ten-year stretch that the stock market has ever seen, but I've never lost my belief that I would ultimately find success as a trader. My conviction has kept me going through the many detours I've taken along the path to my goals. Just as importantly, it has allowed me to enjoy my trading journey even more fully. To strengthen my belief in my ultimate success, I've found some resources to aid me. Continuous learning from other traders has served as an inspiration, as has a wealth of books. Additionally, maintaining an open mind that is receptive to new ideas, developments, and modes of thought has helped me develop a sense of mastery and control. Because I remain mentally flexible at all times, I know that I can adapt and learn to apply myself in a different and better way in a future that may call for it. I know that my quest for knowledge is unending and, at the same time, is a goal in its own right.

Trading is a wonderful business. It is both mentally stimulating and financially lucrative for those who approach it with the correct mindset. For this reason, I have focused in this book on the four main prerequisites to trading success:

- A profit-generating methodology
- Risk control measures
- Psychological mastery
- An underlying philosophical framework

Each of these four elements is a vital component of trading success. As you begin each year, realize that many opportunities will reveal themselves to you. Nurturing an opportunistic mindset that is willing and able to see and profit from change will put you on the path to profits. Applying strict risk control

Chapter 10 | Summing It All Up

measures will ensure that you hold on to these profits. The synergy between the two will allow you to benefit from the truly powerful force of compounding investment returns and position you to generate substantial long-term gains. The right psychological approach helps to smooth the emotional roller coaster and avoid the mental rigidities that are often the root cause of trading disaster. Lastly, employing a valid working philosophical framework will allow you to approach trading with the optimal epistemological foundation. Success springs from having rigorously accurate working theories. Up the irons, unfurl your sails, and let the wind help you ride the investment trends!

APPENDIX A

Resources

Below I've included a partial list of investment resources. Access to sound investment advice has never been easier, and the proliferation of niche investment blogs has given a voice to alternative viewpoints.

Investment News and Data

- Bloomberg.com
- Zerohedge.com
- The High-Tech Strategist
- The Gloom Boom & Doom Report
- Sentimentrader.com
- Pimco.com
- Agrimoney.com
- Mineweb.co.za
- Kitco.com
- *Financial Times*
- *The Economist*
- Dshort.com
- Chicago Board Options Exchange
- Federal Reserve Bank of St. Louis
- Markiteconomics.com

Books

- *Technical Analysis of Stock Trends*, by Robert D. Edwards and John Magee (Orient Paperbacks, 2009)
- *Reminiscences of a Stock Operator*, by Edwin Lefevre (Wiley Investment Classics, 2006)
- *The Alchemy of Finance*, by George Soros (Wiley Investment Classics, 2003)
- *The Black Swan*, by Nassim Nicholas Taleb (Random House Trade Paperbacks, 2010)
- *The Misbehavior of Markets*, by Benoit Mandelbrot (Basic Books, 2006)
- *Market Wizards*, by Jack D. Schwager (John Wiley & Sons, Inc., 2012)
- *Trend Following*, by Michael Covel (FT Press, 2009)
- *Trading to Win*, by Ari Kiev (Wiley Trading, 1998)
- *Linked*, by Albert-László Barabási (Plume, 2003)

Contact

I welcome your feedback and am available for consulting, research, and sharing ideas. I can be reached through e-mail: rob@evertrendglobal.com, and twitter: @RobeverTrend. Thank you, and I wish you well on your road to trading success.

Index

A

American Association of Individual Investors (AAII), 30
Arms Index (or TRIN), 19
Art of War, 145

B

Black swan events, 131
Broad stock market, 41

C

Capital Asset Pricing Model (CAPM), 20
Chaotic nature, 214
Commitment of Trader (COT) data, 36–37
Crisis alpha, 129–131
Critical thinking
    finding flaws and vulnerabilities in market positions, 195
    Karl Popper's adaptive methodology, 192
    Karl Popper's epistemology, 193–194
    overriding goal in mind, 195
    profitable path, 194
    Socrates concepts, 191
    taking responsibility, 195
    tentative acceptance of knowledge, 192

D

Directional Movement Indicator (DMI), 86–87
Double bottom/top pattern
    bear market, 49
    description, 47–48
    dot-com craze, 50
    European bank, 51
    tactics, 48
    triple bottom bear market, 52
Dow Jones Industrial Average (DJIA), 3, 55, 56, 94, 95
Downtrending market, 14
Dow theory, 15–16

E

Equity put-call ratio, 140, 141

F, G

Fat–Tail losses, 143
Fibonacci numbers, 105
Flag pattern
    Cisco movement, 61, 62
    description, 59
    Google shares, 61, 62
    tactics, 60
    U.S. Steel, 63
    Yahoo! stock, 60, 61
FTSE China 25 Index Fund, 96
Futures exchange
    COT data, 36–37
    intermarket analysis, 32–33
    macro trading, 31–32
    patience and discipline, 37–39
    sector and market selection, 35–36

Index

H

Head and shoulders bottom/top pattern
    Citigroup, 55
    description, 53
    DJIA, 55, 56
    large bond bear market, 54
    tactics, 53

I, J, K

Institute for Supply Management, 106
Intermarket analysis, 32–34
Intermediate-term timing tool, 30
Investors Intelligence (II), 30

L

Long Term Capital Management (LTCM), 162–163

M, N

Macro traders, 213
Macro trading, 6, 31–32, 124–125
Market factors
    breadth
        A/D line *vs.* DJIA, 102–104
        bull market top, 103, 104
        McClellan Oscillator, 104
    full stock market cycle, 108–110
    macro analysis, 110–111
    news
        Institute for Supply Management (ISM), 106
        reaction to, 106
        recessions, 107, 108
        stock market, 106
    relative strength, 111–112
    short selling, 112–113
    time, 105
    trades size
        risk tolerance, 113
        stocks sizing, 114–115
    volume, 101–102
Mental trading pitfalls
    deadly A's
        anchoring related to assumption, 152
        assumptions, 151
        energy stock example, 152
    fallacy of intelligence, 162–163
    fighting dominant trends due to skepticism, 153–154
    fundamentalism, 159–160
    guessing *vs.* intelligent investment decisions, 154
    hardwired for trading failure, 147–149
    herd mentality, 156
    market change and public psychology, 158
    reality *vs.* reality should be, 158–159
    risk and reward balance, 164
    tax avoidance, 161
    trading position related to invalid/valid ruling reason, 149
    wisdom and flail about trade, 150
Moving Average Convergence Divergence (MACD), 16, 83–86
Moving averages
    crossover analysis, 83
    200-day simple moving average, 87
    definition, 82
    divergence measurement, 83
    DMI, 86–87
    long-term trend, 87
    MACD, 83–86
    10- and 12-month moving averages, 89, 90
    negative divergence, 83
    S&P 500, 88, 89, 91

O

Overall portfolio risk profile, 136

P, Q

Philosophy, 212
    accepting reality, 165–168
    change leaps
        exponential growth, 173

feedback loops, 176
linear leaps, 174
procyclicality, 174
reflexive participation, 176
control over fears, 170
critical thinking
    finding flaws and vulnerabilities in
        market positions, 195
    Karl Popper's adaptive methodology,
        192
    Karl Popper's epistemology, 193
    overriding goal in mind, 195
    profitable path, 194
    Socrates concepts, 191
    taking responsibility, 195
    tentative acceptance of knowledge,
        192
embracing change, 170–172
failure
    assumption blind, 190
    bad actors, 189
    complex decision-making model,
        188
    Dörner's model, 188
    irrationality, 190
    madman, 189
feeling of ease and symbiosis, 168
fractal world
    art of war, 204
    bell-shaped distribution curve, 199
    equilibrium concepts, 198
    flexibility, 203
    important days and people, 202
    inadequacy of the bell curve, 201
    liquidity, 203
    power law distribution system, 200
    rare events on long-term rate of
        return, 201
history
    Arab Spring uprisings, 180
    Bouazizi's public suicide, 180
    comfort of bad system, 182
    currencies, 186
    debt levels of the largest countries,
        184
    debt ratio problems, 184
    destruction of the Berlin Wall, 181
    Franz Ferdinand assassination, 181
    reasons for not accepting change,
        182
    S&P 2006 Long-Term Baseline
        Scenario, 185
    steady levels of debt restructurings,
        183
network effects
    clustering, 196
    collapse of housing and debt bubbles,
        197
    connected and interdependent
        concepts of world and global
        markets, 197
    efficiencies, 197
    systemic risk, 198
    proactive, positive change, 169
Pitfalls. See Mental trading pitfalls
Power of compounding, 135
Psychology, 212

R

Rectangle patterns
    copper selloff, 46, 47
    crude oil dynamics, 47, 48
    description, 46
    tactics, 46
Relative Strength Index (RSI), 92
Risk control, 210
    eliminating fat-tail losses, 143–144
    equity put-call ratio, 140, 141
    flowing with change, 138
    long-term survivor, 146
    maintaining flexibility, 134
    overall portfolio risk profile, 136
    power of compounding, 134
    selecting indicators, 140
    seperating ego, 144–145
    stop levels and examples, 135, 136
    trading discipline, 137
    treating capital, 142–143
    warning signs, 141

Index

Rounding bottom/top pattern
  description, 56
  Research In Motion, 58, 59
  STEC, Inc., 58
  tactics, 56
  Whole Foods, 57

S

Sentiment indicators, 27
Setups and chart patterns
  broad stock market, 41
  double bottom/top pattern
    bear market, 49
    description, 47
    dot-com craze, 50
    European bank, 51
    tactics, 48
    triple bottom bear market, 52
  flag pattern
    Cisco movement, 61, 62
    description, 59
    Google shares, 60, 62
    tactics, 60
    U.S. Steel, 63
    Yahoo! stock, 60, 61
  head and shoulders bottom/top pattern
    Citigroup, 55
    description, 53
    DJIA, 55, 56
    large bond bear market, 54
    tactics, 53
  macro themes, 41
  rectangle pattern
    copper selloff, 46, 47
    crude oil dynamics, 47, 48
    description, 46
    tactics, 46
  risk vs. reward, 43–44
  rounding bottom/top pattern
    description, 56
    Research In Motion, 58, 59
    STEC, Inc., 58
    tactics, 56
    Whole Foods, 57
  ruling reason, 43
  swing trading, 44
  technical analysis, 45
  triangle pattern
    Apple, 70, 71
    Baidu case, 71, 72
    copper case, 69
    description, 67
    silver market, 70
    S&P 500, 68
    tactics, 68
  wedge pattern
    Amazon, 64
    description, 63
    Natural gas, 66
    Peabody Energy, 65
    tactics, 64
    Toll Brothers, 66, 67
Stock market
  business cycle
    credit and interest rate cycles, 24, 25
    discounting mechanism, 22
    economic indicators, 23
    emotional cycle, 26
    yield curve, 23
  intermediate-term timing tool, 29, 30
  lessons (see Mental trading pitfalls)
  market stats, 16–17
  sentiment indicators, 27
  short-term indicator, 29
  stock groups, 20–22
  stock-sector relationship, 19
  tactical trend trading
    goal, 13
    objective trend determination, 15
    primary trend, 14
    secondary trend, 15
    stock return and volatility, 14
    swing trend, 15
    tactics to employ, 16
    uptrending and downtrending market, 14
  trading at highs, 18
Summing, 207
  acceptance, 209
  anger, 209
  bargaining, 209

Index

change and margin, 211
denial, 209
depression, 209
execution, 207
journey, 216
risk control, 210
trading, 207
winning trader (see Winning trader)
Swing trading, 44
Swing trend, 15
Systematic thinking, 212
Systematic trend following
  best trading practices
    system design, 118
    trading plan, 119
    trading rules, 119
  change and trends, 131–132
  consistent and unemotional trade, 123–124
  crisis alpha and black swans, 129–131
  diversification and risk control, 124–125
  not a black box, 121–123
  portfolio fit
    financial portfolio construction, 126
    inflation correlation, 128
    managed futures and stocks, 126, 127
    portfolio benefit of managed futures, 128, 129
    portfolio diversification, 126
    traditional investment portfolio, 127

T

Tactical trend trading
  buying the best, 8–9
  commitment, 11–12
  futures trading, 5–7
  goal, 13
  method and system, 10–11
  objective trend determination, 15
  power of compounding, 1–2
  primary trend, 14
  risk vs. reward, 9–10
  secondary trend, 15
  stock return and volatility, 14
  stock trading vs. investing
    DJIA, 3
    leadership stocks, 3
    risk control, 4
    sound stock trading, 4
    tax problem, 4
  swing trend, 15
  systematic basis (see Systematic trend following)
  tactics to employ, 16
  trading to win, 7–8
  uptrending and downtrending market, 14
Technical Analysis of Stock Trends, 45
Technical indicators
  Crocs, Inc breakout, 99, 100
  FTSE China 25 Index Fund, 96
  gaps, 73–74
  JDSU price action, 97–98
  moving averages (see Moving averages)
  overbought/oversold indicators
    Apple, 92, 93
    crude oil prices, 94
    DJIA, 94, 95
    RSI, 92
    Transocean chart, 92, 93
  reversals, 79–80
  support and resistance, 81–82
  Toll Brothers' boom and bust cycle, 98
  trendlines, 76
    agriculture bull market, 76, 77
    Financial Select Sector SPDR, 79
    JPMorgan Chase, 76, 77
    STEC chart, 76
Toll Brothers' boom and bust cycle, 98
Trading discipline, 137
Trading rules, 119
Trading-to-win mentality, 212
Triangle pattern
  Apple, 71
  Baidu case, 71, 72
  copper case, 69
  description, 67
  silver market, 70
  S&P 500, 68
  tactics, 68

Index

U, V

Uptrending market, 14

W, X

Wedge pattern
    Amazon, 64
    description, 63
    Natural gas, 66
    Peabody Energy, 65
    tactics, 64
    Toll Brothers, 67

Winning trader, 212
    advantage, 212
    chaotic nature, 214
    macro traders, 213
    mental flexibility, 214
    patient, 214
    positive outlook, 212
    stick method, 213

Y, Z

Yield curve, 25

GPSR Compliance

The European Union's (EU) General Product Safety Regulation (GPSR) is a set of rules that requires consumer products to be safe and our obligations to ensure this.

If you have any concerns about our products, you can contact us on

ProductSafety@springernature.com

In case Publisher is established outside the EU, the EU authorized representative is:

Springer Nature Customer Service Center GmbH
Europaplatz 3
69115 Heidelberg, Germany

www.ingramcontent.com/pod-product-compliance
Lightning Source LLC
LaVergne TN
LVHW040736250326
834688LV00031B/325